A Step By Step Guide To Starting And Running A Successful Horse Boarding Business

By

Sheri Grunska

The Comprehensive Book Of Horse Boarding & Effective Barn Management

Copyright © 2018 Sheri Grunska

All rights reserved. No part of this book may be reproduced, by any means, without written permission of the author and publisher.

Edited by Martha Schultz

Book cover design by
Stoney's Web Design
www.stoneyswebdesign.com

Author cover photo by
Christine Marie Photography

Disclaimer of Liability

The author and publisher shall have neither liability nor responsibility to any person or entity with respect to any loss or damage caused by alleged to be caused directly or indirectly by the information contained in this book. While the book is as accurate as the author can make it, there may be errors, omissions, and inaccuracies.

The purpose of this book is to acquaint the reader who wants to own and operate a horse boarding business through the experience of the author. The information in this book is drawn from the author's extensive experience owning and operating a horse boarding business.

It is not all-inclusive, however, and is not intended to cover all circumstances or every situation which may arise. The author does not make any representations or warranties; either expressed or implied, regarding the techniques discussed and assumes no liability therefore.

Acknowledgments

I want to give a huge thank you to my husband David for working on parts of this book with me. Our business would not be what it is without his knowledge of farm and stable operations. He is the one who does the upkeep and maintenance of everything from broken fences to buying hay and everything in-between. His input to this book is invaluable. Over the years there have been many people who have come into my life who have taught me so much about running a boarding facility, about people and especially about myself. Mistakes can tear us down or they can build us back up if we allow them and become better at what we choose to do for a career and in the process hopefully become better human beings. I also want to thank our wonderful clients at Vinland Stables who allowed me to take pictures of them riding and working with their horses for this book. I didn't have to search far to find plenty of beautiful horses to take pictures of for different chapters and it was truly a fun part of putting this book together. I am also blessed with wonderful neighbors who gave me wonderful photos to help make this book complete.

I want to give a special thank you to Martha Schultz for letting me bounce ideas off of her when it came to this book. I couldn't have written this book without her beside me editing each page many times over.

Writing books is something that I truly love but it can be hard on the ones around you. My family knows now after experiencing life in our home during my last four books that I can become self-absorbed and disappear to the computer for long hours. They have always been patient and I couldn't have written this book without their support. Thank you to my loving, hardworking husband David and my beautiful daughters, Kaeli and Lauren. Forever I am grateful.

Table of Contents

A Step By Step Guide To Starting And Running A Successful Horse Boarding Business . 3

The Comprehensive Book Of Horse Boarding & Effective Barn Management 3

    Acknowledgments 5

The Reason I Wrote This Book 17

~1~ 19

Setting Up Your Barn And Business 19

    Where Do I Start? 20

    Buying Land For A Boarding Stable 20

    Paddocks, Pastures And Ground Condition 21

    Permits And Zoning For Building And Operation 24

    Conditional-Use Permit 24

    Sellers Permit 25

    Department Of Natural Resources 25

    Advertising-Start Early! 26

~2~ 28

The Planning Stages—How Many Of Everything? 28

    Starting From The Beginning 28

    Designing Your Barn And Getting Estimates 31

    Barn And Stable Options When Building 33

    Is Your Barn Horse Ready? 33

    A Self-Contained Barn 38

    The Horse Stalls 39

    Lighting For Your Barn 41

    Water—So Important! 43

    Outdoor Shelters 46

~3~ 47

Designing Your Riding Arenas 47

    The Indoor Riding Arena 47

    Depth Of Arena Sand 48

    What Size Riding Arena? 49

    Different Riding Disciplines And Uses For The Arena 50

  The Outdoor Riding Arena 54

~4~
The Tack Room
  What Size Tack Room Should I Build? 55

~5~
Wash Stall And Grooming Areas
  Designing Your Wash Stall 58
  The Designated Grooming Areas 60

~6~
The Lounge, Viewing Room And Bathroom
  The Lounge/Viewing Room Design 61
  The Bathroom 62

~7~
Hay, Grain And Shavings Room
  The Hay Storage Room 65
  Keeping Hay From Molding While Storing 66
  Grain Storage Room 67
  Bedding For The Stalls 70

~8~
Horse Trailer Parking And Haul-Ins
  Haul-Ins 73

~9~
Designing Your Paddocks And Pastures
  Herd Size And Your Paddocks 75
  Fencing 77

~10~
Farm Equipment Needed

~11~
Hiring Employees
  Employees And Worker's Comp. Insurance 84
  Hiring Employees 85
  Working Off The Board 85

Expectations For Employees 86

~12~

Buying An Established Horse Boarding Business 87

Be Prepared For Turnover 87

Past Record Keeping 88

Unforeseen Expenses 88

~13~

Setting Your Board Rates 90

Unexpected Price Increases For Hay And Grain 91

The Cost Of Feeding Different Size Horses 91

Before You Finalize Your Board Rates 93

Your Rates Compared To Other Boarding Barns 95

Sales Tax And Your Rates 97

~14~

Lawyers, Accountants And Insurance 98

Lawyers 98

Accountants 98

Insurance–A Must Have 99

Care, Custody And Control Insurance 100

Trainers Insurance 100

~15~

The Bank, Your Business Loan, And Your Business Plan 102

The Business Plan 103

Executive Summary 104

Mission Statement 104

Keys To Success 105

The Company Summary 106

Company Ownership 107

Start-Up Summary 108

Services 108

Market Analysis Summary 110

Market Segmentation 111

Market Segmentation Strategy 113
Service Business Analysis 114
Economic Study 114
Competition And Buying Patterns 115
Competitive Edge 115
Sales Strategy 118
Sales Forecast 119
Figuring Out Your Monthly Sales 119
Management Summary 121
Start-Up Funding And Worksheet 122
Important Assumptions 125
Twelve Month Income Statement 126
Cash Flow Statement 130

~16~ 132

Boarding Contracts And Liability Waivers 132

Sample Boarding Contract 133
Emergency Information Form 146

~17~ 148

Barn Rules 148

Your Barn Rules Will Change 148
Can Your Barn Have Too Many Rules? 149
Barn Rules And Safety 149
Learning To Enforce The Barn Rules 150
Different Riding Disciplines And Rules 151
List Of Sample Barn Rules 151

~18~ 160

Riding Arena Rules 160

Arena Etiquette And Rules For Safe Riding 160

Horse Barn Management- The Real Deal 168

~19~ 169

Chores—Making It Easy And Efficient 169

Feeding Horses 169

    The Many Opinions Of How To Feed Hay 170

    Feeding Grain 171

    The Numbering System 172

    Feeding Multiple Supplements 174

    Different Forms Of Supplements 175

    Daily Turnout For Horses 176

    Handling Horses And Turnout Routine 176

    Safety And Handling Horses 177

    Be Clear On Turnout Protocols For Weather 177

    Cleaning Stalls 180

    Cleaning Paddocks And Run-Ins 181

    Disposing Of Horse Manure 183

~20~ 185

Fees For Extra Services 185

    Will Your Board Rate Reflect Extra Services? 185

    Extra Fees For Services Performed 187

~21~ 190

Special Requests 190

    What Is A Reasonable Request? 190

    When A Boarder Chooses To Leave 192

~22~ 193

Employees 193

    Give Good Instruction 193

    Expectations For Employees 194

    Disenchantment With The Job 195

    Being Dependable Is A Must! 195

    Creating A Team 196

~23~ 197

Trainers At Your Barn 197

    Trainers And Your Business 197

    Asking A Trainer To Leave 199

    The Risks That Come With A One-Trainer Barn 200

    The Training Barn VS. The Boarding Barn 201

~24~
Veterinarians
    Veterinarians And Your Business 203
    Professional To Professional 204
    Giving Medications-Is It Worth the Risk? 205
    Ask Your Veterinarian 206
    When A Boarder Refuses To Call The Veterinarian 206

~25~
Farriers
    Will You Allow Multiple Farriers? 209
    The Risks With Just One Farrier 209
    The Pros And Cons Of Free Choice Farriers 210
    Setting Up Appointments And Holding Fees 211

~26~
Barn Hours
    What Works Best For You? 212
    Your Barn Hours Will Fit Their Schedule 213
    A Huge Reason For Burn-Out 213
    Setting Barn Hours Is Healthy For Your Business 214

~27~
The Challenges Of Outdoor Board
    Planning Your Outdoor Boarding 216
    Things To Think About With Outdoor Board 217
    When Outdoor Board Is Not A Good Fit... 221
    Outdoor Board Guidelines 221

~28~
Herd Management
    Mares And Geldings 224
    Introducing A New Horse Into A Herd 225
    There Are No Guarantees In Herd Management 225
    Red Flags And How To Spot Them In A Herd.. 226

- A Little Time-Out Can Go A Long Way 229
- Not Enough Paddocks 230
- Gaining The Trust From A New Boarder 230
- Private Turnout 231
- Educating Will Be Part Of Your Job 231

~29~ 234
Is Your Barn Set Up For The Horse With Special Needs? 234
- Modifying Your Program For The Special Needs Horse 235

~30~ 237
When A Horse Doesn't Fit Your Program 237
- The Barn Manager's Responsibility 237
- When There Are No More Options 238
- Not Every Person Is A Good Fit 238

~31~ 240
When A Horse Needs To Be Euthanized 240
- The Different Reasons A Horse Is Euthanized 240
- The Barn Manager's Role 241
- The Other Boarders And Their Opinions 242

~32~ 243
Barn Owner/Barn Manager 243
- Having A Common Goal And Vision 243
- The Barn Owner 246
- The Bottom Line Is the Financials 247
- Barn Owners Are Often Misjudged 248
- The Barn Manager 248
- Barn Management Job Duties 249
- When You Are Both The Barn Owner And Barn Manager 252
- Are You A Conservative Barn Manager? 253
- Find A Support System 253

~33~ 255
The Many Hats You Will Wear 255
- The Caretaker Hat 255

The Teacher Hat 256
The Rule Enforcer Hat 257
The Medical Hat 257
The Student Hat 258
The Weatherman Hat 258

~34~ 260
Yearly Health Care 260
Veterinarians-Giving Your Boarders A Choice 260
Establishing A Yearly Health Care Plan 261
Deworming And Record Keeping 261
Who Will Administer Dewormer At Your Barn? 262
Deworming Issues 263

~35~ 264
Clinics 264
Keep Your First Clinic Simple 264
List Of Clinics 265
What Do I Charge For A Clinic? 266

~36~ 269
Blanketing And How It Affects Your Job 269
Do I Charge For Blanketing Or Not? 269
The Issues That Come With Blanketing 270
Educating Your Boarders On Blanketing 271
When Horses Destroy Each Other's Blanket 272
Torn Blankets And Drama 273
Storing Blankets 274

~37~ 275
The Multi-Discipline Barn 275
Let's Talk Different Riding Disciplines 275
When A Riding Discipline Doesn't Work 277
Communication And Respect Is Vital! 277

~38~ 279
Has Your Tack Room Become Too Small? 279

    Giving Your Boarders A Designated Space...279

    Keeping The Tack Room Clean..280

~39~

When A Horse Breaks Something-Who Pays?...283

    Who Pays When A Horse Breaks Something?...283

    How To Receive Payment For Damages...285

~40~

Giving A Thirty-Day Notice To A Client..287

    The Wrong Way To Give A Thirty-Day Notice 287

    The Right Way To Give A Thirty-Day Notice 288

    Giving A Thirty-Day Notice By Email...288

~41~

Adjustment Time And Conflict Management 290

    What Your Boarders Will Watch For...290

    Don't Take Offense...291

    Sometimes You Just Need To Say Good-Bye 291

    When Conflict Happens...292

    Your Responsibility As A Barn Owner...293

~42~

Handling A Boarder's Difficult Horse 294

    Have It In Your Boarding Contract! 294

~43~

Billing Your Clients 296

    Creating Invoices For Your Clients..296

    Charging A Late Fee...296

    It's Not Personal, It's Business 297

    Raising Your Board Rates And Service Fees 298

    Giving A Two Month Notice For Rate Increases 298

~44~

What Kind Of Clients Are You Trying To Attract? 300

    What You Want And What Is A Good Fit...300

    Your Riding Disciplines Might Change 301

    Set Your Standards High 301
    If You Build, Your Clientele Will Change 302
    Your Board Rate Will Attract A Certain Clientele 303
    Transition From The Hobby Farm 303
    The Upper-End Barn And Expectations 304

~45~ 305
Boundaries With Your Clients 305
    Figuring Out The Boundaries 305
    The Barn Owner's Responsibility 307

~46~ 309
Why Do Boarders Leave? 309
    When Things Change For A Client 309

~47~ 311
First Impressions And A Clean Barn 311
    Get Rid Of The Junk And Clutter! 312
    A Clean Barn Doesn't Just Happen 313

~48~ 315
Competing With Other Horse Stables 315
    They Say They Do It all! 315
    Smaller Boarding Stables Are Important 316

~49~ 317
Your Barn Will Have Growing Pains 317
    Growing As A Barn Manager 317

~50~ 319
Why Your Job Is So Unique 319
    Do What Is Best For You 320

About The Author 321
Sheri's Books and Website 322

The Reason I Wrote This Book

So, you have a dream…living your life surrounded by beautiful horses, wonderful horse owners and friends, and making money in the process. That was my dream! I wrote this book because there were many times when my dream was falling apart and I couldn't find the resources to help me navigate through it. I wanted to help others understand what to expect and avoid problems through planning. If you are thinking of boarding horses, regardless of the size of boarding operation, you will find this book to be a valuable resource that you will use over and over. My idea was to write a book that was easy to understand in a step by step format to give readers the tools to be strategic in planning their business, understand some of the challenges they will face and deal with unforeseen issues that they may encounter as business owners and barn managers.

This book is a step by step guide to what you will need to get your barn or stable operational and then to keep it running efficiently and consistently. It will open your eyes to the world of horse boarding and all that it encompasses. One of the most often asked questions I get from people who want to start a boarding business is, "Where do I start?" Great question! Most people, including myself, usually start with a couple of horses and then progress into boarding. The way to start is by educating yourself and planning well. I believe this book will give you a good start through information, insights and experiences in the planning, management and ownership of a horse boarding operation.

I have included a sample business plan, boarding contract and barn rules along with many task lists to organize each part of your business. I will talk about many scenarios that will include other equine professionals that work at your barn including veterinarians, farriers, horse trainers and more. I will discuss the weather and how it affects your business year-round (and it will), buying hay, shavings and paying your business mortgage. It is very true when I say that the horses will be the easiest part of your day.

The information in these pages will benefit any size boarding operation. A large boarding barn equates to a large scale effort and risk. A small boarding stable carries lower financial risk but requires the same planning to be successful and can have many of the same issues as a large facility. The problems that boarding barns are known for can happen at any size stable and I hear too many stories of people who had a dream and burn out within the first couple of years. The horse business they started fell apart and they don't know how it happened. My goal is to have you start looking at your horse boarding operation as a business in all areas. Remember that it is a seven day a week job every day of the year. You need to pace yourself and learn from your mistakes and move forward.

I believe we are all in this industry together, and as equine professionals we should be supporting each other and helping each other grow. We need each other to make our businesses strong. I wrote this book to help others that want to board horses for a living start off with a strong foundation and hopefully, not make all the mistakes that my husband and I made when we built our barn and started our business. If I can help one person make a success of their boarding barn then I will have felt that this book was worth writing.

Every area of the horse industry is impacted by the boarding barn and stable and no matter the size; each plays an integral part in the success and stability of the equine industry.

Get ready to dive in because the chapters ahead are going to show you how to set up your boarding business no matter the size and we will start from the very beginning.

Sheri Grunska

~1~

Setting Up Your Barn And Business

No doubt about it, starting any kind of business can seem daunting at times. The responsibility of caring for large animals like horses can add so much more to the stress if you are not prepared for all you are about to embark on. I often hear from barn owners across the country about how they are overwhelmed when they realize how much work it takes to keep a boarding business going. I can hear the frustration in their voices because they were not prepared for the challenges and high cost to keep a barn running and in good working order. I can so relate to their feelings because I was there many years ago.

When we opened our boarding facility in Neenah Wisconsin, we thought we had everything under control. We were approved for a loan to build a 25,000 square foot barn with indoor riding arena and lounge and I was over the moon with excitement. I thought that I had energy that was endless and that I could do it all. I never realized how destructive horses can really be or how challenging it is to work with clients on the same property that you live daily. I had owned horses for a long time but always only managed one or two at a time. Never forty at a time!

I boarded my horses so I never paid attention to what the barn owners or managers had to do on a daily basis to keep everything in order. Even after working at a couple of barns in my life I still never paid attention to all that it really takes to keep everything going. I was the employee and when I clocked out I didn't give it another thought. The truth is that most boarders or employees don't fully grasp what it takes to keep everything in working order or the cost to keep it all afloat. It is no different than me not knowing what it takes to run a restaurant.

Where Do I Start?

I believe the first place to start is with you, your dreams and aspirations. What kind of boarding stable do you want to run? Do you want to casually board a couple of friend's horses or do you want to have a much larger operation? Are you looking to quit your day job and work at home full-time running the barn? Will you have a large mortgage to pay or will your place be completely paid off? Will you have employees or will you and your family be doing all the work? Do you want a full service boarding stable or just offer outside board with a few amenities and extra services. What kind of disciplines do you want at your barn? Trail riders, people who show, speed riders, jumpers etc. As you can see the list can go on and on. There is so much that goes into the whole boarding equation and I didn't have a good grasp on this part of barn management and our business until a couple of years had gone by and we were deep into it.

I suggest starting by thinking about what kind of barn you want. Let's start with size. Size is important because the bigger the facility the more work there is and the cost can be huge to keep it going. Considering a small stable? The one thing I want to stress is that there is a great need for smaller stables. Not everyone likes a large busy barn and the smaller boarding stables often get overlooked.

Buying Land For A Boarding Stable

I often will talk with someone who is either looking for land to buy or has land and wants to build a barn. The one thing many people don't think about when looking at land to purchase is the layout of the land and the ground conditions. It may look great in the summer when the ground is dry but things will change fast once the rain arrives. Find out what type of soil the property has. You can get topographic photos which will show the soil maps with the low areas and the areas that seem to stay wet longer. It will often be hard to tell how the water flows and where the water sits on land that is flat. You can find out more information about the layout of the land in question by hiring a surveyor to take a closer look at the land and help map out how the water is flowing. The more information you can get ahead of time the better for building your barn and planning your paddocks and pastures.

Since we built our barn on empty farm land, people will stop by to talk to us about the process and things we would do differently in retrospect. Our business property is in an area that is very low and our soil is a clay soil which can make for challenging conditions when we get rain. We can have mud in the spring and fall if we get enough rain and it can take a long time to dry because of our soil conditions. This makes it very difficult when dealing with horses and footing.

In our situation we didn't realize how soft the ground would be since it had never had anything on it before but crops. It took about five years before the paddocks could better handle the rain. We have also added a large drain tile to help get the water off the paddocks as quickly as possible which has made a tremendous difference. It definitely is a process that will take time and patience.

Paddocks, Pastures And Ground Condition

If you are having issues with mud then I can promise you that you will have issues with your clients and they will have concerns for the welfare of their horse standing out in the mud. I have experienced this and it is not an easy fix. I will be honest and tell you that when we entered into springtime our first year we were not prepared for the amount of mud we had to deal with. We had created brand new paddocks on virgin farm land and the ground was unbelievably soft and very low in spots. Between the frost coming out of the ground, the cool temperatures, spring rains and of course all the horses, we had a huge mess. It was something we didn't see coming when we were designing our paddocks and putting up fencing the prior year. The ground looks much different once you get horses on it daily. Here in the Midwest where you have all four seasons, mud can be part of the territory with horses unless you are in sandy soil or very high ground. We have worked on our paddocks over the years and added dirt and screenings in certain areas when our finances would allow but we still have a couple weeks each spring where the horses will be inside the barn much more than usual as we wait for the paddocks to dry and become safe for them to go back outside. If you are purchasing an established facility then you can ask the barn owners what the paddocks look like during each season and you can even see for yourself after a heavy down pour. That will tell you a lot about some of the possible issues you might be dealing with.

There are ways to fix poorly draining paddocks that have a problem with muddy conditions but it can be expensive. Taking the top soil off and then adding good dirt and other toppings will make a huge difference but most people don't have the extra money to do this especially after they have started a business. If I could offer any suggestion at this point, I would put in some drain tiles and watch how your water flows for a year or two. The ground will change and often it changes after new construction and the ground settles.

When we first built our barn we had a drain tile put in but it was too small and it couldn't handle the large amount of water. The next year we put in a much larger drain tile and added a large culvert and then dug a huge drainage ditch to take care of our water problem. It was an extra expense we had not planned for, but it was what was needed to stop the flooding.

Digging a drainage ditch and putting in a culvert will help redirect water if you are in a low-lying area.

Where To Build Your Barn?

I have talked to quite a few people over the years who are in the design phase of building their barn and we will often get into a conversation about the location of their barn on their property. When we were in the design stage of building our barn we talked about several locations on our property to build. We didn't want to build it too close to our home so that we could still keep our privacy but we wanted to be able to walk to the barn at any given time in case of an emergency or for something that needed to be done. Location of your barn to your home and paddocks is something to definitely think about.

Location To Your Home

Location is very important because you will have traffic coming in all hours that you are open. You need to consider that trailers will be leaving very early in the morning or coming home in the middle of the night from a horse show or trail ride and if they are driving by your house to enter your property then your privacy or space will be disturbed at times. If your only driveway goes right by your house then you will have vehicles coming and going during the day as well. Because you are going to be working in a job that is seven days a week, you will realize that you need to be protective of your privacy. It is a very unique business in the sense that you can't get away from it unless you leave the property. That is why I suggest building your barn a good distance away from your home so that you can separate yourself from it when you need to. If you are starting from scratch with the entire building project then you can design your site so that your clients are not driving right by your home at all hours. We completely moved our driveway entrance about five hundred feet away from the original driveway location so that our clients can go straight to the barn without ever having to drive by our home and it was worth the extra money to have this done. You may love your job, but the reality is you will have days when you need to get away from it. Privacy is very important especially when your business is on the same property that you live.

Location To Your Paddocks And Pastures

Another thing I want you to think about is the location of your barn in relation to your pastures, paddocks and private turnouts. Our barn is large and holds twenty-seven horses. Hand-walking all our horses outside takes time but what really helps is that our paddocks are very close to our barn so the job can be done quickly. Location is everything when it comes to daily chores. If you are only dealing with a few horses then distance is not much of a factor but if you are hand-walking many horses then it will consume time and energy, especially when the weather is less than perfect. Depending on where you live, seasonal changes will be a huge factor in site planning. We can get heavy snow in Wisconsin and walking horses out in snow has its own set of challenges. Summer storms can move in fast and getting the horses in and out quickly and safely is an important consideration.

Permits And Zoning For Building And Operation

One of the parts of any building project or business venture is the building permits. There is nothing exciting about applying for permits but if you don't do it, you could end up with problems. The easiest way to find out what kind of permits you will need for your business and building project is to go to your county zoning office, city hall or place where they issue permits in your area and ask about local processes and requirements. Permits can be expensive especially if you are building a large barn but it is far better to have everything properly permitted than to find out you are in violation of an ordinance in your area and facing fines.

You will need to find out if your property is zoned for having a business. Boarding horses as a business could mean changing the zoning from residential to agricultural or commercial depending on where you live and the zoning regulations and rules for that area. You will want to make sure you have the correct zoning for boarding horses and this is one of the first things you should check into at the very beginning when you are in the planning phase of your new career venture. Improper planning and non-compliance with local requirements can come with a high cost. I talked to one person who was zoned improperly for her boarding stable and the city wanted to close her operation and it ended up costing her stress and money to get everything corrected so she could stay open.

Conditional-Use Permit

Before we could apply for a loan or start building we needed to make sure the township we lived in would allow us to build a large facility and board horses. We needed to apply for a conditional use permit. Basically we needed approval from the town board to open our horse boarding business. They wanted to know the size of our facility along with how many horses we would have on our property. Most cities and townships will only allow a certain number of horses on a property depending on the amount of acreage you own. If you are going to build small and start out with a low number of horses make sure you have room enough for expansion if you think you will want to expand your boarding operation in the future. The conditional use permit allows you to open your requested business but does not give you permission to change the type of business you are running. For example, if you open a boarding operation and a couple years down the road you decide to get rid of the horses and open a storage business with your barn, you would need to apply for a new permit for that type of business.

Sellers Permit

A seller's permit is required for every individual, partnership, corporation, or other organization making retail sales, leases, or rentals of tangible personal property or taxable services, unless all sales are exempt from sales or use tax.

In simpler words, if you are going to own and operate a boarding business, then depending on the laws of your state and business location you may need a seller's permit. You can find out if you need to have a seller's permit to run your business at your city's town hall, court records building or where they issue permits and business licenses.

Department Of Natural Resources

You will need to provide the DNR with a horse manure disposal plan and the DNR might come to your property to see where the manure storage will be located. We live in an area where there are some wetlands around us and that was important to the Department of Natural Resources to make sure there was no run-off into the wetlands or streams and rivers. We had to apply for a permit and make sure our manure was a certain distance from a stream that runs on the edge of our property.

If I can give a word of advice, make sure you have everything in place with permits before you decide to build or open your horse business. I talked to a woman a few years ago that had opened a boarding barn on her property. As she started to expand she ran into some big problems because a neighbor didn't like all the horses and reported it. It turned out she didn't have all the permits to have her business in the first place. It ended up costing her thousands of dollars more than what it originally would have and she was refused permits to expand her operation.

The Costs Of Permits

Most people that apply for permits for any kind of project usually come home with sticker shock. Permits are not cheap and when it comes to starting a business they can add up fast. I would recommend going to your town hall or city clerk's office and find out ahead of time what kind of permits you will need and the cost of each. You don't want to apply and pay for permits until you get the go ahead from your city or town to build. If you do your homework, prepare properly and adhere to the requirements in accordance with your city or township, usually things move much faster and smoother.

Business License

A business license is a permit or registration required by the federal, state, county, or local government to conduct business. Besides the basic operating permits, you should check to see what other licenses you need for the state and area in which you are doing business. The best place to start is your local city hall or courthouse. See the city clerk who should be able to direct you in the right direction.

Advertising-Start Early!

When we opened our business years ago there wasn't Facebook and I didn't have a business website. All we had back then were newspapers and a weekly bargain shopper paper. I advertised in a weekly paper called the Buyer's Guide and it worked great for the time. I have long since moved forward. Currently I have a website and utilize social media to reach the public and potential boarders. Advertising is important because you need people to find you and know you exist. Facebook is another great tool to use but I believe it is second to a professional website and they both work wonderful together. I have many people who will find me on Facebook but then go directly to my website from there.

Think Globally!

When thinking about advertising I want you to think globally! It may seem strange since you are boarding horses and not selling goods but it is important. I have had many clients who have come to board at our barn from other parts of the country and even the U.K. People move much more often now than they ever have before and that means they are also looking for a place to move their horse. Think big when advertising because you never know when someone will be relocating to your area and they need to find good quality boarding.

I also believe that most people are very visual and that is why a well-designed website with many pictures and details about your stable will help drive possible clients to give you a call and set up a time for a tour. Once they are at your barn for a tour the rest is up to you.

I have talked to a few people that have told me that a website is too expensive to have professionally designed or to keep going each month. I disagree. Websites are very common place now and you can easily make one yourself or hire someone to create one for your business for very little cost. I have had my website for years and the monthly fee is less than twenty dollars a month. It is definitely worth looking into. Remember that you want to make a great first impression and your website will do that for you.

~2~

The Planning Stages–How Many Of Everything?

This is where the fun begins! Trying to figure out what you will need for the complete operation of your boarding stable will be different for everyone depending on where you live, the size facility you want, the riding disciplines of the boarders as well as other factors we will discuss. When we decided to board horses as a business the first thing we had to decide on was if we wanted to make this our full-time career or just a part-time side job. That will make a big difference in the beginning. It is extremely hard to work full-time at one job and try to run a large boarding barn at the same time. Unless you have extra income to hire a full-time barn manager and employees you will burn yourself out very fast. I have talked to a few people over the years who have tried to do both, and I have learned from personal experience that it is extremely difficult to have two full time jobs.

Starting From The Beginning

When David and I first talked about building our barn and starting a horse boarding business, it was our plan for both of us to quit our jobs and work full-time at home. He would quit immediately and I would work for a couple more years after we opened but eventually I would be at the stable full-time as well.

When we were in the planning stages, one of the first questions we had to answer was, how many stalls did we need to be able to make a living at boarding horses?

One of our first problems was we didn't know how much our business loan would be. I also didn't have any idea how much the monthly costs would be to keep our business operating. I had a lot of research to do if I wanted to get a good understanding of the costs to run a large boarding facility.

I have compiled a list of things that are important when you are in the planning stages for a horse boarding business. Initially you will not have exact numbers but will need to estimate on the high side until you have worked through a couple of years' costs through all four seasons. Talk with your banker about what size loan you qualify for so that you can determine the size facility you can afford. Your banker can give you a rough estimate of your monthly mortgage payment. Sometimes this process seems backward, but it is all about gathering information and building a case to support your plan to start your business.

Important things to think about for a start-up boarding business:

- Cost of hay for one year
- Cost of grain for one year
- Cost of water for one year
- Bedding—bulk or bagged shavings for one year
- Fuel for equipment for one year
- Electric for one year
- Maintenance and repairs (an estimate for one year)
- Insurance for all areas of the business including employees
- How much do you want to spend on employees for the year?
- Medical insurance for one year
- Property taxes

This is a simple list of some of the essentials that will keep your barn operating. It is very hard to figure out the cost of electric, gas and even water because every barn is built differently and size is a major component in all of it. A well-insulated barn will stay warmer and you might not need to use heater buckets but if you do need heater buckets during the wintertime then expect your electric cost to be much higher during the extreme cold.

You might have a good idea of how much hay you will need but hay prices fluctuate and a lot depends on the kind of hay you are going to feed. Hay will be your highest expense so it is best to estimate on the high end and have a little left over than to run out or be short on cash to buy more. You may not think this happens to people in this type of business but it happens more than you know and it can become extremely stressful when trying to figure out how you are going to pay for the hay that you need for the horses.

Bedding for the stalls will be your next biggest expense if you have a large facility. Many people like the convenience of bagged shavings but if you are taking care of more than five horses, bagged shavings not only are more expensive but a lot more work. When we opened our barn, I bought a few hundred bags of shavings not realizing how much more money it was going to cost along with the added labor involved to open bags and bed twenty-seven stalls daily. Our bags of shavings were stored in a separate room at the end of our barn and it became problematic when we needed to carry enough bags to put fresh bedding into many stalls. We had to dispose of the empty bags and our large trash cans filled up fast and it became much more work than I expected. We quickly changed to bulk shavings, so we saved money each month and it was much easier and faster to bed the stalls with wheelbarrows full of shavings, which meant we were saving money in labor as well.

When calculating your expenses, make certain to detail everything used on a per-horse basis. Make sure to detail *everything* as it will add up quickly when you have a large stable. Each horse will represent a certain amount of income coming in and expenses going out. This may not sound fun, but I can't stress how important it is. You need to remember that your bank wants very accurate numbers for money coming in and going out. They don't want you to go out of business because you can't make your monthly mortgage payment.

I will discuss the importance of a well-written business plan in an upcoming chapter and that will be the most important thing you do to establish a solid foundation for starting your business. A well written business plan will lay a strong foundation for you and your business.

Designing Your Barn And Getting Estimates

Designing your barn is definitely one of the most exciting things you will do in the early stages of planning. I spent countless hours looking at pictures and I walked through quite a few barns just to get an idea of what I wanted.

Walk through as many barns and stables as you can. The more facility's you look at the more familiar you will become with layout, design and housing for horses. No two barns are the same as you will quickly find out.

The reality of what it cost to build a barn and riding arena can be shocking if you have never had an estimate for a building project, but it is all part of the process. When we were looking for a builder we had four estimates for our barn and they were all completely different in price and the differences were in the tens of thousands of dollars! We made many mistakes in this process and I will be the first to tell you that cheaper is not always better. We took a much less expensive route and it ended up costing us tens of thousands more because of all the major problems we ran into.

When getting estimates make sure you ask about builders insurance and ask to see their building contract ahead of time. I would also get references from previous jobs they have worked on. I encourage you to have your attorney look over all paperwork and contracts before you sign anything and hand over any money. Many things can go wrong during a building project and I have heard horror stories where the builder walked off the job with the client's money and the building not finished. We had many problems during our building project and we were not protected because we had a poorly written building contract.

The inside of Vinland Stables before the stalls were built.

When designing your barn and getting estimates you will need to decide if you are going to have the contractor just put up the shell of the barn or are they going to complete the inside as well. When we built our barn we hired a contractor to put up the shell for the barn, arena, hay and shavings storage. The contractor also hired the electrician to do all the electric work and lights throughout riding arena and stable area. We found a concrete company to pour the cement in all the areas that needed it and we hired someone to build our lounge and tack rooms. One of our biggest expenses was the foundation that the barn would be built on. The piece of property that our barn was going to be built on was a low area and it needed to be raised up almost three feet. That meant a lot of dirt had to be hauled in. Finding a good excavator will make all the difference in the world especially as the barn starts to settle and the rainy season hits.

I have talked to people over the years that have built their barn and then after it settles and the wet season hits, they have problems with flooding. It is very stressful and it is very expensive to fix this kind of problem. You will want to make sure that any excavation is done by a reliable company. The one project that my husband did himself was the building of our twenty-seven horse stalls. I looked at many horse stall kits and when I found the one I liked, he put them in. Installing them ourselves saved us a lot of money.

Barn And Stable Options When Building

Here is a list of things that you will want to think about having for your barn. Some of these items are optional but many of them will be necessities.

- Horse stalls—What kind and how many stalls do you want? The size of the horse stalls is an important element.
- Rubber mats for stalls (Footing for under the mats for drainage—screenings etc.)
- Water buckets or automatic waterers (This will make a difference in how your water is run underground and how the plumbing is put in.)
- Wash stall(s)-inside and outside
- Grooming bays (also used by Veterinarians and Farriers)
- Cross-tie areas
- Tack room(s)
- Storage for hay, grain and other necessities
- Storage for bedding
- Storage for arena equipment
- Lounge and bathroom
- Observation room (This can be your lounge with added windows into your arena)
- Storage area for medical supplies

Is Your Barn Horse Ready?

Here is a list of important items you need to have so your barn is horse ready. I have left out the horse stalls and mats since they are in the previous list and part of the building project.

- Corner feeders for grain and supplements
- Water buckets or automatic waterers
- Salt block or mineral block holders
- Tie rings for the back of each stall
- Saddle racks for cross-tie areas and grooming bays
- Saddle racks for tack rooms

- Halter and bridle hooks for cross-tie areas, tack-room areas, grooming bays and stall doors
- Blanket bars for pads and horse blankets
- Blanket hangers for dirty and wet blankets
- Identification cards for each stall
- Communication dry erase boards
- Horse and paddocks location dry erase boards
- Cross-ties
- Wheelbarrows for cleaning
- Wagon or wheelbarrow to feed hay inside and outside
- Muck buckets
- Pitchforks
- Shovels
- Brooms
- Dust pans
- Water hoses
- Leaf blower (optional but we use ours everyday)
- Garbage cans (large and small) for tack rooms and other areas
- Fire extinguishers
- Hay and bedding

There are many items needed for the daily chores and to help keep the barn clean.

Designing Your Barn For Horses And/Or People

I have had the privilege of touring many beautiful barns of all shapes and sizes. Each barn or stable brings something unique to offer their clients and horses. As you plan your facility you will make many operational decisions that will be determined by whether your focus is on the clients or their horses. Deciding what kind of barn you want will include many individual small touches that you will add. Some barns are clearly designed with the client in mind. Each with every comfort you can think of. Unfortunately some of those special comforts come with a price tag when building.

When we were designing our facility I wanted the horse's comfort to come first. I also wanted a comfortable barn for my clients but I needed to be very practical, especially when I looked at the added cost. You can have a very horse friendly barn and still have it be very comfortable for the people. Our barn is not heated but our lounge and bathroom are and that makes a huge difference during our long very cold winter months. Having a small lounge that is heated doesn't need to be expensive to be welcoming and comfortable. If the lounge is well insulated, then heating it and keeping it warm will be economical and it is something that your clients will appreciate.

Designing Your Barn For Where You Live

I grew up in Southern California where the weather is hot much of the year. Having horses in California is completely different than Wisconsin to say the least. I had never ridden in an indoor riding arena growing up as there was no need to with the warm sunny weather. That is definitely not the case for the Midwest or any area that experiences all four seasons to the fullest. If we didn't have an indoor riding arena we wouldn't have a full service horse boarding business. People who want to ride year round want an indoor riding arena especially during the wet and muddy seasons and the harsh cold winters that we experience. Needless to say, in order for us to stay in competition with other boarding facilities in our area, we needed a large indoor riding arena. Of course, this might not be the case if you live in a warm climate year round.

The same would be true for the stabling of the horses. In our barn we have twenty-seven indoor horse stalls so the horses can stay inside when it becomes extremely cold, wet or rainy. Many people feel more comfortable knowing that their horse is in a dry stall during inclement weather. There are many people who prefer outside board or "rough board" as they call it in the Midwest and providing both options for horse owners is a competitive advantage. Where you live and the type of weather you have year-round will be a determining factor in all your barn and stable design decisions. The cost of building your barn or stable will also be impacted by these factors.

Designing Your Barn For All Four Seasons

If you live in an area that has cold winters and a long, wet springtime, then you are going to want to pay attention to your barn design and site plan layout. Handling horses daily is fairly easy when the weather is calm and the sun is shining. In fact, most farm chores are easier when the weather is great. Once the weather turns and the dry ground turns to mud or snow, chores can take longer and dealing with horses can become more difficult. It is important to consider you, your employees and work flow during the design of your barn. Doing barn chores morning and evening will become exhausting if your barn is not set up efficiently. I have walked through a few barns where the layout is not practical at all for doing daily chores. The barn may be absolutely beautiful and the boarders love it but they are not the ones doing the work seven days a week. I have toured barns where the hay, grain and supplements are kept in a completely different building that is a distance from where the horses are located. This may not seem important unless you live in an area where the weather can be extreme-then doing chores like this will become old very quickly and will burn out you and your employees fast.

Having your hay, grain and bedding all under one roof is important when it comes to doing chores during extreme weather.

If you are designing your barn and live in an area that normally gets a lot of snow then that will be something important to think about during the design phase. Plowing and shoveling snow and moving large snow drifts will be part of the work and a barn that has many obstacles to plow around will make the job much more difficult and time consuming especially when you need to move the snow away from the building.

The one thing you need to think about is that removing snow from the barn area will be important because as it melts some of the water could start to run into the barn. A mid-winter thaw can melt snow and ice and, if the ground is still frozen, the water has nowhere to go. This can lead to flooding in lower areas. That is why having a simple barn shell design with straight lines is so important because snow removal will take much longer and much of it could be manual if you don't have equipment that can get into all the small spaces.

Plowing snow is much easier with a barn that has many straight lines in the design.

A Self-Contained Barn

If you live in an area where the weather is extreme, and rain, sleet and snow are common place seasonally, then I would suggest designing your barn with everything you need under the same roof. Our barn is designed with Wisconsin weather in mind. We are completely self-sufficient under one roof, so that when the weather becomes severe we do not need to go outside for anything to keep the horses fed, watered and stalls freshly bedded. You need to remember more than anything else that if you are going to do this for a business, then the chores will need to be done every day of the year and throughout all types of weather. If your chore set up is not efficient and weather friendly it will become exhausting. It is a good idea to tour as many barns as you can so that you can walk through and get a good look at how they are designed with chores in mind. It will be beneficial to your planning to start looking at things through the eyes of the barn owner, manager and employees who will be doing the daily chores.

Having large overhead doors will make it much easier for your hay and bedding deliveries.

The Horse Stalls

When I walk into a barn one of the first things I look at are the horse stalls and how they are designed. There are some beautiful stall kits but some are not very functional for the basic chores that need to be done every day. There are many types of horse stalls available and I prefer the ones designed for functionality over appearance. When we were planning our stable this was one of the most exciting decisions.

I have created a list of things to think about when selecting stalls for your business. This list is to help you think about the chores and daily use for you and your boarders.

- **Grain door**-The biggest area where I see issues is the door hatch or open area to drop grain. Many stall kits will come with an opening in the grills where you can drop the grain to the corner feeder, but the only problem is that the opening is often too small for most grain buckets. It works great for scoops but not buckets. That is fine if you are only feeding a few horses but if you are feeding many and they have supplements included it will be impractical. You will find yourself opening the stall door instead of using the grain opening to feed their morning and afternoon portions. This takes more time and the grain opening on the stall is not doing what it was designed to do.

If you look you can find stall kits that come with grain door openings that are large and you can open and close them after you dropped your grain and supplements. That is what we use and it has proven to make this part of our chores much easier.

Having a large grain door for feeding grains and supplements is a benefit in many ways. It also makes it nice for dropping apples, carrots or treats into the corner feeder especially if a horse is mouthy.

- **Size of horse stalls**-There are many thoughts about the size of horse stalls and the most common sizes are 12x12 or 10x12 for premade kits. There are also many custom stall designs where you can make the stalls larger but that usually comes with an extra cost. Our stalls are 12x12 and that size has proven to be sufficient for any size horse. Once you start building smaller stalls then you could have an issue with very large horses that come to your barn. Stall size becomes an issue when a barn owner has pre-determined a revenue target for the stable and now needs more horses stalled to meet the goal. The common thought, and I believe misconception, is the more stalls then the more income but that isn't always the case. I believe with more stalls and more horses comes more overhead and labor cost and the extra pennies are not always worth the huge amount of extra work.

- **Blanket bars and stall size**-If you plan on having blanket bars on your stalls then make sure you measure the stall kits to find out if there is room to hang the bars. With many smaller stall kits there is not enough room to hang a blanket bar because when the door is completely open the area remaining is smaller than most standard blanket bars. It is best to double check and make sure the add-ons that you want for each stall will fit in the space allocated.

- **Stall fronts and grill design**-Deciding on stall fronts and grill design is not a simple thing anymore with so many options available. The one thing to think about when looking at grills and stall kits are how the stall grills are put together. Many are welded and I have seen a few kits where the welding is done poorly and there are sharp edges where a horse can easily get cut. Also consider whether the grills are easy to repair if a horse bends one. I prefer stall grills that can be replaced if a horse damages one so you aren't stuck with bent grills that look terrible. This can be more difficult if the grills are welded together. There are kits that are designed so that you can easily replace bent grills to keep your stalls looking nice.

If you are looking for open front stalls where the horse can hang their head over the grill, then you will also find many assorted styles and kits. These are nice for the horse and people love to walk down an aisle and see all the heads peeking over the front. The issue that you need to be aware of with these types of stalls occurs if your aisle way is small or used for a cross-tie area. This can create issues with horses in the cross-tie area if they have heads reaching out to them on both sides. If you have designated areas where the horses are cross-tied away from the stalls, then it is not an issue. The other problem that could become a significant issue is when you have clients that can't control their horse and the horse is pulling them towards every head that is reaching over the stall fronts.
In a perfect world we all would love to have the horses we care for looking over the stall fronts with ears forward and eagerness in their eyes, but the reality is

that with a boarding barn it might turn out to create more issues and unsafe situations than you planned for. I would suggest looking at many different types of stall kits and think of chores and functionality when deciding which kind to buy.

Deciding on your stall design can take time with so many options available.

Lighting For Your Barn

It is important to have good lighting in your barn, especially in the grooming bays and wash stalls. Remember that veterinarians and farriers will be using those areas when they are working on a horse. Good arena lighting is necessary. There are several choices of lighting to choose from and the prices will vary. When we first built our indoor arena many years ago the recommended choice was the high bay metal halide lights. They were very bright but costly to use. It is important to make sure you don't spend extra money on extra lights that you don't need. Asking an electrician or a professional from your electric company to help you figure out how many lights you need for the size arena you have is recommended.

Lighting has changed a lot over the last few years and when it was time for us to change the lights in our arena we switched to LED bulbs which are much more efficient and cost less monthly to keep on. If you decide to use fluorescent lights and you live in a cold-weather climate, make sure the lights are rated for cold weather. Be practical and purchase fixtures and bulbs that are going to be efficient to keep operating costs at a minimum. Depending on the size of your barn and arena, you will be using a lot of lights and the cost to keep them on will add up monthly. Also, don't forget about the outside floodlights for your barn. You will be doing chores often when it is still a little dark in the morning as well as the evening and having good lighting is essential.

Special note-To help save on electricity and costs for an enclosed barn or indoor arena, consider adding skylight ceiling panels or skylight side panels. They are a wonderful way to get more natural light into your barn and they also help cut down the amount of electricity you use and that will save you money.

Be smart about how you design this part of your barn and I encourage you to have a professional walk through your plans with you to make the most out of the lighting you will need to put in.

Water—So Important!

Out of all the things you need to think about when starting a horse boarding business I believe water is near the top of the list. Water can make your job easy or it will make your job extremely difficult, especially if you live in an area that gets below freezing temperatures much of the winter. Deciding on whether you want automatic waterers in your stalls or water buckets is a big decision and each come with a different price tag.

If you choose to put in automatic waterers then you need to make sure your barn will stay above thirty-two degrees so that you don't have frozen pipes or worse, broken pipes! When checking into the cost for digging and piping the water to your barn and adding the automatic waterers, I would make sure you have your barn insulated or heated well enough to keep it above the freezing mark or have an alternative plan when the temperatures drop. I have been to a couple of barns that have a system in place where they can turn off their water when the temperatures become very cold and then they use heater water buckets in the stalls. This kind of system is a great idea but you need to make sure you have an alternative water supply if you turn off the main water to the barn. This might not be a possibility if you are buying an established barn that is not set up like this but if you are building brand new then it is something to definitely check into. Don't forget you'll need electrical outlets in each stall if you are going to use heated water buckets in the wintertime. It is important to make sure they are placed high enough that even the tallest horse cannot reach them. When installing your outlets make sure that the cord for the heated bucket will reach. Depending on the brand of heated buckets, the cords come in different lengths which can make things challenging if you decide to switch brands of buckets down the road.

Having a licensed electrician do all your electric work including the outlets will help insure you have everything in order with safety for the horses being the top priority.

Location of your water hydrant is very important because you will be using it two to three times a day when filling up buckets. When designing your barn, make sure you give this topic consideration and walk through other barns to evaluate how they have their water access set up so that you get ideas. Location is significant when putting in your water hydrants. The same will be very true for filling up large water tanks in your paddocks. If your hydrant is far away from the water tanks, then dragging the hose to the tanks will become challenging work and if the weather is cold and wet then it becomes even more difficult. One of the best investments we made at our farm was when we installed automatic waterers in all our paddocks. The initial cost was high, but it has paid for itself many times over and the labor of filling the water tanks is gone! Heating the water in the wintertime is not expensive at all compared to a hundred-gallon water tank. It is worth checking into.

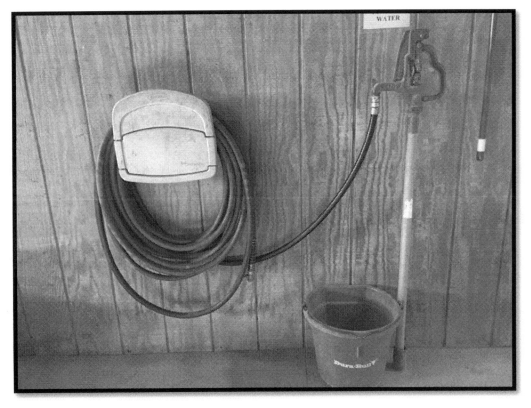

Location of your water hydrants will be important to the ease of daily chores.

There is always going to be costs involved whether you are filling up buckets and water tanks or heating the water during the wintertime. It is a good idea to get estimates and find out how much a heater bucket or large water tank cost on the average to keep heated during a full month of cold weather. If you have twenty-seven heater buckets in your barn like we do, then the cost will add up real quick and you don't want to be caught off guard when the bill comes in.

I believe it takes a year of dealing with all kinds of weather to get a good idea of how expensive it will be to heat your water and the added labor involved. You might start with water tanks and down the road realize it is worth the initial cost to put in automatic waterers outside. The one thing that often gets overlooked is the electric that needs to be run out to the water tanks or automatic waterers. Make sure you talk with an electrician to see what your options are for getting power out to each paddock. If you are digging for a water line then that would be a good time to add the power line as well.

The weather might be frigid outside but the water is luke-warm.

Outdoor Shelters

There are many different outdoor shelter designs that you can choose from. I have seen pre-made shelters that come to your home completely assembled. You can also find many kits where you can order the supplies and assemble it at your place. I don't believe it matters what you choose as long as you set up something that is sturdy and large enough for all the horses to get into easily.

There are a couple of things I want you to think about when you are purchasing run-in shelters. The first one is to make sure you have the corner posts down deep enough into the ground so that you don't have any problems when a storm comes up. My husband and I experienced this first hand when two of our run-in shelters blew completely over after a huge storm because the corner posts were not put deep enough into the ground. I would also suggest adding cement to the hole around the posts to secure it even more. The second thing is to make sure the kit you purchase is well made. Horses are extremely hard on run-in shelters and they will run and kick inside of them and pretty soon your shelter is dented from one end to the other. Even when they use their run-in for a scratching post it can really do damage over time.

Outdoor shelters come in many designs and sizes. The most important thing to think about when purchasing a shelter kit is to make sure it is large enough for the number of horses that will be using it. There is nothing worse than to see horses standing out in bad weather unable to get into the shelter.

~3~

Designing Your Riding Arenas

The Indoor Riding Arena

When we were in the design phase of our indoor riding arena I was surprised at how complicated it quickly became. I wanted to make sure I had the perfect footing for our arena and everyone had a different opinion about the type of sand to use for the footing. I started to take note of the footing in other riding arenas while we were in the planning stages of our barn.

Take your time when planning your arena and look at as many arenas as you possibly can before you finalize what you want. It is one of the most important decisions you will make.

There are many different footings you can use in a riding arena and it can become very expensive. Our riding arena is 80 ft. x 200 ft. in size and the amount of sand that we needed was not cheap. I have been in some arenas where the sand is so deep that it becomes difficult for the horses using them especially if they are not accustomed to moving in deep sand. The depth of sand used in an arena is very important because if the arena sand is too deep it can cause sore and even strained ligaments in the horse. On the other hand, if the arena is too shallow it can equally be hard on the horse with the pounding and concussion of their legs and hooves hitting the ground.

Depth Of Arena Sand

Generally a 2 ½ or 3in. base is a good depth for arena sand. One good option is washed concrete or mason sand as it has very little dust and holds up very well. It still needs to be watered now and then but the upkeep is low. It is also very easy for the horses to move in. You can add a rubber mix to the sand for more cushion and often people will add a clay mix to the sand. If you spend a little more on a good sand mix then you will have fewer issues in the long run. Dusty arenas are a big problem especially in an enclosed riding arena, and washed sand will reduce how often you need to water the arena.

Generally a 2 ½ or 3in. base is a good depth for arena sand. Some riding disciplines will require a little deeper sand.

How Much Sand Should I Order?

This is a question that everyone will ask themselves when they are designing and building their riding arena. Leaving this decision to the professionals who will be delivering your sand seems like the normal thing to do but buyer beware! It is much easier to add sand if you don't have enough then to move the excess sand out of the arena after it has been dumped. This situation happened to us when we ordered sand for our indoor arena and we spent many hours removing quite a bit of sand and we spent much more money than we needed to. We did keep the excess sand in an area on our farm. We have used it over the years when we needed to add sand which has worked out great but it did create a lot more work in the beginning and it was money we could have used somewhere else when we needed the extra cash the most. I encourage you to measure and figure out how much sand you need and if you come up short you can always add more which is much easier than removing a ton of sand that you just had dumped.

What Size Riding Arena?

If I have learned one thing about designing a boarding facility, it is that you can't have too big of a riding arena. In many cases the barn owner realized too late that their riding arena is too small for the number of horses that are boarded at their stable. When determining your arena size I would suggest touring as many boarding barns as you can and find out how many horses are boarded and what the size is of their main riding arena. If you can, ask the barn manager how crowded the arena gets during peak hours and how many people can actually ride comfortably at the same time. I have talked to many people who have built their barn and stable and have come to realize that their arena is too small, causing overcrowding and many other issues. It is hard to enlarge the arena once it is built and the roof is on so good planning is necessary.

Our indoor arena is 80 ft. x 200 ft. and it is appropriately sized for the twenty-seven horses that are housed in our main barn and the seven horses that are part of our current outside board program. Even during the busiest part of the day when the kids come to ride after school there is room enough to ride safely and be out of each other's way. The size of the arena significantly determines cost so a large arena adds to your budget but you will never regret investing in a large indoor arena.

Building a large enough riding arena to appropriately accommodate the size boarding facility you will have is important.

If you are going to be a general boarding operation then I have listed a few things to think about that will be part of daily arena activities and will help you get a good understanding of why size does matter and bigger is better especially when it comes to safety in the arena.

Different Riding Disciplines And Uses For The Arena

- **Trail riders**-Trail obstacles and equipment
- **Dressage**—Using patterns for testing and training
- **Jumping**—Jump standards and equipment
- **Speed**—Barrels, poles and other speed equipment
- **Pleasure riders of any discipline**
- **Carts**—They can take up a lot of space and if you allow carts in your arena you will want to make sure you have plenty of room for others that are riding at the same time.

- **Lunging**–Many people lunge their horse and it will take up a lot of room with the lunge line.
- **Playing with balls and other equipment on/off the horse**
- **Using ground poles**–ground poles will be one of the pieces of equipment that your clients use the most often. They are used for so many training techniques and they can take up space so if your arena is small it can make it challenging to ride around them
- **Lessons**–If you are going to board horses then you will likely have a lesson program, especially if you are a larger barn. The arena congestion and conflicts can occur very quickly if the trainer is giving a lesson and others don't feel comfortable riding around or through the lesson. Having a well-sized arena for a large number of horses will help alleviate this problem.
- **Young horses in training**–Young horses are predictably unpredictable and their training and activities can present unique obstacles in an arena. If your arena is too small then there will not be a good place to work with them away from others and distractions.
- **Clinics**–Many boarding stables will offer clinics throughout the year and having enough area for a clinic is important especially if the clinician is doing group lessons.

The list of considerations for arena planning is a starting point for you. You may not have all these scenarios but if you are planning on a multidiscipline barn then there is a good chance you will have many of them. Think ahead and it will save you much frustration in the long run.

Daily And Yearly Maintenance

A beautiful arena doesn't just happen and to keep it in mint condition takes continual attention and maintenance. Dragging an arena should be done often to make sure it stays level and to keep the footing nice to ride in. I believe dragging an arena at least five days a week will keep it lasting longer with less wear and tear in the long run.

The amount of traffic in your arena will make a difference on how often you need to do substantial maintenance on your arena. A heavy overhaul of your riding arena once a year is highly recommended to keep your arena in pristine condition. This will include pulling all the sand away from the walls and bringing it in towards the center of the arena. Once you have pulled the sand back you can drag and level it out by adding sand in areas that need it. You will have much more sand than you previously thought once you pull the sand that built up over time away from the walls.

Keeping an arena in excellent condition takes daily upkeep and yearly maintenance.

Equipment Needed

The most common piece of equipment to use is a harrow. They are easy to attach to a 4-wheeler or tractor and do a good job. There are a few types of drags on the market and we use a harrow and an Arena Rascal Pro drag. The Arena Rascal drag will let you set the depth that you want to drag the sand where a regular harrow is very limited on the depth you can use. If you are on a budget, then a harrow will do a respectable job. We used a harrow for many years and still keep one for certain maintenance jobs we need to do at our facility. It also helps to have a skid loader or tractor with a bucket to pull the sand back when you are doing heavy maintenance on your arena.

The Arena Rascal Pro is a great piece of equipment for keeping your arena dragged and maintained.

Every horse stable will benefit from having a harrow to maintain arenas and paddocks.

The Outdoor Riding Arena

Your outdoor riding arena will have many of the same considerations as far as usage and size but the footing and design might be a little different depending on where you live and the weather you have. Flooding in outdoor arenas can be a huge problem if you do not have proper drainage and sand to handle the rainy season. The maintenance of the outdoor arena will also vary a bit if you live where the ground freezes during the winter. When the ground becomes frozen hard during winter and then thaws as the days become warmer, the ground will shift and that can greatly affect your outdoor riding arena over time. Not only can the ground move and sink in areas but the wood for the fencing can move and shift and even warp overtime. When you are buying your wood for the outdoor arena make sure it is treated lumber that can withstand the weather and it will last much longer. Untreated wood will rot and become weak very quickly.

If you live in an area that has four seasons then you will probably be adding sand much more often then you will with your indoor arena. If you find out after you have built your arena that you are in a low area and you are constantly flooding in parts of your arena then you will want to add a drain tile to get the water flowing and draining much quicker. The weather can play havoc with an outdoor riding arena so when you are designing your arena make sure to factor in weather, drainage and a well-designed base to handle the seasons.

Making sure your outdoor arena has good drainage for the rainy season is important.

~4~

The Tack Room

Before we built our boarding facility I toured many other barns and I especially enjoyed looking at the tack rooms and taking in the smell of leather and the gorgeous saddles and bridles. These days I always look at tack rooms with functionality in mind and to see how organized they are for the clients. It is amazing to me how many tack rooms are heavily packed with so much tack you can hardly make it into the room. Many are too small for the number of boarders and very disorganized. Another issue I have noticed in tack rooms is that some boarders will have plenty of space for their tack while others have very little room. When it comes down to designing your tack room you should plan adequate room for each boarder at your facility and everyone should have an equal amount of space. If you keep these two things in mind then you will have fewer problems in the future with clients, drama and overcrowding.

What Size Tack Room Should I Build?

The size of your tack room is important to consider and plan because it will either make your job easier or much more challenging as your clients bring in more equipment and other horse related items. Will you have individual cabinets where everything including the saddles needs to fit inside? Will each boarder get one or two saddle racks and what about bridle hooks? If they are allowed to bring their own cabinet what size should it be? What if their cabinet doesn't fit? These are questions you need to ask yourself because they are significant issues you will deal with. Setting limits on what people can store will be important.

To give you an idea of a good tack room size ratio compared to the number of horses at your barn, this is what we have: Our facility houses twenty-seven horses in our big barn. With that many horses we built two large 12ft. x 24ft. tack rooms. Each boarder gets two saddle racks and two bridle hooks. There is plenty of room for a cabinet underneath. After many years of boarding horses, I believe this amount of tack space is sufficient for the number of horses housed in our barn. We also have a smaller barn with its own separate tack room for our outdoor boarded horses and owners in which I have used the same policy and it has worked out great.

When designing your tack room you need to really think about the things you will allow and not allow clients to store in the tack room. If you don't have a policy about tack room storage then you will have people bringing everything possible and stuffing it wherever they can.

Keeping tack rooms organized will help reduce issues between clients.

Using Dehumidifiers

If your tack room is a completely closed room and insulated, then I would suggest putting a dehumidifier in during the warm weather to keep the leather from molding. There is nothing worse than walking into a cold and damp tack room where you can feel the moisture. If your clients' saddles and bridles start to mold, you will have bigger issues. If you want to run a professional business and do things the right way, then make sure you have dehumidifiers running when the warm weather calls for it and your boarders will appreciate it.

~5~

Wash Stall And Grooming Areas

The wash stall is something that is important to have at a boarding stable. The type of weather you have year round will definitely make a difference on the type of wash stall you will design. While boarding horses in Southern California there was no need for an indoor wash stall. We just used a hose outside. In an area where the weather gets cold a wash stall with hot water is a huge plus for any boarding operation.

Designing Your Wash Stall

Your wash stall doesn't need to be fancy, it just needs to be functional, easy to use and easy to maintain. You need to make sure you have a well-built drainage system that can handle the large amount of hair, mud and dirt that will go down it. If you don't take the time to talk to a professional about the proper drainage for this type of business, you might have large plumbing bills later on down the road for repair and maintenance of the drains.

Getting your clients in the habit of cleaning the drain catcher after every wash will help ensure that you won't have plumbing issues. Writing up a list of wash stalls rules is important to help keep the wash stall clean and in operating condition.

The Outside Wash Area

If you plan on having an outside wash area, having a designated place with good drainage is very important. It is recommended to design your wash area with good footing so that it doesn't become muddy with use. You can use rubber mats as an alternative to a gravel bed and they work great. It is important to make sure your outside wash area is far enough away from your building to prevent any water from seeping into the building and also to prevent any accidents with horses. I have seen horses dance around while being hosed off and they will move next to a building and kick out and you don't want them to get hurt as well as cause damage to your building.

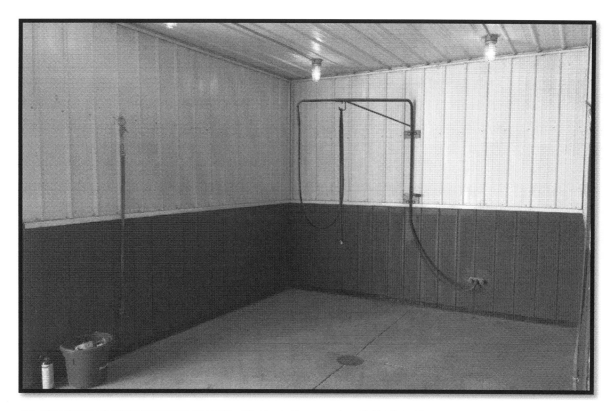

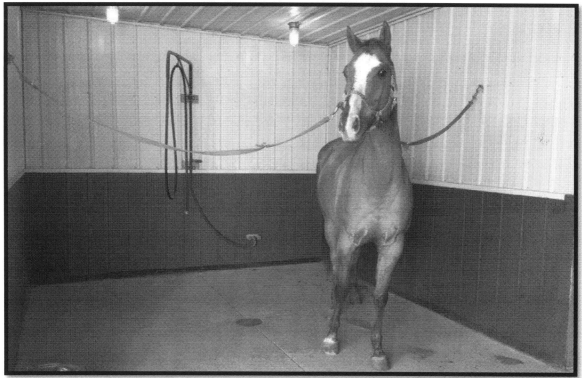

Location as well as proper drainage for the indoor wash stall is important in both making sure the horses are safe while using it and that the plumbing is working well to handle the dirt and hair that will come off the horses being washed.

The Designated Grooming Areas

If I had to build our barn all over the one thing I would change is the number of grooming bays we have. Our facility is large and we only have one grooming bay-which is definitely not enough. We designed our barn with many crosstie areas throughout our aisle way which can be used for grooming. In retrospect, I wished we had built more grooming bays because they keep the horse out of the aisle way and that makes it safe when the other horses walk by. It is advantageous to have grooming bays for clipping, vet calls, farrier work and doing anything that takes time and may result in an agitated horse. When a horse becomes nervous it is nice to know you are not in anyone's way!

Our grooming bay is 12ft. x 12 ft. in size but you easily can make smaller grooming bays and still have plenty of room. In our grooming bay we have extra lighting, electrical outlets that are easy to reach and we also have cross-ties and a single-tie for the horse that doesn't do well or panics when cross-tied. Having designated grooming areas are important and will help cut down on the chaos that can happen very easily in a larger barn.

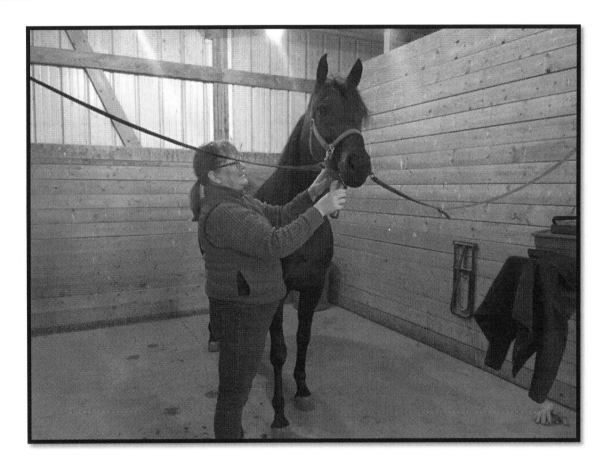

Having designated grooming areas is a plus for any boarding stable no matter the size.

~6~

The Lounge, Viewing Room And Bathroom

Having a lounge, viewing room and bathroom are optional amenities that you want to seriously consider for your boarding business. If you live in an area where an indoor arena is a must then having a viewing room/lounge is a huge asset so that your clients, family and friends can watch riders without having to be in the arena. If your arena is not heated then having an area where people can warm up on cold days will be appreciated by all and will add value to your business.

The Lounge/Viewing Room Design

The lounge and viewing room do not need to be huge or fancy, it just needs to be comfortable for your clients. I have walked into many lounge/viewing rooms in barns and some are very impressive and beautiful but that comes with a hefty price tag. Start off simple and you can create a cozy lounge on a tight budget.

The most important part of your lounge/viewing room will be the windows to the arena. If you are going to put in large windows then make sure you buy high quality thick glass that can withstand a horse touching it. Shatterproof glass is your best option in this setting.

Having designated areas for viewing the arena and people riding, along with conversation and relaxation, will help make sure that the lounge serves everyone's purpose and reduces conflict. A small kitchen area is a feature that will be appreciated.

Working on a small budget will not prevent you from providing a welcoming environment. Almost everything that we have in our lounge from appliances to furniture was purchased used and cost very little. If you are on a budget, then take the time to shop around and you can find some really great deals.

Your lounge/viewing room doesn't need to be fancy, just practical and comfortable. Keeping it simple when on a budget is important.

The Bathroom

Putting a bathroom into a barn comes with an added cost but what a huge asset it is in the long run. If you decide to put in a bathroom, then you will need to have a waste disposal system such as a mound system or septic system. Each state building code will define the requirements for the installation of a bathroom and you will need to ask your building contractor about the building codes and regulations. You might need to have approval from your township or city and they will tell you what the specifications are for an added bathroom.

A bathroom may not be the deciding factor in whether a person comes to your barn or not but it will add to the comfort of your clients and employees and add value to your business.

~7~

Hay, Grain And Shavings Room

When I tour boarding barns and stables I now look at how they are designed from the employee point of view. After many years of feeding horses, turning horses out and cleaning stalls I have come to realize that if you don't have a well-planned design for the daily chores, you will not only burn out your employees but it will cost you a lot more money with the extra time it takes to do chores. This is a huge part of barn management and it is often overlooked.

The type of weather you have will make a difference in how your barn and stable is designed but the one thing that stays the same is creating ease, convenience and organization of doing chores. The more organized your feed program is the less time you will spend in the barn feeding. The same is true for cleaning stalls, bedding and handling horses for daily turnout. Always remember that time is money!

If you live in a state where the weather becomes frigid or it rains often then I would suggest building your barn with hay, grain and shavings all under one roof that is connected to the area where the horses are housed. I have walked through many barns where the hay and shavings are in a completely different building and that makes it especially difficult when you have snow, ice and rain. If you are doing the chores you will quickly recognize the importance of easy access to all your supplies in order to stay efficient when doing chores. If you are renting a barn that is not set up with everything under one roof you may not have options to change it but you might want to look at possible alternatives for doing chores. Discussing issues with the barn owner about possible changes is a good start. It will definitely be worth investigating if you find yourself in this situation.

The Hay Storage Room

When designing the hay room you want to decide what kind of hay you will be storing. If you are going to be feeding large bales (900 lb. squares) then you want to make sure you have room to drive a skid loader or tractor in to stack the hay and move it around when you need to lower the bales on top to the ground.

If you are using small squares, then the room can be designed differently because you can store the hay much higher than the large bales or round bales. With the small bales you will need man-power and most likely a hay elevator.

When designing a new facility make certain that you plan for change. You may find that you want to change the type of bales that you use and you will need to be able to adjust for that change whether it be storage, moving the bales or the equipment needed.

I want to stress how important your hay room will become especially when the weather has been less than perfect. Make this part of your barn design a top priority and remember that you will be doing chores every day of the year and through all types of weather. Do it right the first time and you will never regret it.

Keeping Hay From Molding While Storing

When storing your hay on a cement or dirt floor I would suggest placing long 2 x 4 ft. planks of wood or wooden pallets down as a foundation for your hay. This will keep the hay off the floor and away from direct contact with ground moisture. Ground moisture is not a problem if you are storing your hay above your stable in a hay loft where the floor is made of wood.

Keeping hay off the ground with wood pallets or 2 x 4's will help keep the hay from molding on the bottom.

Grain Storage Room

Having a separate area for grains and supplements is important. You will be feeding grain and supplements twice a day for most horses and you want to be able to do it fast, efficiently and with ease. This is another area where people make it unnecessarily complicated and it just needs to be a well-organized, separate area.

When setting up your grain room you need to decide how you are going to offer this part of your feeding program. Are you going to supply grain only and not allow your boarders to bring in their own grain or will you give each boarder a choice? At our facility we offer three types of grain (for a fee) and allow the boarders to bring in their own grain if they would prefer a different kind than what we offer. With twenty-seven horses in one barn I have many different types of grains and supplements to feed and the grain alone can take up a lot of room. I have organized my grain room so that each storage container is the same shape and size and can hold two bags (100 lbs.) of grain and protects the grain from dirt, moisture and rodents.

Keeping the grain in containers with lids will help keep the moisture and mice out.

Individual horse supplements need to be managed alongside the feed. If you will be feeding many different kinds of supplements then you want it to be well organized in order to save space and time. If your boarders' horses are on multiple supplements it will be helpful to have your boarders bag or container their monthly supplies. This will not only save you time when doing chores but will save you space in your grain room. Don't be surprised when the area you have designated for your grains and supplements becomes full as your boarders try new products.

Having multiple supplements put into easy to open containers and baggies will save a lot of time when doing this part of your chores twice a day.

Keeping Grain From Becoming Wet Or Moldy

When storing grain in a room that has cement or dirt flooring do not put your grain bags directly on the floor. They can get moisture in them though the cement and dirt floor during the wet and humid months and can ruin your grain. Always keep your grain bags on some kind of wood pallet or plastic base to keep them off the ground. Be careful to rotate your stored grain bags in order to make sure that the grain does not spoil or become pest infested. It is recommended to have the client's grain stored in sealable containers that are clearly marked with name and contents.

Keeping the grain in a dry location and off the ground will help insure that it doesn't get wet or moldy.

Bedding For The Stalls

Not only will bedding be one of your largest monthly expenses but it takes up a lot of room. Bedding, whether it be in bulk shavings or bagged, seems to be an overlooked item when it comes to planning storage. I have walked through a few barns where bedding was not thought about during the design process and once the barn was operational the employees quickly realized that access to the shavings was problematic. Creating a storage place with easy access to bulk or bagged shavings is important for the ease of daily stall cleaning.

If you are designing your barn or stable, I would encourage you to think about having your bedding in the same building in which the horses are stalled. I want you to remember that cleaning stalls and laying bedding is very easy when the sun is shining and the weather is great but once the days become cold and it rains or snows every other day you will quickly regret having your bedding in another building outside the barn. It will become physically taxing on whoever is cleaning the stalls daily and that is when people get burned out and start to do a poor job. If you have the resources to build or can add-on to an existing barn to have your bedding under the same roof you will find it very beneficial to streamlining your operations and cost management.

Different Ways To Store Bedding

Consider the delivery and storage of bedding when in your design phase of your facility. Whether you decide to use bagged or loose bedding it is important to plan for a storage location that is convenient for delivery, storage and access. Bagged bedding is generally a more expensive option but can be an excellent solution depending on your needs. In some areas you can have a semi load of bagged or bulk shavings delivered and unloaded in a convenient location so you don't have to go very far to get your bedding.

When we first built our barn I didn't have a realistic view of the work involved with bedding. I purchased hundreds of bags of bedding and didn't think twice about it. I quickly realized the huge expense that came with bagged bedding and bringing the bags to each stall daily was more physical work than I imagined. Transporting and opening bags of shaving for many stalls is back breaking work and it is something most people don't realize until they have done it for a few days. When I started ordering bulk shavings, I cut our bedding bill in half and the labor was cut in half also. That one decision provided significant cost savings in both materials and labor!

No matter what kind of bedding you decide to use, think about your storage location and convenience for your employees because that will become a very important part of your daily chores and stall cleaning.

No matter the type of bedding you decide to use, make sure you have a storage place that is easy to access during all types of weather.

~8~

Horse Trailer Parking And Haul-Ins

Many of your boarders will own horse trailers and will need a place to keep the trailer when it is not in use. If you have enough room and can provide trailer parking it will be a huge benefit for your boarders. Not every stable has the room to store trailers and I don't believe it will make or break a boarding deal but it is a nice perk.

If you are going to set up a designated area for trailer parking I would suggest that each person who owns a trailer gets a designated spot for the duration of the time they board at your barn-unless you change it. I have experienced tension between boarders because they felt someone parked in "their" spot even though at the time no one had designated spaces for their horse trailers. Assigning designated spaces for trailers provides security and consistency to boarders and reduces the risk of anxiety over losing a parking spot or learning to park a large trailer in a new spot.

Having a designated spot for each horse trailer will help keep things organized.

Haul-Ins

If your dream is to start a large facility where you will host clinics and possibly horse shows then you are going to need parking for all the horse trailers that come for the events. Even if you have a small operation and you only have a few people haul-in for lessons, accommodating truck and trailer parking can be problematic if you don't plan for it!

One of the mistakes we made when we built our barn was that we didn't create enough parking area for horse trailers in the front or around our barn. We host many clinics and when the participants arrive it can be very challenging to safely park all the trucks and trailers-especially in the seasons where the ground is wet, soft or snow covered. In the summer when it is hot and dry, it is easy to park trailers on the grass but if we would allow that in the spring or fall the weight of the trailers would tear up our lawn. If you live in a hot and dry part of the country then you probably won't have this issue but in the Midwest it can be challenging during the wet months.

If you plan on hosting clinics or horse shows then it is very important to make sure you have an area designated for truck and trailer parking.

~9~

Designing Your Paddocks And Pastures

One of the most important and controversial parts of your boarding operation will be planning your paddocks (or dry lots) and pastures. You ask: How hard can it be? You will be determining how many paddocks and pastures you will need for the number of horses you will board. You will also need to map out the paddocks and spaces for pastures. Then you plan for the contingencies: new horses needing isolation, old horses, convalescing horses, stallions (if you will board stallions) to name a few. That wasn't too hard so let's move on to the really difficult issues...

- Regional weather
- Soil conditions
- Drainage
- Attitudes and preferences of boarders

The challenging part of planning your exterior land use is that you need to understand and prioritize many elements that are outside of your control. Planning for the contingencies is very important to managing your paddocks, pastures and horses that will be using them daily.

Your stable location will determine what you can offer for turnout. Having horses in a heavily populated, consistently warm and dry state while growing up was much different from having horses in a state where there is plenty of rural space and four seasons. I never experienced pasture turnout or large paddocks for horses until I moved to the country and with that came a huge learning curve. If you are going to start a boarding stable in a large metropolitan area where space is limited, then you will design your turnout much differently than in an area where you have large acreage to work with.

Your herd size will vary depending on the amount of acreage you have for pastures and paddocks.

Herd Size And Your Paddocks

When designing your paddocks or dry lots the first thing I want you to think about will involve the size of the herds. Several elements need to be addressed when determining placement and design of your paddocks. Herd size and placement of paddocks are two major considerations. The lay out of your land will be a determining factor in planning of your paddocks as well. If you know how many horses you are going to board then the next step is to figure out where you are going to put the horses when they are turned out and the frequency and length of turn-out.

I have listed a few questions to ask yourself when you are in the design phase of planning your paddocks.

- Are you going to have large herd sizes or smaller ones?
- Are you going to offer private turnout for just a few or for each horse that is boarded?
- Will you separate mares and geldings or have a few mixed herds?

- Will you offer private paddocks for horses that are on the mend from an injury or health rehabilitation?
- Will you have separate paddocks for new horses coming in that need time to adjust before being put into a herd?
- Will you have very young horses at your barn that cannot be put into a large herd until they become a little older?
- Will you have very senior horses at your barn that need extra care and smaller herd sizes?
- Will you board stallions that require a private secure paddock?
- Will you offer night turnout?

These questions will help you think about the different scenarios including the different horses and their needs. If I can give one word of advice, if you have the space and are putting up fencing-build extra paddocks. You will never regret creating too many paddocks but there is a good chance you will regret not making enough. It's extremely hard to go back and redesign paddocks once the poles are in the ground, the fencing is up and the horses are at your barn. We had to redesign our paddocks twice after we first opened because of unforeseen situations and it disrupted the rest of the chores we needed to get done each day. We will talk about that more in herd management in another chapter.

Once you design how many paddocks or dry lots you need then you need to think about fencing, water and easy access for feeding and ground maintenance.

Fencing

There are many types of fencing used for keeping horses in paddocks and pastures. Of course we all would love to have the long running wood fence that makes your place look like a Kentucky thoroughbred farm but most people can't afford that kind of look and intensive maintenance. There are many alternatives that work great and are much less expensive to install.

Wood Fencing

If you are going to put up some wood fencing then you will want to make sure you have some kind of electric fence line running on the inside to keep the horses from chewing on the wood and pushing on it to eat the grass on the other side. Horses are hard on wood fencing and they will push on it until the fence starts to move and slowly lean out as if it is going to fall over. Electric fencing will usually prevent destruction of the wood fencing as long as it is correctly installed. Wood fencing will have a higher cost to purchase and install as well as requiring significant maintenance but if you have the financial resources it is always a great way to design your paddocks and pastures.

Wood fencing is beautiful but the cost to install and maintain can be expensive.

Electric Fencing

Electric fencing is easy to put up and is inexpensive to use. We have used electric fencing for almost fifteen years and we are still using the same brand that we installed when we first opened and it has withstood the test of forty horses through all four seasons. Electric braid fencing is great because it won't loosen like tape fencing when the winds become strong and it is easy to keep tight with fence tighteners' that are on the fencing when you install it. I have found electric braid to be very safe and if a horse pulls a strand down with their leg they can get away from it fast and easy. Electric braid for fencing is one of the safest fencing options on the market.

Electric braid fencing is easy to install and very reasonably priced.

Electric Tape Fencing

Electric tape fencing looks fantastic when it is first installed because it gives a look that simulates wood fencing. The problem I have found with electric tape is that when it becomes extremely windy the tape can become loose. The same would be true for when the seasons change and the corner poles move in the ground due to mud or frost in the ground. The tension from the fencing can move the poles that are holding the electric tape and soon the tape starts to sag. It can be never-ending, time consuming and difficult to get the tape tight again and back to that first installed new look you once had. I have had friends who started off with electric tape but after a few years of dealing with sagging fencing they switched to electric braid.

With any kind of electric fencing I would suggest making sure you have your corner post dug down below the frost line. Pouring cement down in the hole around the post will help keep the post in place and keep the electric fencing from sagging.

Electric tape fencing is easy to install but can be hard to maintain if the ground becomes soft in the fall and springtime which can lead to sagging tape.

Installing T-Posts And Insulators

T-Posts are an easy and very effective way to put up electric fencing. We have put up a lot of T-posts at our farm and they are easy to move if needed and do not break or rot like wood does. If you are going to use T-posts, then you want to make sure you have them at a close enough distance from each other to keep the electric fencing straight and tight. If you have plenty of T-posts inline and if an electric braid gets pulled down, the whole fence doesn't come down.

There are different opinions regarding the safety of T-posts. If you have been around horses long enough then you know that they can get hurt on anything. If you are going to use T-posts then you will want to make sure the top of the post is covered with a secure cap so that if a horse does come in contact with the posts he doesn't get hurt from the sharp edges at the top of the T-post. I recommend using three strands of electric braid or tape and make sure you have your insulators equally lined up from post to post to give a clean look to your fencing. Your insulators will become brittle overtime due to the sun, rain and change of seasons so you will want to inspect them regularly and always keep an extra bag of insulators on hand for when one gets broken. It will happen more often then you expect.

We have used wood posts with insulators to hang electric fencing as well as T-posts. The type of fence support you choose will determine the kind of insulators you want to use. If you live in an area where you will experience all four seasons, it is suggested to make sure your wood posts are all put in deep enough and set with cement to handle the changing ground conditions. Digging below the frost line is recommended for stability. This will also help keep your wood poles straight during the muddy months.

Make sure to keep extra bags of insulators on hand for when one becomes broken. It will happen more often then you expect.

There are many good types of horse fencing and the type you decide to use will depend much on where you live. Pipe stalls and corrals are often used out west as a great option for individual outside stalls and turnouts. It doesn't matter what type of fencing you use for the horses in your care as long as it is safe and dependable.

Pipe stalls or corrals are a great option for keeping horses in an enclosed area.

~10~

Farm Equipment Needed

When boarding horses there will be many jobs that need to be done daily, weekly or yearly and you will find that you need certain kinds of equipment to help you get the jobs done. I have put together a simple list of the types of equipment needed at most barns and stables and some will be specific to the climate you live in.

- **Hay Elevator**-purchasing and storing hay each year is very labor intensive, especially if it needs to be stacked in a barn. Small bales are very common and most people are familiar with feeding small bales of hay. You will need a place to properly store the hay and getting the hay stacked up high is almost impossible without a hay elevator. Hay elevators can be costly but since many barns and stables are transitioning to the use of the large 900 lb. square bales or round bales it is easier to find a used hay elevator at a fraction of what a new one would cost.

- **Tractor**-A good working tractor that has some power will be one of the most important pieces of equipment you purchase. You will use it for everything from baling hay to bringing the wagons to the barn. You will use it to move manure and dispose of it with a manure spreader. If you have ice and snow then you will use it to spread manure on ice covered paths and paddocks and even to plow snow. A tractor is often used for feeding large bales of hay outside with attachable forks on the front.

- **Manure Spreader**- If you live in an area where you have a lot of farm land then you might get rid of the horse manure yourself with a manure spreader. Spreaders come in many sizes and you can always find a used one to do the job.

- **Skid loader**-You don't need a skid loader but it sure can make your job easier. Skid loaders are very easy to maneuver around and work well for pushing up manure and cleaning out paddocks. They turn on a dime which makes them more desirable for small areas like the inside of a run-in shed. Our skid loader is probably the most used piece of equipment on our farm besides our 4-wheeler.

You can stack large bales of hay or round bales with a skid loader and maneuvering in tight spots is much easier when the hay storage shed is full.

- **4-Wheeler**-We use our 4-wheeler with an attached wagon every day for feeding hay outside and also use it for dragging our arenas with a harrow or Arena-Pro drag. The 4-wheeler will make any job easier and you will be surprised by how much you use it. You will want to plan for some kind of equipment for dragging and maintaining the riding arenas as well as your paddocks.

The 4-wheeler and tractor will be used often on any horse farm.

~11~

Hiring Employees

When starting a horse boarding business, you need to think about the people who will be working at your stable periodically or daily. Your business may start off with you as the only employee but over time you might find you need additional help. The financial part of running a boarding business can include employees. When you design your barn to help make chores easy, fast and efficient you will then save time and money that you would otherwise be paying out to employees to get the daily chores done. No matter who is doing the chores it will affect the barn owner's bottom line.

Doing barn chores day in and day out can be exhausting at times and you will realize quickly that there are many other things that need to be done long after the regular chores are completed. The work load is really never ending when you have horses and there will always be things to fix or change. My husband and I have been doing the barn chores at our farm for many years now and we have become very efficient in our jobs because we don't want to be in the barn all day. We have learned to streamline everything so that we can finish our chores early and then we can work on other things that need to be taken care of before the evening chores begin.

Employees And Worker's Comp. Insurance

The most important thing you need to have set up before you hire your first employee is worker's compensation insurance. Working around horses and handling horses can be dangerous at times and an accident can happen anytime. I can't stress enough how important it is to carry worker's comp. for your employees.

Worker's compensation is a form of insurance providing wage replacement and medical benefits to employees injured in the course of employment. All it takes is one person getting seriously hurt while working for you and you could lose everything. Many business owners don't carry worker's comp. insurance because it is expensive and they don't want to pay for it. If you are going to run a horse business then do it right and get insurance. You have too much on the line not to have it. The cost if there is an accident can be catastrophic and you would have to pay out of pocket for the medical expenses. It happens, so you need to be prepared.

Having boarders work off their board for a reduced board rate is very common but you need to understand that if they get hurt you are still liable! It doesn't matter if they say they are doing the chores in trade for reduced board because you are still liable and will be held responsible. Barn owners need to treat all workers as employees and give them a paycheck so they are covered by worker's comp. and you are protected.

Worker's compensation is calculated according to how much you pay out to your employees. The more you pay employees the more you will need to pay into worker's comp. The payments are usually established based on what you estimate you will be paying employees annually. Rates are adjusted at the end of the year depending on what your actual incurred labor expenditures were spent in labor for the year. When purchasing worker's comp. insurance, your agent will explain in detail how it works and how it will be set up for your specific business.

When looking to purchase worker's compensation insurance, you can ask your equine business insurance carrier who to contact. They can also help you through the process and answer any questions you may have about how it works.

Hiring Employees

When hiring employees to work at your barn you will quickly find out that the basic chores like cleaning stalls and feeding hay is something that most people can learn to do easily. Finding people who can handle the horses properly when walking them outside for the day or bringing them back in can be challenging. I am very careful when I hire people to handle the horses at our barn because I know that some of our horses are very difficult to handle and I don't want accidents or horses getting loose because the person did not know what they were doing. Make sure that the people handling horses have horse knowledge and know how to handle even the most challenging horses safely and effectively. If you are not careful in this area then you could be opening up your stable for many accidents that didn't need to happen. I want you to remember that who you hire at your barn is a direct reflection on you and your business. How they treat the horses and talk to other boarders will say a lot about you as a barn owner and manager. Be cautious and smart in who you hire and it will go a long way in promoting the type of boarding facility you have.

Working Off The Board

I believe it is much better to pay your employees an hourly wage then trying to figure out a board rate reduction. When you do a trade of board for work that is done, then it always seems like the hours worked become confusing and either party can feel they are getting the short end of the stick. Simply stated, the potential for conflict is not worth it.

As a business owner it is much better and strongly recommended to pay an hourly wage and when they get their paycheck they can use that as money to help pay their board. They are still getting a reduction in board but it is just being handled in a more accountable, professional and businesslike manner. It will also reduce confusion on how many hours were actually worked and that will result in less conflict for both parties.

Expectations For Employees

If you have never had employees before then you are about to learn a lot about yourself and being the boss. There are going to be times when it is not fun being in charge but that is true for any person that is running a business. You will have employees that will be reliable workers and can do almost anything without being supervised. They are on time every day and are very dependable. And then just like any other business, you will have employees that are late to work every day and don't think there is anything wrong with showing up ten minutes after their start time. You will have employees that feel that work time is also social media time and spend much of their work time on their phone. It will be up to you to identify and address problems when you see employees wasting work time on their phone or taking many extra breaks.

For some reason many people don't look at mucking out stalls or doing chores as a "real job" and they do things that they wouldn't do if they were working at another job. It is your responsibility to set expectations right from the start and let them know what is allowed and not allowed while working. If you do this in the beginning you will weed out the people who really don't want to work and then you will attract others that would love to work at a barn and they will do a good job. It is not worth the headaches you will have to keep someone on that can't follow your work expectations.

I would encourage you to write up a description of what is expected with the job and what is not acceptable while on the clock. Also providing a description of safety practices when cleaning stalls with horses in them and handling horses is important. Getting your employees on track right from the start will set the tone for a positive and well-run boarding business.

~12~

Buying An Established Horse Boarding Business

Purchasing an existing boarding business will come with its own set of challenges. I often talk with people who have purchased an established boarding facility and one of the largest hurdles they need to overcome has to do with making changes to the business. Many times the purchase of a boarding facility will come with the clients still boarding there and many of them will have been at the same place for years. This can make change very challenging. Let's face it, most people don't really like change even when those changes will be a good thing. We become very comfortable in how things have been for a long time and it is hard to break that cycle.

If you are buying an established boarding business it is important to evaluate all aspects of the operation before determining if changes would be beneficial. Some barns need so much work that the owners have to practically start from the beginning while others only need some cosmetic work. Fixing up a barn with fresh paint and cosmetic improvements will be the easy part. The existing boarders will love those kinds of changes. The tough part will occur as you start to look at how the barn is run. Creating new barn and arena rules will be a huge undertaking if the barn has very little or no previous experience with rules. Changing the feeding program and how chores are done in the morning and afternoon may be another challenge. Making these changes will most likely come with some disagreement from the staff and boarding clients. Nonetheless, you must now look at the business as your financial investment and you don't want to start losing money right from the start.

Be Prepared For Turnover

When I work with a new barn owner and we are talking about the changes they are going to make to the existing program I always tell them that they need to be prepared for turnover. The truth is they are going to lose some boarders because they will not like all the changes. It is no different than any other business and you need to be mentally and financially prepared for this.

One of the most important things you can do as a new barn owner is to keep the communication open and provide frequent updates to your current boarders about changes. Be willing to take the time to listen to concerns and answer questions honestly, directly and clearly. This is the time when they need to have a clear understanding of what is going on and give them time to adjust and soak it all in. Even though you might lose a few clients I believe most people will hang on to see what happens with the new changes and they might come to find out they like it much better. It just takes time, patience and care.

Past Record Keeping

The best thing you can do is ask for the financials and record keeping from the past five years if the previous barn owner has any. Unfortunately, many boarding businesses do not keep the best records, but try to find out as much as you can about the expenses going out and revenue coming in. This should also include how much was paid out to employees. If the records are not accurate or complete then you will want to work off of your own list taking one issue at a time to work on. It will become overwhelming if you try to do all of it at once, so prioritizing issues in order of importance will get you moving in the right direction.

Changes take time, so if you purchase an existing business, you need to understand that it could take months to get things in basic order. Once you go through all four seasons you will most likely make more changes and adjustments that come with extreme weather often experienced during summer and winter. Give yourself a couple of years to get a really good understanding of how the operation works in all types of weather. As purchasing hay will be your biggest expense (next to your business mortgage) it will be important to understand the price fluctuations from year to year depending on the growing season. This, of course, is a variable that can affect your board rates and how much money is left over after the bills are paid.

Unforeseen Expenses

Horse barns will come with many unforeseen expenses. You can walk through a barn in the summer when the weather is beautiful and the ground is dry and think you have gone to heaven. The barn looks amazing and you are ready to become the new owner. Then the rains come in the fall and all of a sudden you have water coming into the barn or stable area and the stalls or riding arena are starting to flood. It happens and if you are in this situation then you will find out fast that you are going to be spending extra money to fix a huge problem. The same will be true for equipment that has not been maintained and needs work that you didn't anticipate and even the arenas and grounds on the property that need work. There will often be costly surprises when taking ownership of an existing boarding business.

Part of evaluating the purchase of an existing boarding business is to make sure you look at the fine details of the operation. It is critically important to your success to make sure you know what you are getting into. You will already have enough work on your hands with all the known changes required so don't let unforeseen issues compromise your success.

~13~

Setting Your Board Rates

One of the most important decisions you will make has to do with what your board rates will be. Before finalizing your board rates for your business, I strongly encourage you to develop a business plan that details all of the elements of your operation including estimated cash flow even if you are not seeking a business loan. A well-studied, well thought-out business plan will help answer some of your questions about your cash flow including some unanticipated expenses that you may incur.

One of the challenging parts of starting a new business and determining your board rates is that you will not realistically have a good understanding of your expenses for a couple of years of operating through all four seasons. For example, I had not given a thought to how much higher our electric bill would be in the winter months and I was shocked when our bills arrived. The same can be true for fuel for tractors and anything you use on the farm. You will do a lot of estimating at first and estimating on the high side can provide a degree of financial safety.

When we opened our new facility many years ago we set our board rates too low. I had nine months to get clients to sign on while we were building our barn so that we would be full on opening day. When I was advertising I started out with a well-planned board rate but as time passed, I lowered our board prices. The rate changes were the result of my insecurities as a new barn manager and caretaker of other people's horses. That was a huge mistake! Once we were into our first year it was evident we were not bringing in enough income. We experienced many unforeseen expenses and despite having a full barn, we still had a budget deficit. At that point we couldn't just raise the board. We decided it would have been a terrible move for our business and it would have made us look incompetent in our knowledge of running a business. We had to operate with a loss for that first year because of that one major decision. I kept my day job and my husband also worked part-time so we could pay our bills. It turned out that we would need to do this for a few years. We paid a high price for that one mistake.

I have come to realize that this mistake is very common with many new business owners. I have talked to a few people throughout the years who have gotten themselves into the same situation. They started off too low in their boarding rates and quickly realized it and now were scrambling to find extra ways to bring income into the business without raising the board rates too much.

Unexpected Price Increases For Hay And Grain

Purchasing hay is another unknown expense from year to year. Remember that hay prices will be reflective of the growing season for that year. For example; if the summer is very hot and dry in your area there is a good chance the hay prices will increase because growers are not able to harvest as much hay. The same could be true if the summer is very wet and the farmers can't get the hay to dry properly. That is when the quality goes down so much that the hay ends up being only usable for livestock. We have had our hay prices fluctuate a few times over the years and it was because of weather and fuel prices. I encourage you to think ahead and check with a few suppliers in your area regarding prices. The more knowledge you have about hay and prices the more prepared you will be to handle negotiations when purchasing hay. Hay will be your largest expense next to your business mortgage.

Grain is another commodity that can fluctuate in price. You will need to decide if you are going to include grain as part of your board or charge separately for grain. If you are going to include it as part of your board rate then you need to have good current knowledge of grain prices. When we first started our business the grain prices were relatively low (compared to what they are now) and I included four pounds of grain daily in the board rate. A couple of years after we were opened for business there was some massive flooding in the region where the grain is grown and a significant percentage of the grain crops were destroyed that year. That natural disaster caused the cost of grain to increase back then and it has never gone down. As a result, we were losing money monthly in this part of our business. I changed our boarding policy and offered two options to boarders; providing their own grain or having me supply the grain at an additional cost. It is much easier now as I know exactly what I am paying each month so I never lose money with this part of my business. It is beneficial to keep up on the conditions, events and other things that might impact the grain prices.

The Cost Of Feeding Different Size Horses

When you think about your hay program and the many horses that will live at your stable you will want to consider the different size horses that will board at your barn and how that may affect your profit margin. I have gone to barns where only a certain amount of hay is allowed daily and if you want more hay for your horse you need to pay for it. I have also been to boarding stables where they charge according to the size of the horse. Based on my experience I feel this is a misconception that many barn owners have. If you have a smart and well thought-out feeding program in place and your board prices are set high enough, your board should be adequate to cover the hay requirements of different size horses at your facility. Unless you are running a stable that only allows draft horses you will not lose money. If you are only feeding draft horses then you should have this figured out already into your finances and have an appropriate board rate to cover the cost of all the extra hay a draft horse will eat.

You are potentially going to have large horses and small ponies and if you have a general boarding operation with many breeds then over time it does balance out. You will have young growing horses, horses that come to your barn underweight and need to gain weight and many horses that need to lose a few pounds. Some horses will be worked heavily while others haven't been ridden in years. You will have older horses that need the extra hay while others go on a grain mix because they don't digest the hay as well anymore. We have had many different ages and breeds of horses at our barn throughout the years and we have never charged extra for more hay.

If you start charging according to the size or age of the horse, your life will become unbelievably complicated and create additional stress for yourself. If you run a general boarding facility where any age or size of horse is welcome then it will balance out. You will not make as much money on the draft horses but you will make extra on the small horses and even more on the ponies if they pay full price. Some horses will eat less and some will eat more and you will find that you are not losing money if you set board rates correctly in the beginning.

Unless you are a breed specific type of boarding facility you will have the pleasure of taking care of many different horses in many shapes and sizes!

Accounting For Wintertime And More Hay

When figuring out your board rates you want to take into consideration the wintertime and your feeding program. As the temperatures drop the amount of hay you need to feed will increase. It will take you a couple of years to get a good idea of how much hay you will go through during all four seasons. Make sure you plan for the additional hay needed for the winter feeding program to assure the horses maintain their weight and are not losing weight due to the cold. You might be able to modify your feeding program in the summertime if you have enough acreage to allow the horses on pasture. Some facilities have enough pasture that they can cut down on the amount of hay fed during the summer months which, of course, will save money.

Plan to feed more hay in the wintertime especially if you live in an area that gets much colder weather.

Before You Finalize Your Board Rates

When you work through how much to charge for boarding you need to think about some key components to how you set up this part of your business. I am going to give you a list of some often overlooked but extremely important things to think about when setting your board rates.

- **Will the horses at your barn stay in all the time or will they go outside each day?** This is one of the most important questions you need to ask yourself because many other decisions will be based on this decision. There are a few riding disciplines that choose to leave their horses in all the time except for short periods of turnout. If you are going to accommodate the clients who want their horses kept stalled, then you need to realize that your operating expenses will be higher so your board rate needs to be increased to cover your costs. With the horses stalled most of the time you will go through much more bedding, have more wear on the stall and incur many additional costs of care.

- **Who will do the chores and how much can you pay out for labor?** If you choose to have a barn where the horses will be left inside most of the time, then your labor cost is going to increase dramatically when it comes to stall cleaning and daily chores. The stalls will be much dirtier and it will take longer to clean them daily. You will need to have a good handle on this part of your business and the time it will take to do the chores otherwise you could be losing a lot of money each month. If you are the one doing chores there is still a cost associated with your time. Don't make the mistake of thinking that your time and work is free–it is NOT! Regardless of whether you do chores or you have employees doing chores you need to document cost for the purpose of accounting. Don't lose sight of the fact that the longer it takes you to clean and do the daily chores the less time you will have to get other things done that need to be tended to on a daily basis.

- **What service amenities will you include with the board?** I encourage you to sit down and write up a list of the service amenities you will include with board. Clients may be expecting certain services so your board rate needs to detail what you include and what services are available at an extra cost.
  - Will grain and supplements be included in the board rate?
  - Daily turnout?
  - What will your barn hours be?
  - Will you medicate if needed?
  - Will you blanket as part of the board?
  - Will you put on bell boots and leg wraps before turnout if asked?
  - Will you include holding horses for veterinarian and farrier appointments?
  - How many days a week will stalls be cleaned?
  - Is there turn-out and stall cleaning on holidays?

I encourage you to be very clear to potential boarders of the services provided under the boarding contract and the services that are outside of the contract. You should also share those areas of care that are optional and available at an extra cost and those that are not available at all.

- **What will you offer as riding amenities?** You are going to want to think about the type of boarding business you will have. Do you want a high-end show barn or a more casual riding atmosphere? Will your barn be open for riding disciplines of all types? Will your barn or stable offer trainers on site? Will there be arena equipment to use like jumps, or poles/cones etc.? What is the size of your arenas? How many arenas will you have for people to use? Are there trails on site or places to ride outside? Will your barn be heated? Will you offer a lounge and bathroom on site for people to use?

I have given you some things that I feel are important to think about when determining your board rates. You need to remember that people will compare board prices and what you offer but, in the end, what matters most is knowledgeable, dependable and consistent care for their horse. You can't be everything to everyone and you will wear yourself out trying. There is no perfect barn that has everything but your clients will be willing to make compromises on amenities if the care is impeccable and they don't have to worry about their horses. Don't underestimate the value of consistent quality care of the horses that will be at your barn. It is the most important thing you have to offer.

Your Rates Compared To Other Boarding Barns

You will need to do some detective work and find out what other comparable boarding stables in your area are charging. This doesn't mean that you need to stay in the same price range as them but you want to be knowledgeable about your competition and what the market can handle in your area. After all, if you are offering the same exact boarding amenities as another facility five miles away and your rates are a hundred dollars higher you might have a problem getting people to move over to your place.

The great news is that there are absolutely NO two boarding facilities that are the same. Each one will have their own layout and what they offer for amenities might be similar but definitely not the same. The layout of the land and area to ride will be different for all of them and so on. Don't be nervous to be the most expensive boarding facility in your area, just be smart about how much more expensive you are going to be than the others. We have a couple barns in the area that are more expensive than my facility but are comparable. Then we have a barn about forty-five minutes from us that is the most expensive barn in the valley and their rates are almost two-hundred more than what we charge for board. They also cater to a limited clientele and they are a upper level competition barn and breeding facility. They have a special niche and it works well for them. You will also find what works well for your stable and what makes it different from the competition in your area.

I have compiled a list of things to look at when comparing other boarding barns and prices in your area to help you get a good look at pricing. One rule of thumb-the closer you get to the large cities the higher the board rates tend to be for the same amenities. I live ninety minutes from Milwaukee and the price difference of what I charge for board and what they charge for board is huge. It is because those facilities are closer to the city and they have a much larger group of professionals with a higher income, less available land and more competition. Location will be an important consideration when you think of starting your boarding business.

List of amenities to look for in other boarding barns:

- Size and number of outdoor riding arenas
- Indoor riding arena and size
- Size of stalls and what kind of footing in stalls (Rubber mats, sand etc.)
- Feeding program and what they include in the board rate (ie; Type of hay and how much, grain, supplements, salt block etc.)
- How do they feed and do chores daily? Round bales, large square bales, free choice or small individual piles for each horse.
- How much acreage to ride on or trails nearby?
- Herd sizes and size of paddocks and pasture if available?
- Outside shelters
- Private turnout
- Water availability year-round (heated water in wintertime)
- Barn hours
- How often are stalls cleaned?
- How often are horses turned out and for how long?
- Tack room size as well as saddle racks and space for each client?
- Grooming areas and how many?
- Wash stall (Hot and cold water)
- Round pen
- Trailer parking
- Heated lounge and bathroom
- What amenities do they offer? (ie; giving medication, leg wrapping, blanketing, walking, holding for farrier etc.)
- Trainers available on site?
- Choice of veterinarians and farriers?
- How often are the paddocks cleaned and dragged?
- How often are the arenas dragged and maintained?
- Are things fixed quickly when broken?

- Is there someone that lives on site?
- Are there activities like clinics offered at the facility?
- Are fans allowed in enclosed barns during hot weather?

This list will get you to start thinking about what other barns offer and how their price reflects what they have for amenities. Remember that you can offer all the greatest amenities but the most important factor in boarding is still the quality and consistency of care that you provide the horses.

There is an immense value in the reputation for quality care given to horses at your barn. That value should not be ignored when setting your prices. Also, don't underestimate your value as a barn owner and manager.

Sales Tax And Your Rates

Each state will have different tax requirements for businesses. This is something that you need to check with your accountant on and find out what your state requires. The tax rate will also vary from state to state. In the state of Wisconsin, horse boarding businesses are required to pay sales tax on the income they receive each month.

When establishing your boarding fees, you will want to decide if the sales tax will be added on to the total monthly fees or figured into the monthly rate and taken out of the board total. I have seen it done both ways. It can become very confusing when computing your profit margin if you are taking taxes out of the regular board fees but not including all the extra charges and service fees added on during the month. It is much easier to make mistakes if you don't have an exact accounting each month of where all your money and taxes are coming from. I recommend treating it like any other service business where you add the sales tax on at the end of the total charges, so you know exactly what to pay out each month to your state. There is less room for error when it is done this way.

~14~

Lawyers, Accountants And Insurance

Lawyers

When starting a horse boarding business, I strongly encourage you to find a good lawyer. I didn't realize how important having a good lawyer was until we needed one during our building project. Since that first time I have needed to contact my attorney only few times over the years because of situations that have happened involving clients and his counsel was invaluable. Legal issues are nothing to fool with without professional help.

If you are going to build from nothing but empty land then make sure you have a lawyer look over all land purchase agreements, building contracts and even loan information that the bank gives you. You want to make sure you understand all of the contract language and issues and that you are protected in every way. If your plans are to turn your barn into a boarding business or you are renting a facility, you will want to make sure your attorney looks over all your supplier contracts, boarding contracts and liability waivers.

I have heard many people say that they can't afford to hire a lawyer to look over things like boarding contracts but, in reality, you cannot afford not to. You have worked hard to get your business up and operating and you can be exposed to great financial risks if something serious happens without the necessary legal protections in place. Be smart and expect the unexpected. Having a good lawyer will be worth every penny spent. Don't fool around when it comes to this part of your business. Please take this seriously and you will never regret it.

Accountants

With the ease of filing taxes online many people choose to do their own taxes. If you have a business then I would suggest you find an accountant to handle your income taxes and quarterly reports. Unless you went to accounting school you will get overwhelmed pretty quickly, especially when there are changes to the tax laws. Besides filing monthly sales tax and quarterly reports there is so much more that goes into keeping your business financially fit. You are going to be so busy with your daily business responsibilities that it is very easy to let this part of the business fall behind. That is when people can easily get themselves in trouble when trying to manage the complexities of business accounting and taxes.

When looking for an accountant make sure they have knowledge of the horse industry and how it works. You don't want any mistakes made that could financially cost you down the road.

A few years ago several barns in our state were audited and many of them had to pay back sales tax because they were not paying it at all. I talked to one barn owner who told me that her accountant never told her she needed to pay sales tax and the end results were financially disastrous. Every state will be different, and you need to check with an accountant that knows the laws for your state. Don't get caught having to pay five years' worth of sales tax because your accountant didn't know the laws.

Insurance—A Must Have

Business insurance is something that you need to have and it's never fun to purchase but it's a necessity. You will probably cringe every time you write your check to pay your insurance company but after the check is sent and you head out to the barn you will relax because you know you are covered. I am in shock at the people who have horse businesses and do not have any kind of insurance. They are gamblers, taking a chance that nothing will happen.

I have learned a lot about insurance companies and finding the right coverage for our boarding business because I have used three different insurance companies over the years and they were all different in coverage and cost. I have learned one very important lesson through my dealing with insurance companies: Make sure your insurance company understands the horse industry! The first company I hired many years ago didn't understand horse boarding and the terms that were used in the paperwork, so I had to explain much of it to the agent. That should have been a red flag for me, but I hired him anyway. Down the road I changed to another company that didn't have knowledge of how the horse industry works and I found myself again explaining the terms in the questionnaire to the agent who was filling out the paperwork. Yes, I am a slow learner at times!

I finally got smart and switched companies and went with a company in my state that only does horse properties and equine businesses. What a huge difference. Not only did they explain things to me and showed me the areas of my business that were not covered correctly but they also saved me money and I am now paying less than I was with the first two companies. My advice is to find an insurance company that deals with horse structures and equine businesses.

Care, Custody And Control Insurance

If you are taking care of other people's horses then you are going to need CCC insurance or otherwise called Care, Custody and Control insurance. This insurance is essential coverage for all horse operations which involve non-owned horses. This would include boarding, breeding and training.

This coverage fills the void in your regular business insurance and is coverage in case of injury or death of a non-owned horse because of your negligence. If you have a lawsuit brought against you then this insurance will cover the defense cost. This coverage does not however apply to horses that you own or lease.

When you talk with your insurance agent you will be asked a series of questions related to your type of equine business and then he/she will write up the proper CCC insurance for your business needs.

I cannot stress enough the importance of having the proper insurance for your horse business and that includes Care, Custody and Control. Equally important, make sure your insurance agent knows more about the horse industry than you do when it comes to insurance. You have worked hard to start your business and you are now an equine professional and need to protect your investment and your future. Acquiring insurance and understanding your coverage is important to the protection of your business and if something happens you will be glad you wrote that check and are covered. You know that anything can happen when it comes to horses so don't take any unnecessary risks.

Trainers Insurance

We allow different trainers to give lessons and train horses at our barn. It is a huge asset to my business, but each trainer is required to carry their own liability insurance and provide proof of coverage before working out of our stable. There are many barn owners that do not require insurance from trainers that work out of their barn and they are taking a huge risk. All it takes is one bad accident and not only will the trainer be sued but there is a very good chance the barn owner will be sued as well. It is just how things usually go when someone gets hurt: The insurance companies take over and liability falls on everyone involved or associated.

As the barn owner it is your responsibility to make sure all trainers carry the proper insurance when they work out of your barn and that means having your boarding business listed as an "Additional Insured" on their certificate of liability insurance.

Without your business name listed you will not be protected under their insurance if something bad happens. Many insurance companies do not charge extra to list an "Additional Insured" for the first add-on and usually all your trainer needs to do is call their insurance company and have your barn added. It is a very easy and necessary process in protecting your interests.

Most insurance companies will contact you yearly during renewal time to fill out a questionnaire. They will want to know if you have had any accidents involving people on your property and if so, did it involve a horse? Did the person need to go to the hospital? They will also want to know if any horses were seriously hurt or died on your property over the previous year. This incident information can be important when your insurance rates for the year are established. Therefore, it is so important to carry comprehensive insurance and make sure your trainers carry their own liability insurance.

~15~

The Bank, Your Business Loan, And Your Business Plan

When applying for a loan to start a business of any kind the bank will look at your loan application in a much different way than they would a home loan. There is so much more that goes into it and they will look at it as a much higher risk. Finding a bank that does agricultural loans is even more challenging. Let me start off by saying that boarding horses is a risky business in the banks eyes. It is not the same as a farmer asking for a loan for farming equipment for his dairy business. The truth is that horses are a luxury and not something we need to have to survive and if you are seeking a large loan then you are really going to need to do your homework. A comprehensive, well-written business plan will be an important document to help your banker understand your financial position, projected cash flow and, ultimately, the potential risk of providing you a business loan.

When we were first seeking a business loan many years ago we were turned down several times. Even with our land as collateral many banks didn't want to touch it. I finally went to a bank that had an agricultural loan officer who understood farming and rural business and he was willing to work with us. Now, years later, I always tell someone who is asking about applying for a business loan, to find a bank that works with farmers and agricultural loans. There is no guarantee but you have a better chance with someone that understands the farming community and the distinct parts that make up rural life and that would include horses.

Commercial mortgages usually have higher interest rates and shorter terms than residential mortgages. When we first applied for our business loan, our ages were factored into the decision for the length of the loan. Our original business loan was approved for twenty-three years so that it would be paid off by retirement age. Once you have been approved for a business loan and you have moved forward with your business, you will be asked yearly to provide a financial report and a copy of your income taxes. The lender might also ask to come to your facility for a tour.

The Business Plan

In its simplest form, a business plan is a guide or a roadmap to your business. You are sharing your business ideas and how they are attainable and you are giving your detailed plan for reaching them. A normal business plan (one that follows the advice of business experts) includes a standard set of elements. A plan should include components such as descriptions of the company, product or service, market analysis, forecasts, management team, and financial analysis. Business plan layouts and outlines can vary but should include detailed information that supports your business opportunity. (This is detailed in the next section.)

If you are becoming overwhelmed by some of these words, relax, because I am going to explain them to you in a simple version and relate how it pertains to your horse boarding business. The bank wants to get to know you on many levels and that includes who you are, your background, experience and how knowledgeable you are in your chosen field of business. You are being interviewed so they can decide if they want to loan you a large amount of money for your business. You need to remember that the bank is not in business to lose money and they are going to get to know you very well during this process. There will be times when you feel like you are under a microscope and you will need to be okay with that. The truth is many businesses go out of business during the first couple of years and then the bank needs to figure out what to do with the building and everything inside. Either way, they usually take a loss if they can't sell the property and it turns out bad for everyone. Banks do not like risk, so it is so important to present a well-written business plan and show them that you have seriously considered every part of your business. You also need to convince them that you have the perseverance and fortitude to carry through on your business plan effectively for future years.

A well thought-out business plan is something that will be a guide to keep you focused and on-track to meet your business objectives. I didn't understand the importance of a business plan until a few years after we opened our boarding business. Putting together our business plan made me think of things that I wouldn't have thought of before, like the kind of clients I hope to attract, client retention objectives and what I wanted my mission statement to be. These subjects alone will start to mold what kind of horse boarding operation you want. They are the beginning steps for so much more to follow.

When I was first asked many years ago to write up a business plan for our boarding business, I have to be very honest and tell you that I didn't know what one was! I was in for a huge amount of learning when it comes to running a business and all that goes into getting it off the ground.

I have compiled a list of sections that are on a business plan. I want to emphasize that your bank may ask for some specifics that are not listed here and that is where you need to have good communication with the banker to make sure you have everything detailed at an appropriate level as it relates to your specific business.

Executive Summary

The executive summary will be your lenders first glimpse of you as a potential client, so it needs to be well written, concise and informative while targeted to "sell" your business plan to the bank. It should not exceed a page or two. Remember that many lenders will read ONLY your executive summary when determining if you should get a thorough review for approval so make the summary your best presentation!

In writing the summary there are several points that are commonly covered. You will want to provide an overview of your business plan so your reader knows what to expect in the full plan. Catch their attention with some key points and keep it brief but compelling.

So, what do you include? You want to describe the following points:

- Business information; name, address, etc.
- What will your business provide and what problem will it solve?
- How you fit in the competitive market.
- What are you seeking–what is the loan amount requested? How will it be used?
- Brief financial projection- cash flow over year/years.
- Distinguishing business elements–why will you be successful?

Present the information in the order of importance for the bank. Each element should be a separate paragraph.

<u>Write the Executive Summary AFTER having completed your business plan.</u> It is only when you have gone through the diligent exercise of your plan that you will be able to write the summary with precision and good reasoning. This will be the first segment of your business plan, but it is written last–it seems counterintuitive, but it has been proven to work.

Mission Statement

Your mission statement tells everyone that reads your business plan about your boarding business. It will tell others what you are passionate about and how it will positively affect all those that come to your facility and community around you. You can include some of your goals as a boarding stable, the philosophy of care for the horses and your customer service values for working with clients.

Mission statements often include some emotion and passion. This offers the banker an insight into what you want to do and the depth of passion you have for your endeavor. If you read many mission statements from different businesses, you will find that a well-written mission statement will make you want to do business with that establishment because it has tugged at your heart strings while conveying a very professional business image.

Keys To Success

In this section you will list the things that are going to make your boarding business successful. When we first wrote ours, I could only think of four keys to success. Now, years later, I would be able to write down an exhaustive list. Once you are working your business daily, you will realize all the extras that come up that will help make your business successful. Here is a short sample list of some key points to get you thinking.

1. **Provide quality horse care.** This is where you will want to explain in depth your idea of good quality care and how it will set you apart from the other boarding businesses.

2. **Maintain a 100% lease rate.** The bank knows that there is a very good chance you will not have a hundred percent lease rate all the times. They are familiar with rentals and you are renting out stalls. Just like apartment complexes, you might have an empty stall now and then. It's the idea that you will do everything in your power to keep your barn full and you are willing to go the extra mile to fill those stalls that is important to them. The one thing that the banker will want to hear is that you plan on having a waiting list. A realistic waiting list is security for you and the bank feels better knowing you will work hard to have clients waiting to board at your barn.

3. **Maintain reputable and honest relationships with your clients, other equine professionals and the community.** The best thing for a business is honesty, integrity and a great work ethic. When you run your business with these things in mind it truly will show and your business will stand out.

4. **Provide a return on investment that would allow your barn and business to offer more amenities as it grows.** You are going to want to compile a list of things you would like to provide your boarders in the future. Growth, change and improvements can be good indicators of a successful business and will show that you are willing to use some of your profits to improve your business and benefit your clients.

5. **Promoting and marketing will be a high priority.** You are going to need to market your business and the bank wants to know that you are going to work hard to promote your name and strive to become a familiar name in your industry and community. Marketing beyond your locale will be important to your success and you

will want to share your plan in this section. Remember that a good quality website can bring many clients from all over the world. One of my past boarders lived in England and her family was moving to Wisconsin and she found me through my website. After talking with her she relocated here from England and soon her horse followed. Think globally and the bank will love that you are thinking big. It's not just about your surrounding areas anymore. People move more now than they ever have before and you need to take advantage of it.

6. Keep current on new equine programs that involve the best care in feeding and nutrition, medical care and daily horse keeping for the betterment of the horse and their overall health. Horse care standards change and so will some of the things that happen at your barn regarding the care of the horse. It is important to stay current on changing trends in horse care. Changing your care protocols and managing updated feeding programs will demonstrate your commitment to excellence. Keeping current is a plus in not only the banker's eyes but also your clients. As the equine industry moves forward so does knowledge of how to care for horses. Learning and moving forward with it is good for any business. Your business advantage will be to make changes in your operations in accordance with the advancements in science and the equine industry and promote your business as a "best practices" facility.

This is a brief list of some ideas for keys to success that are great to think about whether you are applying for a loan or not. Getting and idea of what will make your business successful will also start to lay the foundation of the goals for your business and that is healthy for any new or existing business.

The Company Summary

The company summary or overview is an essential part of any business plan. The company description outlines vital details about your company such as where you are located, how large the company is, what you do and what you hope to accomplish. So, in the case of your horse boarding business, you would describe the details of your future operation including how big your facility will be and where you will be located. You can add how your horse business will affect the community and surrounding areas and even how it will make an impact in a growing equine industry. If there is a need for the services you offer then share it and how you will help fill a void in your area.

Here is a list of items you will want in your company summary:

- Your business name
- Your business structure (i.e. sole proprietorship, LLC, S corporation or partnership)
- Your business management team
- Location of your business
- The business history-when it started and the successes you have had already
- A description of your operation and how it will fill a need in your area
- Your future plans to expand and how it can benefit your clients and the community

This is a short list and each business plan will vary a bit in the order of information that is given.

Company Ownership

This section of your business plan doesn't need to be long. This section will include short biographies and the key people who will be running the horse business. Include the benefits and knowledge each person will bring to the business including experience in their field, their successes and their responsibilities in your business. Be very clear and descriptive about each person's roles in the business. Explaining who is running the business and what they bring to the table is of great interest to any banking institution. This descriptive process will start to open your eyes about what your role will be in your business as well as anyone else that is managing your boarding barn with you.

Here is an example of the roles my husband and I have at our facility: My husband and I both run our boarding facility together but we each have very different and distinctive roles each day. We may both do the morning chores together but he handles the feeding of hay, while I take care of the grain, supplements and medicines that need to be given. He takes care of manure and waste management and the constant maintenance and upkeep that come with a horse operation. I handle the ordering of all supplies, including hay, grain and bedding and anything else that we need. I handle all tours and most issues that come up with our boarders. We each have our distinctive roles and what we feel the most comfortable doing.

Start-Up Summary

In the start-up summary you are going to show how much capital you are seeking and where the money is going to be used. Basically you are going to make a list of things you will need to get your business off the ground.

This section is so important not only for the bank to see but also for you, whether you are seeking a loan or not. Once you start listing all the items large and small that you need for your boarding business it will truly open your eyes. You will begin to think of things you never thought of before and it all adds up quickly.

When writing your start-up summary it is important to be as detailed as possible. When you are preparing this part of your business plan, keep the communication open with your banker because each bank will be looking for something slightly different in a business plan and your banker could ask for specifics in certain areas that others may not. Accuracy in your estimates is critical because mistakes will impact every part of your business and this is where businesses run into trouble and run out of money.

We made that mistake when we were itemizing our potential expenditures and we missed many items, so once we were operational we realized our errors. Our first year ended up costing us much more than we anticipated. Remember that it is the small stuff that you will do every day for chores and to run the business that will be important but often is overlooked in the planning process. Most new start-up businesses do not have extra money and are tightly budgeted, so it is important to be as detailed as possible. "The devil is in the details!"

It is important to itemize all the items that a stall will need to be useable such as the wood, stall grills, buckets, corner feeders, salt block holders, mats for stalls etc. If you are putting up fencing, then put down how many rolls of electric braid or any kind of fencing you are going to use. Include the number of saddle racks and bridle hooks and every single item that will need to be purchased for the tack rooms and stalls. List everything that will be needed in your barn, stable and outdoor areas. There is nothing worse than to have an opening date only to find that you are short on supplies that you overlooked and short of cash. Don't let that happen to you!

Services

The products and services section of your business plan is more than just a list of what your boarding business is going to offer. If you need to get funding to build a new facility then the service section needs to showcase the quality, value, and benefits your horse boarding business will offer.

I have compiled a sample list of what your service section might include to give you an idea. For each item you list you will want to write a short description. Relevant detail is important because you are trying to sell your business and yourself to the bank. They need to feel assured that you know what you are doing and that there is a need in the area for what you are offering. You are entering a service oriented business and the bank wants to know that you are ready for this.

One more thing to think about-There is a very good chance that the person you are working with at the bank is unfamiliar with horse boarding terms and they might not have ever looked at a business plan for a boarding operation before. The more descriptive you are the fewer questions they need to ask and the more receptive they are likely to be. Make it easy for them to understand.

Possible amenities to be offered

I have compiled a list of possible amenities to be offered by your business. Your list will vary depending on the type of boarding stable you will have and what you will offer at your facility. Remember to describe what each term means.

- Full board or stall board
- Outside board or rough board
- Personalized feeding program including hay and grain
- Will feed supplements and give medications
- Stalls cleaned daily
- Horses hand walked daily for turnout
- Daily check on each horse for health, injuries and other possible issues.
- Small herd size in the paddocks
- Heated water in wintertime
- 80 ft. x 200 ft. lighted indoor riding arena
- 70 ft. x 120 ft. outdoor riding arena
- 100 ft. x 250 ft. outdoor riding arena
- Large pastures with shelters
- Private turnout
- Foaling stalls
- Trailer parking
- Heated viewing room and lounge
- Bathroom with shower
- Grooming bays in several areas of the barn
- Rubber mats in stalls
- Wash stall (Hot and cold water)
- Separate grooming bay area for veterinarian and farrier and emergencies

- Owners will live on site and provide emergency care to any horse at any time.
- Stable will contract with trainers and other equine professionals to offer lessons, training and events like clinics for our boarders and the community. We will also include educational workshops and clinics that will benefit not only our boarders but also the 4-H, FFA and Horse and Pony Clubs in the area.

I have given you a short list of suggestions and your list could go on and on depending on what you want to offer. It really is "the sky's the limit" on what you can offer at your facility and this will give you a good starting point and from there you will mold your business plan specifically for your business.

Market Analysis Summary

This section might be overwhelming at first if you are not familiar with this term but, simply put, you are going to provide a detailed overview of the boarding industry in your area and statistics to support it. Basically you want to show there is a need for a horse boarding operation in your area. The market analysis should include your target market, your competition and how you plan to establish your business as part of the horse community in your area.

This is what your market analysis section in your business plan should include:

- **Horse boarding industry and future outlook**-You will want to give detailed statistics that define the horse industry, including growth in your state and immediate area, trends in the horse industry and what the outlook looks like for the future of the horse industry.

- **Who is your target client/boarder you are trying to attract?** You should include data on the type of clients you are targeting such as; riding discipline, age, gender, income level and lifestyle. For example: If you are looking for boarders that are serious show competitors and show on the A circuit, then you are going to show that there is a need for that type of boarding facility in your area. The same would be true about riding disciplines. If there is a need for a hunter/jumper boarding barn in your area, then you need to show that. If your barn is going to be a high profile barn where the board will be substantially higher than other barns in your area, then you will need to show that there is a need and clientele that will contract for board. Also, you will want to find out how far people are willing to drive for quality care horse boarding. If people are not willing to travel the distance to see their horse, then you will have issues with filling the stalls. Location is everything.

- **Competitive Analysis**-Who is your competition? You are going to want to know who your competition is and so will the bank. What are their boarding rates and what do they offer? Are they full with a waiting list or do they have empty stalls? How many barns have indoor riding arenas for inclement weather or cold winters in your area and explain why that will be a huge asset. Some of your biggest selling points will be what you offer that others may not have or overlooked.

Finding out information about other barns in your area can be challenging especially because you are not going to want to ask another barn owner some of these sensitive questions that you need to know. You will need to be creative in finding out if there is a need. It is a specialized type of business in a unique industry but with websites and social media it is now easier than ever to find out what other boarding operations offer.

Doing Your Research

Each state will have some sort of state horse council that keeps records of the horse industry including the number of horses in your state and even the financial impact the horse industry has in your state. That is a great place to start your research. When we were working on our business plan I started placing ads in the local newspaper to see what the response would be. That was long before Facebook but you could do the same thing today with so many more avenues to find out what the need is. We also contacted local veterinarians in the surrounding areas to find out how many horses they service in a year's time. The same is true for farriers and other equine professionals like horse trainers. Another resource is the breed circuit horse shows in your state along with 4-H horse shows. Show participation and attendance is an effective way to find out about the interest and activity in your area. You can also get information from state horse councils about trail rider numbers and the places they trail ride and camp in each state. The research is endless and for each person that owns a horse a good percentage will need a place to board that horse and that is what the bank wants to see.

Market Segmentation

In this section you are going to take your broad target of future clients and then break it down in smaller sets of target clients and consumers that have common needs. It is about identifying the specific needs and wants of your customer groups (In this case-horse owners) and then using those insights to determine services which meet customer needs.

In the horse industry and the horse boarding world, the large market will be horse owners and the smaller subsets are the different types of horse owners looking for housing for their horse and how that fits in with what you will offer at your stable.

I am going to give you a sample list of what Market Segmentation looks like for any future horse boarding business. I have listed different groups of possible clients to get you to start thinking about who you are trying to attract to your barn.

- **Children**-If you have a boarding stable then many of your clients will be children and their parents are looking for a safe place for their child to ride under the supervision of knowledgeable trainers and equine professionals operating the stable.

- **Teenagers and College Age People**–Many young people are wanting to enrich their horse experience to include showing and competition of various kinds. They want to compete on a more competitive level and the programs at your barn will help them achieve their goals.

- **Single Adult Horse Owners**–This group of horse owners are looking for interaction with other adults and for many the social aspect of horse ownership is equally important to horsemanship.

- **The Serious Adult Competitor**–This is a person who needs to train year round and they need a facility that can give them the space, equipment and time to work their horse adequately for competition.

- **Trail and Pleasure Riders**–If you are starting a stable that caters to trail riders then include them as part of your target clients. Include why your facility will attract trail riders and the amenities you offer specifically for this group of riders.

- **Owners of Older Horses and Horses with Special Needs**–There is definitely a special group of people who own older horses and special needs horses and are looking for a place with extra care and attention to the specific needs of their horse. If you are able to offer a program that caters to special needs horses then you want to make sure you target this group that is often overlooked.

- **The Horse Trainer**–If you are building a facility that offers year round training then you will attract many horse trainers. If this is something that you are planning on, then these equine professionals need to be added to your market segmentation. A good trainer is an asset to any boarding business, and while the relationships may bring additional management challenges, it will bring clients to your barn. It is a win/win for both the horse trainer and the barn owner and needs to be mentioned in this section.

- **Owners of Brood Mares and Babies**–Another very specialized group of horse owners are people who want to breed their mare. Many facilities do not offer the proper housing for pregnant mares and young babies. If you are including this into our boarding program then you will want to list this group and include why there is a need for this type of boarding program in your area.

As you can see there are many different groups of horse owners and I have only listed a few for you to get an idea of what market segmentation looks like.

Market Segmentation Strategy

In this section you are going to develop a plan and strategy on how to attract your target market of boarders. In this section I would include what is available near you to help attract clients to your barn and how that will benefit those clients. For example; if you are trying to attract trail riders then a huge asset would be trails that are connected to your facility, which is a huge plus for people who don't own a horse trailer. Another example would be having a tack store close by for the people who show and need to pick up last minute items before heading out to the horse show. In our area, we have a huge venue that holds horse shows almost weekly throughout the summer that is well-maintained and has a covered arena so that horse shows can go on no matter the weather. That is a huge plus for local horse owners that want to show nearby and it has been an added asset for our boarding facility.

In your Market Segmentation Strategy section you can add a closing statement to tie in with attracting customers. If there is a market need then share it, along with what you have to offer that future customers will notice. When I was writing up our business plan I included that I had started marketing our target audiences a year in advance of opening. The best thing you can do is to be detailed about your strategy because the bank wants to feel confident that you have really thought this out and you know who you want for your future customers and understand what they want so you are able to retain clients.

Service Business Analysis

A boarding business is service oriented and entails many responsibilities to keep things running smoothly, efficiently and financially responsibly. This analysis is a report of a business that is service based and focused on horse boarding.

In this section you want to be very descriptive about what your barn will offer and how it will help your clients and even the community. Your boarding barn will also affect many other equine professionals and when working in harmony it will run like a well-oiled machine. Some examples are the hay supplier, bedding and grain supplier to start. Your business will also be entwined with the veterinarians in your area as well as the farriers. You will affect the business of horse trainers and equine massage therapist and this is a small list to start with.

You will want to describe the work that will be involved in keeping the business running efficiently from chores in the morning to closing the barn at night and how this will affect your clients. You can include the many things you will do to distinguish your business as an exemplary boarding operation.

An example of a service you offer would be, hand walking each horse out each morning and looking each horse over to make sure they are free of cuts, abrasions and in good health before they are turned out for the day. The same practice would be true for evening chores when bringing in each horse for the night. This is a significant selling point to many boarders because many stables do not offer this simple service. You will want to elaborate on the activities you will offer your boarders and the services that will be included in board as well as optional services available.

Economic Study

I would recommend doing a current economic study on the horse industry and how the industry is growing. When I wrote up my business plan I researched the statistics in the American Horse Council Foundation to find out exactly what the growth was for this industry and how it would impact my business. There are many sites that offer statistics for all parts of the equine industry and the associated financials for every part of the industry. I would check with your state horse council and start there and then broaden the analysis to the entire country. This part of your research will truly open your eyes. When we did our research it was many years ago and I am sure the numbers have grown dramatically in some areas of the country.

Competition And Buying Patterns

Know your competition! To be honest, when I was writing up my business plan I didn't understand the competition in the area. I was the new kid on the block so to speak and I had a lot to learn about the barns in my area. I encourage you to do your research and learn what other barns and stables are offering for amenities and what their fees are for board. Do your research to find out what people are looking for in comparison to what you will offer at your stable. Figure out what you are going to offer to distinguish your stable from others in the region. It's plain and simple but needed and it will be an eye opener once you do your research. This discovery process will help you refine your objectives and clarify your competitive advantages. Clearly state how you are competitively positioned in this section of the business plan.

Trends

The longer you are in the business of boarding horses the more trends you will see come and go. It is the nature of any business. What was once a huge attraction for boarders at one barn may have long gone by the wayside. It is a crazy business and you never know what will catch someone's eye and you need to remember that people talk and the horse community is small and impressionable. I encourage you not to get caught up in the trends of the day and instead concentrate on your distinguishing services and quality care for the horses at your barn.

Between continuity of quality care and good customer relations, your business will be set apart by a high retention rate, satisfied boarders and healthy horses. When that happens and your reputation strengthens, the bank will be happy to see your yearly reports.

Competitive Edge

When I prepared our business plan years ago the banker wanted to know what our experience was with horses and what our competitive edge was. I always tell people it's like stepping into the Shark Tank! This is where you need to sell yourselves based on your knowledge and experience. The truth is that no bank is going to lend you money to start a horse boarding business if you have no experience with horses and caring for them. It is no different than any other business.

When you are thinking about what your competitive edge is, I want you to analyze and then describe the unique characteristics of your boarding business that will provide the foundation for long term financial stability. It is not just about the physical amenities you offer. Your barn amenities may bring people to your barn but they will not be the reason boarders stay. It is *YOU* that will keep the boarders at your barn. When writing up this section you will start off with the amenities that you will offer and what specifics will set you apart. It can also be important to discuss your philosophy of care, commitment and your distinctive personal touch. For example, I have been told many times over the years that people can set their clocks by how we do chores. We are very consistent and that gives comfort to our boarders and takes away the fear and stress that many boarders feel. Are you easy to reach and do you reply back in a timely manner when a client is trying to reach you? Things like consistency and prompt responses are very important to clients and the bank will also view them favorably.

Your Past Boarding Experience

Your past boarding experience is an important benefit because you know what it is like to be on the client side of the business and you may have experienced many of the same concerns that your future clients have experienced. Many boarders may have experienced horses not being fed enough hay, not having water at times or dirty water to drink, and stress in the herds with no capability to change, to name a few. Boarding barns that promise the world and don't follow through on their promises is an issue that many boarders are faced with. If you have boarded your horse and experienced any of these problems then it will make you much more aware of your clients' wariness. I have just given you a few examples, but the list is endless.

Your past boarding experience is a great teacher and will help you start to develop a list of things you will offer and do to set your barn apart and give you a competitive edge.

Ask The Right Questions About Competitors

If you take your time and do the research on what other boarding stables offer and how they compare with your business, it will help define the direction you want to go with your horse business and help you take advantage of competitive positioning. I have compiled a list of questions you are going to want to answer about your competitors.

Here is a list of questions to ask regarding your competition:

- **Where are your competitors located in proximity to your boarding business?**
  The bank will ask how many boarding stables are in your area and how close are they to your facility?

- **What are the competitor's strengths?**
  What do the other barns offer? Do they have an indoor arena or many acres to ride outside? Do they offer full-service boarding or just outside board? Do they host horse shows and clinics? Find out what is going on at the barns in your area.

- **How do the barns in the area compare to what you are building in terms of quality, appearance and how they are designed?**
  Are the barns in your area nice or do they look run-down? Do they have a professional appearance or look more like a hobby farm?

- **What are other boarding stables price structure compared to yours?**
  What are the rates of other boarding stables in your area and what is included in the board fee?

- **Are the boarding facilities in your area full?**
  There is a good chance the bank will want to know if the other barns in the area are full. It most likely will not make or break a deal but if the other barns are struggling to find boarders then it could raise some questions about your stable and how you will keep it full with clients and horses.

- **What are your supply sources for products such as hay, grain and bedding?**
  I can remember our banker asking us who we were going to purchase our hay from and how the other barns in the area supply their hay. Hay will be your most expensive cost monthly (next to your business mortgage) and the bank will want to know if you plan on growing your own or purchasing it. The barns that can grow and harvest their own hay will save a lot of money. I know most people don't have the land or equipment to make their own hay and in many regions the hay is shipped in. The bank needs to know that you have a good supply chain planned or established for your major supplies, especially hay, grain and bedding. The bankers will need to have confidence that you have a financial plan and resources to financially handle the costs involved, especially if the hay needs to be shipped in from another area.

- **What are your competitors marketing activities?**
  Do a little detective work and find out what other barns do for promoting their business. Do they have a website or do they effectively use social media sites? Do they host clinics and horse shows? Do they sponsor 4H, FFA or Pony Club activities? There are many ways to market your boarding stable and get the word out to the community. Even advertising for an open house is a great idea and it gets the public to your stable.

Remember that you are selling yourself and your idea to the bank. If you are good at something, then let them know. If you are a horse trainer and have had a waiting list for two years, then comment on it in your business plan. Let the banker know you are an expert in your field and that you are willing to work hard (harder than you have ever worked before) and that you are good with not only horses but people. After all, the people part will be the key factor in getting new clients to sign on. Promote yourself confidently along with your reputable experience because you need the bank to believe in you.

Sales Strategy

The sales strategy is an important part of your business plan because it shows your road-map to attract future clients to your horse business. In this section you will identify the steps you will take to reach your target clients. You will want to think about the best ways to reach people who are in the market for a place to board their horse. Also, it is important to remember that there are many people who own horses that may not be happy with where they are currently boarding. You want to make sure you are utilizing all methods of communication to make people aware of your boarding business and benefits. People will move their horse if they learn of a new and positive place to board. They just need to know you are there!

Examples of tools to use for a sales strategy are:

- **A well designed website is huge in attracting future clients.**
  I believe people underestimate the power of a professional looking website. Creating and maintaining a well-designed website for the public will help support your image and philosophy of care. It is a required element in marketing your business effectively. Do not overlook the importance of keeping your website updated so it provides current, accurate information and provides a reason for the consumer to return to your site for additional information over time. Your site should be viewed as a valuable resource in their horse ownership experience.

- **Facebook**
  It is easy, free and it gets the word out very fast, especially if you are promoting an open house or an event. It's a fantastic tool. I would suggest linking up Facebook to your website that way people will find you on Facebook and it will drive them to your website. Having the two different sites work together is a win/win in every way.

- **Having a professional looking flyer or brochure is good and you can distribute them strategically.**
  You need to remember that not everyone goes on Facebook or even the internet. It may seem like the world is on social media, but they aren't. Having brochures placed in the local feed stores, tack stores and vet clinics is a good way to gain visibility.

- **Word of mouth from your satisfied boarders is one of your best sources of information distribution about your excellent horse care.**
  There is no better advertisement than word of mouth! Our barn stays full because we give great care and our boarders have many friends who own horses and they talk. I have received countless new clients over the years because someone at my barn told someone else about the care we give and encouraged them to check it out. It doesn't get any better than that and this is a fantastic sales strategy!

Sales Forecast

If you look up the definition of a sales forecast you will find something along this line;

Projection of achievable sales revenue, based on historical sales data, analysis of market surveys and trends, and salespersons' estimates. Also called a sales budget, it forms the basis of a business plan because the level of sales revenue affects practically every aspect of a business.

If that sounds like a mouthful then you are probably feeling like I was years ago; a little overwhelmed at this point. I want to simplify this section for the type of business you want to go into and get you to understand that your sales forecast will have some estimated guesses in this section unless you are purchasing an established boarding business. There is truth in the statement that the sales budget or forecast affects almost every aspect of any business. After all, without good knowledge of how much money is needed to keep your business going and a valid projection of how much money is coming in, there is a good chance you are going to have a bumpy ride.

Figuring Out Your Monthly Sales

If you are going to start a boarding business, then you need to start figuring out the costs that are involved with the construction and start-up and that will mean getting estimates. At the same time, you are going to have to decide how many horses you want to board at your place and the amount of income each horse will bring in. This is where many people get stuck. It is difficult to determine how many horse stalls are needed to pay the bills because you don't know how to accurately determine the per stall/horse cost of bedding, feed, labor and miscellaneous costs. This is where you need to estimate costs on the high end for expenses so that you don't end up short in revenue.

Take your time and do your homework. This might mean many conversations with the builder and many modifications and price adjustments until you get an estimate that is in the ball park for what you can afford. Another major decision is what your monthly board rates will be and you are going to have to know what the market can withstand for stall board and outdoor board rates in your area.

Once you have the number of horses you want to board then you will multiply that out to get your gross income for one month of board. Then multiply that by twelve months to get a yearly estimated gross total. That is a very simple starting point to see if you are in the ball park. Then you need to add up what you are estimating your monthly bills are going to be to keep the operation going and you need to include everything including sales tax if that is included in the board. Insurance is another big one that people will forget to figure into the costs. It all adds up quickly and if you don't have a good idea of some of the numbers then estimate high to cover yourself.

I have compiled a list of things that need to be considered when figuring out the sales forecast and monthly expenses for running your operation. Your bank will also include anything that is not listed and that could and probably will include other personal loans. Each banking institution will have their own way of doing things when it comes to business loans.

Here is a list of some of things to think about for your sales forecast:

Revenue

- Income coming in–Indoor stall board monthly total
- Income coming in–Outdoor board monthly total
- Extra services offered each month such as blanketing fee or holding fee for vet or farrier.
- Selling of miscellaneous items i.e.; Horse tack and other accessories, horse dewormer and medications, first aid accessories etc. (Many barns sell items that a boarder might need in an emergency)
- Clinics and horse shows
- Training and lesson revenue generated by the trainers that work out of your barn.

Expenses

- Monthly business mortgage
- Hay and grain
- Bedding
- Accounting
- Advertising
- Fuel
- Insurance
- Office supplies
- Barn supplies
- Repairs
- Property taxes
- Business phone
- Utilities
- Water
- Auto expenses
- Farm equipment expenses
- Employees

This is a simple list to get you thinking of what your income and expenses (cash-flow analysis) should include. When setting up your business plan your bank might want you to include other expenses. I cannot tell you enough how important it is to get a correct estimate of what your monthly expenses will be and to estimate on the high end if you are unsure of what the actual costs will be. There is nothing worse than opening your business and a few months down the road finding that you are not bringing in enough money because your expenses are higher than you expected. A shortage of money can destroy your business if you are not careful. David and I worked second jobs for much of the first five years because of some of the expenses we had not planned on or accounted for. When they say starting a business is both high-risk and demanding work it is very true. Do your homework!

Management Summary

The bank will want to know your experience in running a horse facility and how you are going to manage the day to day operations. The management summary section of your business plan will describe how your boarding business is structured and details who is involved. You will also elaborate on your external resources and explain how your business will be managed.

You will provide background information on the experience, role and value of each member of the management team. This is a good time to write up job descriptions and your experience. When I wrote up this section I already knew that my husband would be handling most of the physical work (including the heavy equipment) even though we would both clean stalls and handle the horses both morning and afternoon. He would take care of the day to day repairs and other chores that are done daily on any horse farm. I would take care of the financial bookkeeping, paper work, tours and most of the client communications. This is where you will really begin to define your roles and responsibilities. Role definition is very important in the day to day operation of any business.

In this section you will want to provide a resume that includes relevant experience, qualities and experiences that will increase your chance of success. For example; document the value of your equine industry contacts in your area, your factually demonstrated skills of organization and dependability and quality horse management. Think outside the box—if you are creative, flexible and hardworking then share it. You need to remember that bankers read business plans every day and you want to present a distinctive, compelling story. The horse industry is unique and there is a good chance your banker doesn't get too many business plans for a horse boarding operation so be detailed when it comes to what the management team will be doing and explain it in a way that the banker can easily understand. You are selling yourself and they want to know that the management team is capable and committed.

> *You are selling yourself and they want to know that the management team is capable and committed because the reality is, the job will become very hard at times and you need to show the bank that you can handle it.*

Start-Up Funding And Worksheet

This section answers the question, "What do you need the money for?" In other words, it shows all the purchases you will need to make in order to open your doors for business. Make sure you have included everything. It is better to over-estimate what you will need so you aren't underfunded.

Preparing your financial statements for your business plan can be challenging and even scary if you don't have a business background. I have included a simple list of things you may want to include in your projections for start-up costs. You will need to also check with your lender on how he would like you to format this section and if there is anything additional to be included in this worksheet.

Here is a simple list of start-up costs:

- **List all barn and stable costs**-You need to be extremely detailed and that means including everything from stall kits to mats for the stalls. It will mean saddle racks, bridle hooks, brooms, wheelbarrows, screws, bolts and more. Detail everything imaginable that you will need.
- **Equipment used to run and maintain the business**-If you are going to purchase a 4-wheeler or tractor then you need to include these items. They are important to keep the business running and your bank will want to discuss this with you as well.
- **Initial supplies and materials**-You are going to need hay and grain for your start-up and most likely bedding if you are doing stall board. You will want to start off with a full barn of hay and other commodities like grain and bedding when your doors open.
- **Advertising materials (Business website, Logo design, flyers and brochures)**-There will be some start-up cost for advertising, especially if you are going to design a website. Even the simplest form of advertising takes money and time to execute.
- **Miscellaneous costs you need to open your boarding business**-Every new business has unplanned expenses, especially in the months leading up to opening day. There will be many unanticipated expenses, so your bank will talk to you about start-up cash allocations for those expenditures.

The most challenging part is trying to figure out what your costs will be and making sure they are realistic. Some of the best advice I read about the start-up funding said, "It is always better to over-estimate expenses and under-estimate income."

Terms And Definitions
Here is a list of some terms and definitions that you will want to become familiar with if you write up a business plan and are putting together a Start-up Funding worksheet.

Start-up Expenses–Start-up expenses are the expenses you will need to start your horse business. For example, some of our start-up expenses were the cost of all the materials for inside the barn. The fencing, water buckets and corner feeders, tack-room saddle racks and bridle hooks, brooms, wheelbarrows, etc. Also include insurance, legal fees, accountant fees and even employee training if you are going to have employees when you open. Hay, grain and bedding should be listed in start-up costs.

Start-up Assets-Start-up assets include the cash you have on hand, equipment, land, buildings, inventory, and any other items you own that have a value. If someone approached you to buy your horse barn, those items you could sell are considered your assets. For us, the building itself was an asset and the horse stalls were a permanent part of the building and they were included in the start-up asset category.

You will want to discuss this section with your lender if you are not entirely sure what is included as an asset or expense for your business. There will be variations depending on whether you are building a new barn or trying to get a loan for an existing barn and business which could make a difference in your presentation of expenses and assets in some areas of the worksheet. Remember that it is always best to ask your lender how they would like it to appear on the business plan. They would prefer that you ask in order to have it done correctly. The lenders are there to answer your questions and help you work through all of this.

Long Term Liabilities–Long Term Liabilities are notes or loans that are due beyond a one year period.

Break-Even Analysis-Your business's break-even point represents the sales amount (income) that is needed to cover all your costs. It is the amount of revenue you need to generate to cover your fixed and variable costs.

The analysis is done to determine the point where the income received will begin to equal the costs associated with receiving the income. The break-even analysis will calculate what is known as a margin of safety and that will tell you and the lender how much the revenue can fall while still staying above the break-even point.

I cannot stress enough how important it is to keep the communication open with the lender you are working with. They would much rather have you be honest and ask questions while you are determining numbers for your business plan, especially if these terms are new to you. When we first started, I had no idea what many of these terms meant and I had to learn as I went along.

Important Assumptions

Putting a business plan together is all about looking into the future and forecasting and defending assumptions. It is used to identify the most important assumptions in a company's business plan, to test these assumptions, and to accommodate unexpected occurrences. There are going to be unexpected outcomes. There are in every business. The success of your business is dependent upon accurate information and estimates which help explain and define those areas that present financial risk.

I have compiled a list of questions to ask yourself that will help you with this section. Determining the important assumptions is a critical part of every business plan.

Is there a need in your area for another horse boarding business? This is probably one of the most important questions a lender will ask and you should have a solid answer and facts to support it. You can't assume that there is a need because you love horses and you believe everyone else feels the same way. There are many people who love horses but not enough to own one.

Can the people who own a horse in your area afford the rates at your facility? This is where you need to have reliable information about the board rates at other barns as well as their occupancy history. There are many boarding stables that offer less expensive board rates but as board rates increase, you will find fewer barns in the higher price scale. This is true for most areas. Having a good idea of what your board rates will be will help determine what category of boarding facilities you will be included in and it will also give you a clearer idea of how many competitors you will have. Knowing how the economy is in your area is also important. If you are in a growing area that has good income jobs and professional businesses, it will be easier to find clients that can afford the monthly board.

Can your business turn a profit? This might not be an easy question to answer but if you gather accurate estimates and create a strong business plan, you will have a reliable analysis of your opportunity for success.

Are you the right person for the job? This is a critically important question and the lender wants to know if you have what it takes to run a horse boarding operation. It will be a life transforming endeavor that you may not fully appreciate until you are fully committed, and then there is no backing out. The lender wants to make sure you have a realistic understanding of what you are getting yourself into and have the commitment and strength of character to stay with it. He will want to know about your people skills and how good are you at handling unexpected situations.

It is important for you to realize that the lender wants to get to know you and see if you have what it takes to run your business, even under adverse conditions. All businesses present challenges and they see many businesses go under because the owners can't handle the pressure.

Twelve Month Income Statement

The income statement will show the projected operating expenses for your business. It will give a summary for each part of the business over a period of time and it is very common for a bank to ask for a twelve-month income statement.

Your statement will be detailed by each month of the year with projected numbers in each category to give you a final projected income for the entire year. There are many templates online that you can download to help you create a professional looking twelve-month income statement.

Here is a list of items that should be on your income statement for a boarding operation. Some of them will be modified to fit your business model. For example-if you don't offer outside boarding, then you would not list it as one of your activities. We offer outside board, so we broke it down into outside board and inside stall board. It is important to be specific in the types of boarding options you will offer at your business.

Revenue-This is the money that you will be taking in each month from your business.

- **Outside Board**
- **Inside Stall Board**
- **Occupancy %**-This is your projected goal of the percentage of stalls filled each month and a then a final total for the year.
- **Miscellaneous Services**-This is where you would list a projected income for optional services offered at your barn.
- **Trainer Fee**-If you are going to make money training horses and giving lessons then you will want to give a projected income for this part of your business. If you are not a trainer but will make an income off of the lessons and training that trainers are doing at your barn then you want to include this also.
- **Clinics and Horse shows**
- **Goods sold**—If you plan on having a small tack store at your place then you will want to list a projected income for items sold.

Expenses—Your twelve month income statement will also include all your expenses. It is usually presented after your projected revenue section.

- **Rent/Mortgage**-If you are building you might not have hard numbers for what your business loan payment will be each month. This is something that you will need to discuss with your lender. They should be able to give you a base number for the amount of a loan they would be willing to lend.
- **Salaries/Bonuses**-If you believe you will have enough money coming in each month to pay yourself, then give an estimate here. Don't be surprised if you don't have enough money to pay yourself each month in the beginning, as this is common with start-up businesses. In our situation, we had money coming in from seconds jobs that we worked outside our business. The bank wanted to know what our income was from those other jobs and how long we expected to work those second jobs.
- **Accounting and Legal Fees**-Many larger boarding facilities will have an accountant to handle much of the paperwork for employees and taxes. Talk to your accountant and find out what an estimated fee would be for the work you want done for your business for the year. You may not have monthly legal fees, but you should have a cost estimate included as a precautionary measure.
- **Advertising**-Most websites are going to cost a monthly fee. If you have a website designer with recurring fees, then summarize and include them.
- **Insurance**-Include what the annual business insurance will cost for the year. This should include Care, Custody and Control Insurance. You will also want to include business vehicle insurance.
- **Office Supplies**-Include all office supplies. Ink and paper costs can add up fast when printing invoices and information for your boarders.
- **Barn and Stable Supplies**-Start making your list now of things you will need to open your barn and keep it running the first year. I can guarantee that you will miss something and be running to the hardware store a few times during the first year.
- **Fuel**-Estimating the fuel you will use to run all the equipment and your business vehicles will be challenging. Think through your day and the chore routine and how often you will use your tractor, skid loader and 4-wheeler etc. This is where your past experience will be helpful in deciding how much fuel you will use for the equipment to do daily or monthly jobs.
- **Hay**-If you have been working at other horse barns then your experience of feeding horses will benefit you in determining how much hay you need for the first year. My husband was very good at keeping track of how much hay we were going through and he actually kept a log of the amount of hay we used for a year (for our four horses) and then he could multiply that out for forty horses. I would encourage you to estimate high in this section until you have actual experience as to how much hay you will need annually for the number of horses you board.

- **Grain & Supplements**-The cost of grain and supplements will depend on what you include in your boarding. If you include grain in your monthly board then you will need to decide how much grain is the maximum you will include for each horse. For example, if you offer up to 4 lbs. of grain daily then you want to figure the cost using that number so that you are not losing money each month. I know that not all your horses will use four pounds of grain daily but you need to estimate to cover the maximum consumption cost. You don't want to come up short on money and it is better to overestimate and be able to use the extra income in another place than become overextended.
- **Bedding**-You will need to decide what kind of bedding you want to use. Bulk or bag shavings will each come with a different price tag. Your estimates of cost will also be determined by how heavy you bed your stalls. Estimating how much bedding you will go through each month will definitely include a little "guesstimating" during the first year and through all four seasons. For example, we use a lot more shavings during the coldest part of winter and even during a couple weeks each spring when the horses are in more often due to mud. I didn't realize this until we went through a couple of seasons and I looked back at my records at the amount of extra shavings we purchased during certain times of the year.
- **Repairs**-You are going to have repairs. It is part of any working farm or stable and estimating will be challenging and past experience will help in this section. Estimate high!
- **Phone**-Out of all of the items you will be estimating, your phone bill will probably be one of the easiest to figure out. Unless you are traveling outside the country or going over your data usage, your bill should be the same most months.
- **Utilities**-Since we were building a new barn it was hard to know what our utilities were going to be with all the lights in our barn. Our biggest concern was the arena lights as they would use a lot of energy. I would recommend asking your electrician or your power company what amount of power consumption you should anticipate They have specialists that will ask you what type of lighting you are putting in and the number of lights you will have installed and they can figure out the cost of use estimate for you.
- **Water expense**-If you live out of the city limits and have a well then you might avoid a water bill expense. But if your business will be in a municipality where you will be using the city water then you might have a large water bill. Do your research! Water will be one of the most important parts of your business and you will use a lot every day. You don't want to get yourself into a mess where you can't pay your water bill because you didn't estimate enough.
- **Auto Expenses**-If you have a business truck or vehicle then you will want to list any monthly payments attached.

- **Property Taxes**-If you are building a structure then your property taxes will go up. When we were trying to find out what our property taxes were going to be we went to our county office and looked up the public records of property taxes for similar facilities in our area. That gave us a starting point.
- **Depreciation**-It is the decrease in value of an asset over a period of time. In our case it would be our new barn. This is something that I would definitely talk with your loan officer about and once you have an idea of the cost to build your barn then you or your accountant can develop an annual depreciation schedule based on the current laws.
- **Taxes—Payroll**
- **Taxes—Other**
- **Entertainment**
- **Health Insurance**
- **Dues and Subscriptions**
- **Travel**
- **Other**

Putting together the income statement will take some time and serious thought. Do not overestimate your projected revenue. This is where so many people can create an incorrect projection of cash flow very easily if you over or underestimate costs in major areas. The biggest reason why owners get themselves into trouble is that they overestimate revenues and the actual expenses were much higher than predicted. This happened to us when we first started, and it can be very stressful if you cannot pay your bills. Finding a strategy for earning money to make up the income that you are short each month can be very difficult.

There is a huge difference between an established business and one that you are starting from empty farmland. With an established boarding business you should be able to look at the revenue stream and expenses from the accounting books of the previous owners and that will give you and the bank a good idea of cash flow. The one big problem with this is that often times the barn owners are not keeping clear and concise records and you might not get a valid picture of cash flow.

Starting a new business without benefit of history presents a risky proposition for banks to evaluate. It makes it much more difficult for the bank to decide if it is a safe business opportunity to invest in. Make certain to help them, and yourself, by providing comprehensive, realistic financial estimates based on factual data.

Cash Flow Statement

Cash flow is the money that comes in and goes out of a business. It is the cycle of cash in and cash out that determines your financial stability and soundness of your business. When you show this in a cash flow statement it will give a much clearer picture of how your business is doing.

When we were preparing our cash flow statement we again didn't have hard numbers to use so we had to estimate. It helped that our lender understood agricultural loans and the type of business we were embarking on. If you are purchasing a business that has already been in operation for some time, then you should be able to look at their past cash flow records. Keep in mind that any records kept are only useful if they are accurate and detailed, so it is critical to your success that you do your own work in creating a cash flow statement. Shortcuts in this process will create high risk for your business. The biggest problem will be if they kept good records for their business.

In our business plan we had a one year and three year cash flow statement. The bank wanted to see both and we estimated three years out. Once you get to this point in your business plan you are going to start to get a real good idea of the costs and what it will take to get your boarding business up and going. I believe writing up a business plan is beneficial whether you are seeking a loan or not. It will truly open your eyes to what it will take to run your business.

The Last Part Of Your Business Plan

The last page of our business plan included a well-drawn picture of the barn and indoor riding arena that we wanted to build. It gave the lender a good visual as I went over every detail of the building and how it would be used. I believe it's a huge benefit for any business plan and it brings it all together.

Waste Management

You need to remember that it is NOT just about the building. It is about the daily operation. Where will you store your hay, grain and bedding? What will you do with moldy hay and grain and the garbage that will accumulate from your business? What will you do with your manure? Do you have a place to store it? What about manure run-off? If you need to pay someone to dispose of it, how much will that cost and how often will it need to be done? We live in a day where the environment is so important and it will be vital to have a plan for waste management.

Looking Professional

The day to day life of running a horse boarding barn is not glamourous and most of the time I wear worn out jeans and work boots. My barn clothes are work clothes and they usually have bits of hay and mud attached to them, but it is all part of the job.

That is okay for cleaning stalls and doing chores but when you are presenting your business plan to a bank, look professional. Make sure your business plan is presented professionally with easy to read graphs and charts. If you don't know how to create graphs and charts yourself then pay someone to do them for you. Have it professionally bound and it will show the lender that you are serious and you took the time to really make a good impression. You only have one chance to create a great first impression. Remember you are asking someone to loan you a large amount of money and to trust that you will work hard and pay it back. Take the time to do this part of your presentation right the first time.

The Waiting Game

Being approved for a business loan can take a long time. It is nothing like a home loan that can get approval in a day or two. It will be treated in a much different manner and you will feel like you are in the shark tank at times. Be prepared to wait and expect to have several meetings with your loan officer to answer questions and provide additional information, as needed. If the bank is giving you serious consideration you might be at the bank discussing your operation and answering questions with some frequency. This is all part of the process of the bank's due diligence. Being very responsive to the bank's requests will be worth your efforts if your loan is approved.

One more note-David and I were turned down several times from different banks before we were finally approved by one. The best thing we did was talk directly to an agricultural lender. That made the difference for us. Most loan officers will be unfamiliar with horse boarding businesses of any kind, so they will not understand a lot of what you are talking about and it will be a hard sell for a conventional lender. When you are approaching a bank, ask if they have an agricultural loan officer and work with that department. That will start you in the right direction.

~16~

Boarding Contracts And Liability Waivers

When we were in the process of building our barn and I was trying to get everything in place, the one thing I didn't have was a boarding contract. This was many years ago and social medial wasn't around yet and I didn't feel comfortable asking other barn owners for a copy of their contract. I did what most people do, I went online and searched for "Boarding contracts." Sure enough, there were plenty of sites out there that sold pre-made boarding contracts, so I ordered one. I had a boarding contract, so I thought I could check this off my list. I would use the pre-made contract and all would be good. At least that is what I thought. I was very wrong. This is where you should heed the words "buyer beware."

I want to start this chapter off by making it very clear that just because you purchase a boarding contract online doesn't mean it is written correctly for your business or the state you do business in. The contract might not provide you with the language necessary to provide your business with the needed protections in law.

A well written contract will help you to avoid misunderstandings and will protect your financial interests. I strongly encourage you to have your boarding contract written or reviewed by an attorney that understands this type of business and the laws in your state. A pre-written boarding contract might be inexpensive to buy, but it could cost you a lot in resolving legal issues if it does not properly protect your interests. I can't stress enough how important this part of your business preparation is.

Unusual Situations Not In Your Contract

A new situation came up recently that made me aware that my contract was missing a very important section that I needed to have corrected at once. I had my boarding contract for years and it was out of date in certain areas and needed to be updated. I called my attorney and he went over my contract and revamped it. It is a good idea to have your attorney look at your boarding contract every few years to make sure it is current with the laws in your state and dealing with the needs of your operation and clients that will board at your barn.

I know that some people will hesitate to hire an attorney because they are worried about the cost. It is far better to have a well written contract that your attorney reviewed than to find yourself in a situation where you are at financial risk. This would include resolutions from simply getting paid through the complexities of asking a boarder to leave immediately for cause. It happens more often than you would expect, so you need to protect yourself in all situations.

Sample Boarding Contract

I have listed some parts of a boarding contract that I feel are very important. You will design your contract to fit your business and you can put anything in it that you would like. I am giving you some examples of what is in our contract that will give you a starting point. Please note that these examples are based on the requirements for the state of Wisconsin and some of the sections might need to be worded differently for other states. Again, have an attorney read your contract before one horse or boarding client comes on to your property.

I have also included the reasons why I have each section in my contract and share some examples.

Sample Boarding Contract

WITNESS THIS AGREEMENT this _____ day of _____, 20_____, by and between (Your barn name here), hereinafter referred to as "Stable," and the individual or individuals undersigned, hereinafter referred to as "Owner." Address of Stable is (Your complete barn address here).

This short first paragraph is important because it states the name of your business and address and sets the definition of how the boarding contract will be described between you, the barn owner, and the client.

1. Fees, Term and Location. Owner acknowledges and accepts those terms set forth in the rate schedule as posted by Stable, whether said rates be daily, weekly or monthly. Payment shall be due in accordance with that rate schedule on a timely basis. In the event the subject animal is removed from the premises for any reason and returned, this agreement shall be deemed reinstated at the then current rates. Stable reserves the right to notify Owner within the fifteen (15) days of the horse's arrival if the horse, in Stable's opinion is deemed to be dangerous or undesirable for Stable's establishment. In such case, Owner shall be solely responsible for removing the horse within seven (7) days of said notice and all fees incurred during the horse's presence upon the premises. This Contract shall be deemed terminated and concluded upon the payment of all fees.

This first section (paragraph 1) of the boarding contract sets the parameters of what your rights and protection are regarding new horses coming into your facility. It also sets the guidelines for the monthly board payment arrangement.

The longer you are in business the greater probability you have of dealing with a horse that needs to leave immediately. When we first opened, we had a new family that purchased a horse and they were not very knowledgeable about horses. The horse was delivered and within twenty-four hours I knew there was a serious problem. The horse was trying to lunge opened mouthed at anyone that came near him and after three days nothing changed. The owners had the veterinarian come out to evaluate him and we all agreed that there was a chance the horse might have been drugged, evidenced by the radical change of behavior from when they had seen the horse originally. At that point no further test was required and I had to tell the owners that the horse couldn't stay at our barn. We felt this horse would be extremely dangerous to anyone that came close to him. In the many years of boarding horses at our barn we have only had this situation happen one time. We were fortunate to have had a section in our boarding contract to protect us in this situation.

The boarding fee is due, in advance, on the first of each month. All other fees and charges are due on the first of each month following the date of the invoice. All outstanding boarding fees and all other outstanding invoiced fees and charges are subject to a finance charge from the fifth of the month at the rate of 5% per day, 1825% per annum, until paid in full. In addition, Stable shall be entitled to enforce a lien against said horse and Owner's property on the premises as further described below. The initial monthly boarding fee and charges applicable to the services as set forth below shall be $_____ per month, plus tax. Owner acknowledges and agrees that Owner shall be responsible for all costs of repairing or replacing all property of Stable damaged or destroyed by Owner's horse and shall make timely payments as set forth above.

This section is extremely important and you want to make sure the new boarders coming into your facility understand it. You will post the board rate and if you are going to add sales tax over and above the board rate then you need to make this very clear. Many boarding businesses do this differently and some will incorporate the sales tax into the board rate. You can set this up either way. I have found it so much easier to keep things straight with sales tax when it is added on after the board rate and other fees for the month.

You are going to want to state a day that the board is due in full and you will want to have a "grace period" included. If you don't have this section clear and concise then I can guarantee that you will have many clients paying late and you will be calling them asking for the board check. You also need to have your late fee included in this section. I have ours set up with a 5% late fee and I had my attorney make sure that we were within the laws of Wisconsin for collecting late fees. Each state will be different so you need to have your attorney check this for you to make sure you are doing everything legally when it comes to collecting a late fee.

The last section of this paragraph includes that any damages and repairs will be covered by the owner of the horse and how the payment will be handled. You need this in your contract because as long as you have horses on your property things will get broken. Horses are very hard on everything and it will be prohibitively expensive for you to be paying for all the repairs. Remember that it is a business first.

2. ***Description of Horse to be boarded.***

Horse's Name: _____ ***Date of Birth*** _____
Breed: _____
Color: _____
Sex: _____
Distinctive Markings: _____
Date of Arrival: _____ ***Date of Departure:*** _____
Veterinarian 1st Choice: Name: _____
Phone: _____
Veterinarian 2nd Choice: Name: _____
Phone: _____

You are going to want a section in your boarding agreement that includes the description of the horse boarded. It may not seem important, but if you have an issue with a boarder you want to make sure your complaint is about the horse described on the boarding contract. Some of your clients or horse trainers will have multiple horses and one (1) boarding contract to include all their horses could leave you in a difficult situation if you are trying to prove a case against one particular horse and the name of the horse and description isn't on the contract. This is something to think about and you will want to ask your attorney about this.

3. *Feed, Facilities, and Services.* *Stable agrees to provide adequate feed and facilities for normal and reasonable care required to maintain the health and well-being of the animals. Owner acknowledges that Owner has inspected the facilities and finds them in safe and proper order.*

This section of your contract protects you, the barn owner. Sometimes boarders will initially be happy with your stable but may become dissatisfied due to an unexpected experience or interaction. They may be unhappy with the care you are giving their horse, or they now have an issue with how something is designed with the facility, fencing, how you feed or water. This paragraph acknowledges that they approve of how you feed and care for the horses daily and they cannot seek restitution for something that they decide they don't like or disapprove of. Make sure you are very thorough when you give your barn tour and describe your daily chores. Stable tours are so very important! This is where you need to show your prospective clients your entire facility and answer all their questions.

4. *Risk of Loss and Standard of Care.* *DURING THE TIME THAT THE HORSE(S) IS/ARE IN THE CUSTODY OF STABLE, STABLE SHALL NOT BE LIABLE FOR ANY SICKNESS, DISEASE, ESTRAY, THEFT, DEATH OR INJURY WHICH MAYBE SUFFERED BY THE HORSE(S) OR ANY OTHER CAUSE OF ACTION, WHATSOEVER, ARISING OUT OF OR BEING CONNECTED IN ANY WAY WITH THE BOARDING OF SAID HORSE(S), EXCEPT IN THE EVENT OF NEGLIGENCE ON THE PART OF STABLE, ITS AGENTS, AND/OR EMPLOYEES. This includes, but is not the limited to, any personal injury or disability the horse Owner, or Owner's guest, may receive on Stable's premises.*

The Owner fully understands that Stable does not carry any insurance on any horse(s) not owned by it for boarding or for any other purposes, whether public liability, accidental injury, theft or equine mortality insurance, and that all risks connected with boarding or for any other reason for which the horse(s) in the possession of, and on the premises of Stable are to be borne by the Owner. Stable strongly recommends equine mortality insurance be obtained applicable to the subject horse(s) by Owner.

The Standard of care applicable to Stable is that of ordinary care of a prudent horse owner and not as a compensated Bailee. In no event shall Stable be held liable to owner for equine death or injury in an amount in excess of five thousand dollars ($5,000) per animal. Owner agrees to obtain equine insurance for any animals valued in excess of five thousand dollars ($5,000), at owner's expense or forego any claim for amounts in excess of five thousand dollars ($5000). Owner agrees to disclose this entire agreement to owner's insurance company and provide Stable with the company's name, address and policy number. Failure to disclose insurance information shall be at Owner's risk.

In this section you want to make sure that the owner of the horse understands that you do not have insurance coverage for their horse if the horse gets hurt or dies unexpectedly. This is important because as long as you are the owner of the facility whether be it boarding, breeding or training, there will come a time where a horse is injured or, worse yet, dies. At the point you are going to be dealing with a lot of emotion from the owner and there is no way to predict how the owner will respond. The difficult part of this kind of situation is that the horse owner will be dealing with many unresolved questions and issues.

The only time you would be responsible is if you were negligent in the care of a horse at your barn. In that situation you would be responsible and that is why you want to make sure you have "Care, Custody and Control" insurance to protect you in case you have been found negligent in a situation regarding the injury or death of a horse on your property.

5. <u>Hold Harmless.</u> *Owner agrees to hold Stable harmless from any and all claims arising from damage or injury caused by Owner's horse(s) to anyone, and defend Stable from any such claims. Owner agrees to disclose any and all hazardous or dangerous propensities of horse(s) boarded with Stable.*

When talking to a potential client that is going to be signing your boarding contract, you need to learn as much as possible about their horse's behavior. For examples, do they have any bad habits like biting, kicking, aggressive behavior toward people and/or other horses? If someone gets hurt due to an issue with a problem horse then you need to protect your business and that includes finding out everything you can about the horse.

This also means that the owner of that horse takes full responsibility for any accidents to people and or horses caused by their horse. This would also include herd management and riding with other boarders in a group setting.

You will certainly have situations where someone buys a new horse and they do not know all the behaviors of that horse. In that case you will find out together what some of the horse's issues are and create a game plan for that horse. In any case you need to protect yourself so that you are not held responsible as the barn owner or manager if something happens due to the behavior of a particular horse.

If the owner of the horse is aware of a serious vice or habit that could be dangerous then they need to disclose it, and if they do not, then you have every right to ask them to remove the horse immediately.

6. *Emergency Care.* *Stable agrees to attempt to contact Owner should Stable feel that medical treatment is needed for said horse(s), but, if Stable is unable to contact Owner, Stable is then authorized to secure emergency, veterinary, and blacksmith care required for the health and well-being of said horse(s). All costs of such care secured shall be paid by Owner within fifteen (15) days from the date Owner received notice thereof, or Stable is authorized, as Owner's agent, to arrange direct billing to Owner.*

STABLE SHALL ASSUME THAT OWNER DESIRES SURGICAL CARE IF RECOMMENDED BY A VETERINARIAN IN THE EVENT OF COLIC, OR OTHER LIFE-THREATENING ILLNESS, UNLESS STABLE IS INSTRUCTED HEREIN OR ON OWNER'S INFORMATION SHEETS, BY OWNER THAT THE HORSE(S) IS/ARE NOT SURGICAL CANDIDATES.

Owner agrees to notify Stable of any and all changes of address, emergency telephone numbers, itineraries or other information reasonably necessary to contact Owner in the event of an emergency. In the event Owner departs for vacation or is otherwise unavailable, prior to departure Owner shall notify Stable as to what party is authorized to make decisions in the Owner's place with regard to the health, well-being, and/or medical treatment of the horse(s).

It's Murphy's Law—if the owner goes away on vacation their horse will need a vet! I want you to be prepared because some time during your boarding career you will run into a situation where you have a very sick or injured horse when the owners are on vacation and you can't reach them. This means you will need to make the decision on what to do for the horse.

When you are reviewing your boarding contract with your new clients make sure you explain this section to them and talk to them about what they would want done if they cannot be reached. You should have each new client provide written instructions in the event that surgery is recommended. This is important in the case of a serious illness like colic or severe lacerations where surgery might be recommended and immediate decisions are necessary.

When I have boarders go on vacation and they know I won't be able to reach them, they will write me a letter giving me permission to make all medical decisions and they leave their credit card on file with the veterinarian of their choice. It makes things much easier for me and the veterinarians involved.

You will definitely need an "Emergency Care" section in your boarding contract to protect you in all situations.

7. *Limitation of Actions.* *Any action or claim brought by Owner against Stable for breach of this Contract or for loss due to negligence must be brought within one (1) year of the date such claim or loss occurs.*

This is a pretty straightforward paragraph and it simply puts a limit on the amount of time a boarder has to take legal action for something that they feel has happened to them or their horse on your property.

8. *Hoof Care/Shoeing, Vaccinations, and Worming.*

- *Owner agrees to provide the necessary hoof care/shoeing of the horse(s) as is reasonably necessary, at Owner's expense.*
- *Owner agrees to provide Stable with all health records with regard to the horse(s). Owner agrees to have the horse(s) vaccinated on a regular schedule, and in the event same is not accomplished and proof of same presented to Stable within thirty (30) days from the date of such services or veterinary treatment, Stable is authorized to arrange for the such treatment, but not obligated to do so: such expense shall be the obligation of Owner, and upon presentation by Stable of the bill for such services rendered, including service charges, and bill shall be paid within fifteen (15) days from the date the bill is submitted.*
- *Stable shall deworm horse(s) on a regular rotation schedule, cost of deworming will be added to board for that month and is Owner's responsibility. Copies of the rotation schedule are available in the office. If you do not wish for the Stable to deworm your horse(s),*

there must be a prior agreement between Stable and Owner regarding an acceptable alternative.

You should have the farrier, vaccinations and deworming protocols for your boarding stable established before your new boarders arrive. Once you have a plan on how you want to handle this part of barn management then incorporate it into your boarding contract. You may think you won't need to have this in a boarding contract, but you do. I have had a few situations over the years where I was dealing with horses with neglected feet and owners who didn't want to provide farrier care. I also ran into a situation years ago where a new client didn't believe in vaccinations or deworming and refused to do either. You are going to want to make sure you have care protocols stated in your boarding contract and discuss them with your new client at the time they are reviewing it. It is very important that you discuss annual care standards and compliance requirements with all prospective boarders, as well as new clients.

9. Ownership-Coggins Test. Owner warrants that he owns the horse(s) and will provide proof satisfactory to Stable of the negative Coggins test upon request.

Every new horse that comes onto your property needs to have a current negative Coggins. Most people understand this, but you may have someone that is moving to your barn who doesn't know what a Coggins is because their horse has never been tested and it wasn't required where they were previously boarded. You will need to explain to them that their horse cannot step foot off the trailer onto the premises until you have seen and read the Coggins report. This might mean that the horse's arrival date at your stable will need to be rescheduled until after the test results have been received.

10. Changes or Termination of This Agreement. It is agreed by the parties that Stable may change or terminate this Agreement at any time, regardless of the rental period. Owner shall be solely responsible for removing the horse within seven (7) days of a notice of termination and for all fees incurred during the horse's presence upon the premises. This Agreement shall be deemed terminated and concluded upon payment of all fees. All notices must be issued in writing unless otherwise agreed upon by the parties. The posting of updated rate schedules in a conspicuous or open place in Stable's office shall constitute notice of any and all rate changes or rules and regulations changes as may be deemed appropriate by Stable. Owner may terminate this Agreement upon thirty (30) days prior written notice and payment of all fees incurred during the horse's presence on the premises. This agreement shall be deemed terminated and concluded upon payment of all fees.

This is a very important section of your boarding agreement because you want to make sure you have control when a situation between you and a client is unresolvable. You hope it never happens, but if the relationship becomes unmanageable between you and a boarder, it is better that the boarder and horse vacate sooner than the customary thirty days' notice. You need to have the power to invoke this clause.

I have found myself in this situation a couple of times and it is safe to say it happens to barn owners at one time or another. Protect yourself by having this contract well-written, because if you don't, it can create unnecessary stress and drama while the boarder is still at your barn.

11. Rules and Regulations. *The Owner agrees to abide by all the rules and regulations of the Stable. Such rules and regulations may be changed by the Stable at any time upon posting in a conspicuous or open place in the Stable's office.*

Some barn owners will post their barn rules in their boarding contract, but I have found that your barn rules will change often, especially during the first few years of business. I believe it is much easier to have a separate sheet for your barn rules so that you don't have to keep modifying your boarding contract. You can also give your new clients two sets of barn rules. One set they will sign and date, (and give back to you for your records) showing that they have read the rules and understand them and the other set is theirs to keep.

12. Right of Lien. *The Owner is put on notice that Stable has a right of lien as set forth in the laws of the State of Wisconsin, for the amount due for the board and keep of such horse(s), and also for storage and services, and shall have the right, without process of law, to retain said horse(s) until the amount of said indebtedness is discharged. However, Stable will not be obligated to retain and/or maintain the horse(s) in question. In the event the amount of the bill exceeds the anticipated unregistered value of the horse(s). In the event Stable exercises Stable's lien rights as above-described for non-payment, this agreement shall constitute a Bill of Sale and authorization to process transfer applications from any breed registration as may be applicable to said horse(s) upon affidavit by Stable's representative setting forth the material facts of the default and foreclosure as well as Stable's compliance with foreclosure procedures as* *required by law. In the event collection of this account is turned over to an attorney, Owner agrees to pay all attorneys' fees, costs, and other related expenses for which a minimum charge of $250.00 will be assessed.*

This section protects the barn owner if a boarder has stopped paying their board. In a few situations a client of mine couldn't pay the board but I was still feeding and taking care of the horse. I have also heard many horror stories that are similar and a few stories where the owner abandoned the horse and was never heard from again. YOU NEED TO PROTECT YOURSELF so that you don't end up with horses that you don't want or need. This section will give you the right to keep the horse stabled at your barn until all fees are payed in full.

If you encounter a situation where a boarder has stopped paying their board the first thing you need to do is contact your attorney, explain the situation and make sure you handle the situation legally. You want to protect your interests while properly managing the question of horse ownership. It is important to have an attorney look over your boarding contract and make sure this section is correctly written for the laws of your state so that you have the power to put a lien on the horse and even sell it if that is the only resolution.

13. *Property in Storage on Stable's Premises.* *Owner may store certain tack and equipment on the premises of Stable at no additional charge to Owner. However, Stable shall not be responsible for the theft, loss, damage or disappearance of any tack or equipment or other property stored at Stable as same is stored at the Owner's risk. Stable shall not be liable for the theft, loss, damage, or disappearance of any tack or equipment taken to horse shows or clinics. Vehicles and horse trailers stored upon the premises will be subject to a $_____/day storage cost for all delinquent accounts.*

While running a boarding business you may periodically experience a boarder who is upset because something of theirs is missing. I hope it never happens at your barn but the reality is the longer you board horses the better the chance that something will end up missing. Even in the most organized and secure tack rooms things can be misplaced, lost or stolen and you don't want to be held responsible. The same would be true for damage to any tack, equipment and even horse trailers parked on your property.

You might find yourself in a strange situation where a boarder has left your facility with their horse but they have left their tack, saddles or even a horse trailer. If you think it won't happen, be prepared. I have had everything left at my barn from brushes, halters and blankets to saddles and even one horse trailer. It is amazing what people will leave behind especially when their personal life is going through changes and they don't care about anything else.

14. *<u>Inherent Risks and Assumption of Risk.</u>* *The undersigned acknowledges there are inherent risks associated with equine activities such as described below, and hereby expressly assumes all risks associated with participating in such activities. The inherent risks include, but are not limited to the propensity of equines to behave in ways such as running, bucking, biting, kicking, shying, stumbling, rearing, falling or stepping on, that may result in an injury, harm or death to persons on or around them; the unpredictability of equine's reaction to such things as sounds, sudden movement and unfamiliar objects, persons or other animals; certain hazards such as surface and subsurface conditions; collisions with other animals; the limited availability of emergency medical care; and the potential of a participant to act in a negligent manner that many contribute to injury to the participant of others, such as failing to maintain control over the animal or not acting with such participant's ability.*

- *Owner also understands that they MUST WEAR A HELMET at all times while riding a horse if under 18 years of age.*
- *Any and all riders other than Owner MUST SIGN a Release of Liability PRIOR to riding and handling any horses on property.*
- *Owner also understands that APPROPRIATE RIDING SHOES MUST BE WORN while riding. To clarify, appropriate riding shoes all have heels. Riding in tennis shoes or any flat soled shoe is not allowed.*
- *Owner expressly releases Stable from any and all claims for personal injury or property damage, even if caused by negligence (if allowed by the laws of this State) by Stable or its representatives, agents or employees.*

> ***WARNING***
>
> ***UNDER WISCONSIN LAW, AN EQUINE PROFESSIONAL IS NOT LIABLE FOR AN INJURY TO OR THE DEATH OF A PARTICIPANT IN EQUINE ACTIVITIES RESULTING FROM THE INHERENT RISK OR EQUINE ACTIVITIES.***
> ***Wis. Stat. §895.481***

If you are running a horse boarding operation of any size, then you need to understand that it is not a question of *if* there will be an accident but *when* there is an accident. Horse/people accidents happen and even though most people understand the risks involved with handling and riding horses you still need to protect your interests by having this written into your boarding contract. This will include the specific equine laws for your state as well. You need to realize that you might not be sued by the owner of the horse but there is a good chance if they are hurt badly, you would be sued by the husband, children or other family members who want someone to take the blame for the accident of their loved one.

The insurance companies will also consider all parties remotely involved to be held responsible for costs and losses and include all participants in any lawsuits. Make certain that you are protected by having a strong contract that covers these occurrences. Have a good attorney write this section up for you so that you don't need to worry about risk exposure when something happens.

15. Entire Agreement.   This contract represents the entire agreement between the parties. No other agreements, promises, or representations, verbal or implied, are included herein unless specifically stated in this written agreement. This Contract is made and entered into in the State of Wisconsin, and shall be enforced and interpreted in accordance with the laws of said State.

Your boarding contract helps protect you from legal and financial exposure. If a client tries to go after something that you verbally discussed, it will not hold up as part of this contract. That is why it is important to have your boarding contract as detailed as possible. A lengthy boarding contract is fine. The contract is written to protect you, the barn owner, and the business that you have worked so hard to build.

16. *Enforceability of Contract.* *In the event one or more parts of this contract are found to be unenforceable or illegal, the other portions hereof shall be deemed in full force and effect.*

When I first was looking at boarding contracts I didn't know where to go. Remember, this was many years ago and I was a very new business woman without any business experience. I did what most people do; I purchased a boarding contract off of the internet. I was naïve and assumed because it was on the internet that it was a well-written and legal boarding contract. I was very wrong! Over the years I have had my boarding contract reviewed and updated by my attorney. Even though my first boarding contract was poorly written, most sections of it were legal for the state of Wisconsin. The one section that was not legal was the section on collection of money for board each month and the late fee attached. I didn't find out until later when I finally had my attorney go over it that it needed to be rewritten. So even though that one section was not legal the rest of the boarding contract still was.

OWNER (OR AUTHORIZED AGENT)

*By:*_____

*Date:*_____

OWNER'S PARENT OR GUARDIAN (IF OWNER IS A MINOR)

Print Name:

_____*Date:*_____

Address: _____

*Telephone: (Work)*_____

- *(Home)*_____
- *(Cell)* _____

Received by: (Name of your barn and business including LLC/Corp. etc.)

By: _____

Print Name: _____

Title: _____

As with any contract, you are going to want all parties involved to sign and date the contract and complete all blank spaces. When drawing up a boarding contract you can specifically design it for the type of operation you will have including breeding and training of horses on your property.

I can't stress enough how important it is to have your boarding contract complete and ready to go before the first horse comes on to your property. I also recommend making a copy of the signed contract for each client so that they can look at it at any time if they have a question. I have had a few situations over the years where a new client will move to my barn and is so happy to be there, then something happens that upsets them and they want to know their rights as a client. The first thing they will do is call me and ask to see a copy of their contract. That is the first sign that something is wrong. If you provide clients with a contract copy right from the start, then they can reference it anytime if they have a question or concern.

Online Boarding Contracts

If you purchase a contract online and they advertise that it is completely legal for the state you do business in, **don't** take that as complete truth. You are responsible for your business and that means you need to have a good attorney verify that the contract is legal for the state you are doing business in. At the end of the day the responsibility will always fall back on the business owner.

Emergency Information Form

Along with your boarding contract you should have an emergency information form completed by each client. This will be your go-to information sheet for any type of emergencies. Here is a sample of what should be on your emergency information sheet.

- **Full names of the owners**
- **Address, City, State and Zip Code**
- **Phone numbers including home, cell number and work numbers.** An emergency contact beside family is always good to have.
- **Horse Identification including**–Name of horse, Date of birth (if known), Breed, Color, Sex, Distinctive markings and date of arrival.
- **Emergency Surgery and Veterinary Care**-Have the owner of the horse write down what their wishes are in case of an emergency like colic surgery or other life threatening situation.
- **Veterinarian information**–It's always good to have two veterinarians listed if the veterinarian of their choice doesn't do 24-hours service. If there is an

emergency you want to make sure you have a vet clinic that will come out any time of day or night and on the weekends or holidays as a back-up.
- **Farrier information**-It is good to know the owner's preferred farrier in case of an emergency, especially if the owner cannot be reached.
- **Additional information and services desired**–This is a great place to write down the special services or information that you will need to know for the feeding program or if there are any health concerns.

When A Different Contract Is Needed

If you are running a boarding business and want to offer other services like overnight boarding for travelers, then you will want to have a short-term contract written up for special situations where horses are boarded for a short period of time. The same will be true for clinics where people will be trailering in for overnight, as well as horse shows. I would ask your attorney to look at the type of contracts you need for the unique activities you will offer, as well as very short boarding stays.

~17~

Barn Rules

Barn rules are a must for any boarding barn. Without them you will have chaos, and with that comes drama and stress both for you as the barn owner and manager, as well as the boarders. People may not like rules but they will appreciate them because rules help to maintain a safe riding and working environment. Rules are only of value if they are enforced fairly and equally. Everyone needs to adhere to the rules to maintain a safe, clean and enjoyable environment for all equine activities.

The truth is that a well-run barn has rules and when rules are established it sends a message to your clients and the people outside your facility that you run a very professional operation and business. Barn rules are important to have no matter the size of your business and you can easily have the same issues with only a few horses and clients as you would with a large facility.

Your Barn Rules Will Change

When we first opened our boarding facility, we didn't have barn rules in place. I didn't even give it much thought at the time because I didn't realize all the problems that could occur. Once we attained full occupancy, creating barn rules became a necessity. It is hard to imagine all the issues that can evolve in a new boarding barn. Once you are dealing with issues daily it becomes apparent that rules to govern behavior are very important to a drama-free environment.

Over the years our barn rules have changed quite a few times. I have added many rules and even gotten rid of a few. It is safe to say that your barn rules will need updating every couple of years. You might not make a whole lot of changes throughout your time in business but I can guarantee that you will add some during that time.

Can Your Barn Have Too Many Rules?

I really believe a better question to ask is…Do your boarders understand why you have the rules you have? Now I can't say that every rule a barn owner puts in place is reasonable because, let's face it, we have all heard some pretty crazy rules. As a good barn manager your job is to educate your boarders on why you have the barn rules you have. Every barn will have different rules and different ways of doing things. I believe common sense plays an important part in all this. Having your boarders pick up after themselves is a very important and standard rule to have. Giving guidelines for horse safety within the arena or anywhere else on the property is also smart. Sometimes a problem occurs when the barn owner or manager becomes a control freak and doesn't give the boarder room to breathe when in the barn. If your rules are unreasonable for your boarders and they seem unhappy, then it is time to re-evaluate your program. Finding a healthy balance is very important.

At the end of the day you are not going to be able to make everyone happy, so the best thing you can do is design your barn and rules for what works for you, your staff and your family. Clearly defined rules will help maintain safety and reduce extra work and drama throughout the day.

Barn Rules And Safety

Many of your boarders will be new horse owners or only have limited experience with horses and boarding stables. When you have a new horse owner at your barn there is a good chance they will not realize everything that can go wrong. They might not realize how dangerous a horse can be when it is spooking, and they don't know what to do. The same would be true in the horse herds. I had a situation where a boarder was kicked by a horse because they unknowingly created a competitive situation with the other horses in the same paddock. They were feeding treats to their horse in the middle of a herd and their horse and another horse got into it. Heels started flying and this person was kicked badly. Needless to say, after that situation I now tell our boarders not to feed treats to the horses in the middle of the herds. Anything can happen quickly and you don't want to be the one to have to call a loved one and tell them there was an accident. New horse owners don't have an understanding of horse behavior so it is better to educate them about why you shouldn't feed treats around other horses. This example might not seem like a rule you would want but it is something to think about if you ever find yourself in this situation.

No Surprises For New Clients

Start all your new clients off right with very clear expectations about your barn rules and it will make things much easier in the long run. The one thing you need to remember is that your barn is your home also. This is where you work daily and also live and you are the one who will be there long after everyone has gone home for the day. All boarding stables will have different rules. Don't try to copy what others are doing for their barn rules, instead do what is best for your operation and clients. You will be much happier in the long run and so will your clients. Your stable will not be the right place for everyone, but the right clients will find you and they will stay for a long time because they will appreciate the way you run your barn. It is much easier to have boarders that are happy with your rules than to constantly hear complaining because someone doesn't like the rules you have. Do what is best for you and your business!

Learning To Enforce The Barn Rules

Get ready because this will be one of the most difficult and tiring parts of your job! Having barn rules and enforcing them will seem exhausting at times. You will have moments where you feel like you are the police, watching what everyone is doing and it is not fun. There are going to be situations that need to be addressed and it is your job as a barn owner or manager to take care of it. It is part of having a well-run business. You will learn to be professional and tactful in discussions with your clients about rules. It is not easy at times and it will take you out of your comfort zone, but it is all part of running a business. You need to remember that it is not personal, it is business.

I have talked to a few barn managers who struggle with this because they are concerned about the boarders becoming angry with them. You can't control how your clients are going to take things, but you can control how you respond. Do the best you can and it will get easier the more often you are put in a situation where you need to discuss barn rules.

It is also very important to understand that if someone refuses to follow your barn rules then there might come a time when you need to discuss their options and that they need to find another place to board their horse. It can be a frustrating time for any barn manager but you need to set a standard for all your clients to follow without exceptions or favoritism. Remember that this is business first and a well-run business enforces rules with equanimity.

Different Riding Disciplines And Rules

When you are writing up your barn rules you will have a core set of rules that will apply no matter what kind of stable you operate. Cleaning up after yourself and rules governing safety are standard in most barns. The rest can vary depending on the riding disciplines you have at your barn and even the size of the facility and arenas.

If you are primarily a hunter/ jumper barn where jumps will be set out most of the time, then you might have a set of rules for proper protocol when jumping horses. The same would be true for speed riders that use barrels and poles. If you have people who love natural horsemanship and use many different tools (tarps, objects to help desensitize etc.) you will want to make sure that their equipment does not hinder others from using the arena. If you have a multidiscipline barn where there are many styles of riding and training methods, then things can become complicated quickly if you do not have well thought-out rules and protocols for using the arena. On the other hand, if you help your clients understand the reasons for your rules and guidelines you are likely to have good compliance and avoid issues and discontent between riders. I know this because we have successfully instituted and enforced rules throughout our boarding career.

When creating your barn rules I believe it is best to have regular barn rules and then a separate set of riding arena etiquette and rules. This will be a much better and clearer way of presenting it to your boarders.

When you purchase your business insurance your agent will ask you many questions about your horse boarding business and some of those questions will pertain to your barn rules. Your insurance might reflect a price rate depending on what you allow and don't allow at your barn. For example, my insurance agent wanted to know what kind of dogs I allow on my property and I have been asked breed specific questions about the dogs and if they are allowed in the barn and if they are leashed, etc.

There are many considerations when formulating barn rules and it may be worthwhile asking your insurance agent about the areas of risk that you need to be aware of when your boarding business is open.

List Of Sample Barn Rules

I have compiled a list of barn rules to give you a starting point in developing rules that support your business style and protect your interests. These are suggestions and you will design *your* barn rules around your business. Your rules will need to be re-evaluated and modified periodically if issues evolve. You will add rules in the early stages of operation but then may modify or eliminate some rules as you stabilize your client base and business. An ongoing review of rules is beneficial and reflects your interest in meeting the needs of your clients, the horses and your business interests.

Barn Rules And The Reasons For Them:

1. No smoking on premises at all.

This rule is clear, but you still need to have signs posted. There are many people who smoke and they may not realize that smoking around a horse barn is not safe. I have seen people smoke right next to a stack of hay bales and not think twice about it, so having this rule will save you the stress of dealing with smokers.

2. No dogs allowed in the barns or riding arenas at all. You may bring your dog out to the stable and walk them but they need to stay on a leash at all times.

Dogs and horses would seem like a natural combination but when it comes to a boarding stable it can lead to many problems. The problem starts because many of your clients own dogs and will want to bring them to the stable. Many dogs are not well trained and do not listen to their owners. The dogs may not be accustomed to horses, barn cats or other people and can pose a safety problem when they react adversely and have unpredictable responses. I had a situation where a person brought their dog to the barn and the dog ended up chasing a barn cat through the arena while people were riding. As you can guess the dog spooked a horse and I had to deal with the very upset client. I was very lucky that no one was hurt.

The essential point about dogs on your property is if something bad happens and someone is bitten or a horse spooks because of a dog, the liability will always fall back on the barn owner. It doesn't matter whose dog it is, it is still the barn owner who is taking all the risk. This is where you will want to check with your insurance carrier and see how you are protected for this kind of situation.

3. Riders under the age of 18 must wear a helmet at all times when riding.

As a barn owner you can choose to make helmets a rule or not for young riders but there is a good chance your insurance premium will be higher if you allow people under 18 to ride without a helmet. This is an individual choice for the barn owner and you will need to check with your insurance carrier and see how this will reflect your rates. Each state will be different when it comes to the helmet rule.

4. Correct footwear with a heel must be worn while riding. No sandals or tennis shoes at all while riding.

The longer you are running a boarding barn the more interesting behavior you will see including peoples' attire when riding. I have had a few situations over the years where I have seen people come to ride in everything from sandals and tennis shoes to rubber muck boots. I have also experienced situations where a rider fell off their horse, had their foot slip through the stirrup and hang up their leg resulting in the risk of being dragged by the horse. These cases could have been tragic but the horses stood quietly while someone helped dislodge the rider. Some of your boarders, especially new horse owners, will not realize all that can go wrong in an instant and it is your responsibility to educate them so they have safe riding behavior.

5. No running or yelling in the barn areas as this could spook a horse.

If you have visitors at your barn then you will have some running and yelling at times. Kids will be kids and you will need to remind people that loud noises and running can be disturbing to the horses and create unsafe conditions in the barn and arenas. This is a good sound rule to have when it comes to safety.

6. Observe barn hours:

I am a huge fan of barn hours. (I will talk more about barn hours in a different chapter). If you choose to have barn hours, then you need to have them listed in your rules. If you don't have them listed in your barn rules, then you risk having people at the barn all hours of the day and night.

7. All visitors must sign a waiver release form prior to riding or handling a horse on the property.

When operating a boarding business, you will need to have liability waivers signed by all visitors who will be doing anything with the horses on your property. Your boarders need to understand and comply with this requirement without exception. Make this easy by having your liability waivers readily available. Remember that your entire business is at risk if something catastrophic happens and you do not have the liability waivers signed.

Have a designated location for liability forms and a folder for holding signed forms. You can also email all your boarders a copy of your liability form and they can print it off and drop it in the folder at the barn in order to make it easier for them. This works especially well for unexpected visits from friends or family coming to see the barn and horses.

8. No riding in any stable aisle way.

This rule may not apply to every barn and stable. At our stable this rule is in place because we have a long aisle that has a cement floor. This rule exists because I had people riding down the aisle and I realized it created an unsafe situation for the riders as well as the people with horses in crossties. I felt it would be a liability issue to allow people to ride down our cement aisle.

If your barn is open concept or dirt aisle, this may not present risk or a problem for your situation. This is one of those situations where you might not realize you need a certain rule until you have been in operation for a while.

9. Never leave your horse unattended in the crossties. If you need to step away from your horse then please make sure someone is nearby to watch your horse.

If you are going to use crossties in your aisle, then I strongly encourage you to have this rule. Horses can become turned around and tangled in crossties and some horses will panic and spook. Crossties can break, horses can get loose and bad behavior can create dangerous situations when horses are unattended. For example, horses can kick out at other horses as they are passing by and this can be extremely dangerous for horses and people.

You need to remember that your clients will not always be aware of all the things that can occur. It is up to you as the barn manager to make them aware of these types of situations so that you minimize the risk of injury to people or horses.

10. Never tie a horse to stall grills. Damages including repair and replacement of the damaged grill will be the boarder's responsibility.

If someone ties a horse to a stall grill it is very likely that you will have a bent or damaged grill. After spending a lot of money on your new stalls and appreciating their new appearance, it can be very upsetting to experience damage due to horses being tied to them.

I have seen it at many horse shows where people will tie their horses anywhere and to anything without regard for property. If you want to maintain your barn's appearance you will want to have this rule, be watchful and enforce it. When your barn looks nice it supports a professional appearance and confident management. People notice those kinds of things, so when your stalls are damaged it reflects poorly on your business.

11. When getting your horse from the paddock or pasture make sure all gates are securely locked after you come out.

Boarders need to be vigilant about checking and re-checking paddock gates when exiting the paddock to reduce the risk of a horse getting loose on the farm. At some point as a barn owner, you are sure to experience the gut wrenching words…"Loose horse!"

It is important to train your boarders how to exit the paddocks safely and how to always check the security of the gates. The type of gate latch you have for your gates can also make a difference on the ease and reliability of locking. Just remember, some horses can get out of almost anything!

12. Clean up after your horse, BEFORE YOU LUNGE OR RIDE. This includes sweeping up the crosstie areas and placing the sweepings in the muck bucket. Clean up all manure in the riding arenas after use.

This is a big one! You are going to be dealing with many people at your stable and if you don't get them in the habit of cleaning up after themselves, there is a very good chance that your barn will become a mess very quickly. If you are going to only board a couple of horses then it is not such a big deal, but if you plan on having a larger facility then you will be shocked at how quickly your barn can look like a disaster zone. You will have many boarders that will be very clean and even clean up other people's messes but you will also have boarders that will not clean up unless they realize it is a rule. It is just the reality of dealing with people.

The best thing you can do is to make it a rule and then you won't find yourself becoming frustrated when your place is a mess. This is a common complaint I hear often from other barn owners and if you have this rule then you also need to enforce it. Reminding people to clean up is often a necessary part of management. Most of your boarders will appreciate a very clean barn and help encourage compliance. A clean and well-organized barn is a real advantage for any business.

13. Adult supervision required for all young children. A minor needs to have permission from the barn owner before being left at the barn alone without supervision.

As the barn owner you will establish the rule that states the age at which a child can be left alone with their horse at your stable. If you don't set the age parameters you will have some parents that will drop their child off and leave them unsupervised. People will ask me what a good age is to start leaving a child alone at the barn. There is not a black and white answer for this. It is difficult to determine the age at which a child can manage their horse independently. A lot will depend on the child and the knowledge they have for safety, horsemanship and their maturity level. The other part of the scenario is the horse.

Some horses are bomb proof and extremely quiet while others are hot and spook and become agitated easily. There are many parents that don't know a lot about horses and buy a horse that is not suitable for the skill level of their child. When this happens and the person can't handle the horse, it can easily lead to many safety issues. If the rider is young or inexperienced a parent or trainer needs to be present at all times.

Very small children should always be watched and supervised by an adult. Over the years we have had situations such as our toilet being plugged up, markers used on the walls and even hay bales cut open because parents were not watching their young children. Your boarding business is not a playground where anything goes! The people who come to your barn need to understand the rules and their responsibilities.

Do not allow a breach of this rule!

14. Do not put your horse in another horse's stall without the owner's consent. If you have permission to use a different stall then leave it exactly how you found it. Make sure it is clean from all manure and top off the water bucket if your horse drank from it. Please leave the stall better than you found it.

This is one of those rules that you would not think about if you are just starting out in the boarding business. I never gave this a thought until I started having problems with trainers and some boarders putting their horses in stalls that were not theirs to use. The stalls had been cleaned for the day and the water was topped off and now the person renting the stall walks in and the stall is a complete mess. Few boarders will be pleased with someone using their stall, especially if it is left dirty. <u>They rightfully become protective of it just like renting an apartment except it is for their horse.</u> The first person they will complain to is you as the barn manager. You need to remember that they are paying for a stall and part of the amenities is a clean stall with a clean, full water bucket for their horse. Your boarders will become very protective of their stall, as they should because this is where their horse lives.

Again, this might not seem like a big deal and in many boarding barns it may not be. I was a boarder for many years and I would be upset if I came out and another horse was in my stall. I have heard this complaint from people who have boarded at other barns and it makes the establishment look poorly managed and unprofessional. This is a totally avoidable issue when your rules are clearly defined.

15. All horse hair clippings and loose hair should be put in designated garbage cans. NOT in tack room garbage cans.

This rule is probably not a very common rule but I have known a few barns that want the horse hair all put in a separate garbage can. The reasons for this might vary, but for us it was because the horse hair in the tack room garbage would attract mice. Horse hair is beautiful on your horse but once off the horse it becomes a mess. The loose hair floats and pretty soon you will have hair all over your tack room. Mice love horse hair and will use it for making nests. Mice can be very destructive and can damage tack so it is essential to deter them from making your barn their home.

16. The wash stall needs to be cleaned after each use to prevent clogging of the drain. Immediately after you are finished using the wash stall please sweep up all debris and put it in a muck bucket. Please hose down remaining debris. After the stall is clean, remove the drain and empty it of all dirt. You might need to hose off the drain if it is covered in mud. If there is any standing water in the aisle way it needs to be swept into the drain. Please double check to make sure both the hot and cold water is turned completely off.

You will need a rule about keeping your wash stall clean. By detailing the cleaning process you will have a consistent standard of what "clean" means. If you don't provide and explanation of "how to clean" then there is a very good chance you will be calling the plumber to come and fix a clogged pipe. We had to call a plumber early on in our boarding business and it was on a Saturday, of course! After I paid the bill for the emergency call I decided right away that I needed a new rule added to our list.

You need to remember that some of your clients will not care if the wash stall is clean or left dirty for the next horse. They will wash their horse and move on to the next thing. It is up to you as the barn manager to make sure that cleaning the wash stall becomes a maintenance habit for all boarders.

17. When bringing your horse into the barn from the paddocks please stay on the path at all times. If you walk your horse on the grass when the ground is soft or wet, it will tear it up. There are designated areas for you to hand graze your horse.

This barn rule is largely determined by location and weather. For example, our boarding business is in Wisconsin where we have very wet spring and autumn seasons and, at times a wet summer. Our facility is in a low-lying area with a soil substrate that has a lot of clay in it. In other words, we can get muddy very fast. In order to keep the grass around our barn and home looking nice we don't allow horses to be on it.

There are places for people to graze their horse and ride them but we want to keep our lawn looking nice for the public, so we don't allow horses on it. If you live in a dry region then you probably won't have this issue. You need to remember that horses are heavy and their hooves will push into any soft ground around them and they will tear it up very fast.

18. Turn off the lights if you are the last one to leave the barn. Make sure all arena lights are off as well as the aisle lights. Working together to conserve electricity will help keep the board rates down.

The most important thing you need to get your boarders to understand is that the board rates are made up of more than just hay, grain, stall cleaning and daily turnout. Your board rate will include other business costs such as your insurance, electricity, fuel and much more. If the lights are on when no one is using the barn or riding arena, then the meter is spinning and your monthly bill will reflect it. You might need to remind your boarders of this from time to time. It is no different than being mindful of power conservation in your home to reduce your electric bill. You might need to post signs in designated areas in your barn to remind people to turn the lights off as well.

Your Barn Rules Will Evolve And Change

I have given you a short list of barn rules as a starting point to get you thinking about the not so obvious issues that will come up. If you are starting a new boarding stable your list will probably be short until you get into full operation with horses and people. Be prepared to adapt your rules because you will experience significant changes during the first couple of years in operation and a few thereafter.

It is important to be mindful that many of your boarders will have had previous boarding experiences at other barns before coming to your stable. Every boarding stable has their own set of barn rules and different ways of doing things.

Some of your boarders may come from a facility that had absolutely no rules at all while others came from a stable where the rules were never enforced. Give your new clients time to adjust to how you do things at your stable. You might need to explain some of your rules and why you have them, so take the time to answer questions, so they understand your objectives. Starting your relationship with your clients with a good foundation will make your job much easier.

~18~

Riding Arena Rules

Arena Etiquette And Rules For Safe Riding

Your stable will have rules but you also need rules for your riding arenas. Rules for your riding arenas will help preserve order and avoid chaos. There is nothing more stressful than boarders not getting along because of conflict in the riding arena. If you don't think this happens, then you are in for an awakening. There will likely be a few times when you will feel like the referee at a soccer game trying to restore order and keep the peace.

Your arena rules will vary depending on the riding disciplines you have at your barn. In the beginning you might have difficulty coming up with reasonable rules, but once you are in full operation you will recognize the issues and develop rules that will be sensible and effective. Make sure to inform boarders as the rules list evolves and changes are made.

Your indoor riding arenas will usually have a few more rules because you are in an enclosed building and the dynamics of the area around the arena can impact safety. Some riding arenas have stalls on one end of the arena and some are completely enclosed with only one or two entrances and exits. Safety issues and rules will depend on the design of your barn and arena, as well as activities.

Many issues between boarders will start in the riding arena. The best way to keep the peace in your arena is to create rules that are appropriate for the type of facility you have. You will have a basic set of safety rules, but you will also have arena rules developed for the routine use of your arena. If you have a hunter/jumper barn where the jumps will be set up much of the day, then you will want rules for making sure everyone is safe when you have riders jumping and when additional riders are in the arena. If you have a barn where you have pleasure/trail riders and also riders who do speed events, then you will want to set some guidelines so that the different disciplines avoid conflicts when using the arena at the same time. Common courtesies and common sense will often prevail in these situations, but rules are the foundation of equitable use of the arenas. This is something that you will adjust as you get through the first couple of years and especially if you don't know what kind of clients, breeds and riding disciplines you will have.

Many years ago we had an issue with carts in the arena. I had a boarder who drove a cart and I had another person who was very nervous about bringing her horse into the arena when the horse and cart were working. There were some words exchanged between the two people over the horse and cart and they both came to me upset and seeking resolution. This was a part of barn management that I was not prepared for but I knew I needed to help facilitate it with a positive outcome. In a situation like this you need to realize that you won't make everyone happy and it might even look like you are taking sides because one of your clients probably will not like your decision. It is part of running a barn and you need to be an effective leader and move forward. In this situation with the horse and cart, I decided that carts were allowed to be used in the arena and that the horse and rider would need to adapt to it. Since then we have several horses that pull carts at our barn and it has never been an issue again unless there is a safety issue that I need to address concerning a horse and cart situation.

I have compiled a short list of riding arena etiquette and rules for safe riding. These are some of the rules I use at my barn and this will give you a starting point to create your own set of riding arena rules. It is okay to add on to your list and change it as you experience new issues that you didn't think of in the beginning.

Riding Arena Etiquette and Rules for Safe Riding:

1. When entering the indoor arena be sure to announce your entrance WELL BEFORE you enter. Call out, "Coming in" or 'Door" and listen for a reply that it is okay to enter. Riders inside the arena will either say "OK" or "Stop, wait a minute." Remember they don't know you are entering the arena and they might be riding by at the same time you are entering.

This is the most important rule we have for our indoor arena. You will want to make sure you have this rule enforced if there are blind spots where the entrance is located or if there are design considerations that block the view of the arena. We had a situation many years ago where someone came walking through the entrance without yelling "Door" and a young rider was coming by at the same exact time. Her horse spooked and she fell off and broke her arm. Since that accident, I make it a priority to educate my new boarders about this rule and get them to understand its importance.

2. Lunging horses—Only two horses can be lunged at the same time in the indoor arena. If you find that two horses are already being lunged in the arena, you will need to wait until one is done before lunging your horse. Please be aware of where you are lunging your horse. If other people are

already riding or having a lesson and you come in, please ask them, "Where would be a good area to lunge my horse?"

When horses are being lunged they take up a lot of area with the lunge line and it makes it very difficult for people to ride around them. Please communicate with each other.

When you have horses being lunged and horses being ridden together in an arena, it can become a safety hazard if the arena becomes overcrowded. Our arena is 80 x 200ft. in size, which is very large, but once you put two horses on lunge lines, it becomes crowded and can make it tight to ride around the perimeter.

I have this rule at our barn because I have seen three people try to lunge their horses while others ride and it doesn't work well at all. Some of your boarders are not going to recognize the hazards so it is up to you to bring it to their attention.

Lunging horses is a common practice but the lunge line will also take up a lot of space. Keeping the number of horses lunged simultaneously to a minimum will help keep everyone safe, especially if your arena is small.

3. When passing another rider from behind, always pass on the inside (not between the rider and the wall). When meeting another rider coming towards you, pass so that your left shoulders meet. The *"Inside"* of the arena is towards the center. The *"Outside"* is by the wall.

There is a good chance this terminology will be confusing to some of your new clients, especially the ones that have never used a riding arena before. The best thing you can do is to give them a visual so that they clearly understand it.

Taking the time to explain arena terminology will be vital in keeping everyone safe especially new clients who may have never ridden in an arena before.

4. If the arena is crowded please call out your direction of travel if you will be traveling across the diagonal of the arena or need to do lateral exercises on the wall. Please be courteous and understand that when the directions are called out by a rider it is your responsibility to free up the requested area until the pattern is completed and that it is only temporary.

This is a rule that you will need to explain to some of your new clients and a visual will be helpful. If you have a large riding arena with low traffic then this may be a non-issue, but in a smaller arena with several riders, congestion and frustration can occur quickly if people feel they have been cut off. I have seen this happen in our large arena and people can be quick to complain. As the barn manager, you will be the one they complain to so it is better to have this kind of rule in place early on. Many riding disciplines work on the diagonal as part of their training, and educating will be part of your job if you have riders that are unfamiliar with this term and arena protocol.

When someone is riding on the diagonal, it is important for others to allow them to move forward until they are on the other end. Communication is of the utmost importance when riders are doing different maneuvers in the arena.

5. Stop your horse and stand still whenever a rider is having trouble controlling their horse.

This is a great practice to get into and it helps keep everyone else safe especially when a rider is having trouble controlling their horse.

6. Do not stop in line of travel of another rider. If you need to stop/dismount please do so in the center or corner of the arena.

Making this rule a standard practice for all riders will significantly help rider safety. Some riders will halt their horse while unaware that another rider is coming up behind them and create a dangerous chain reaction. Riders can become so focused on their riding that they forget that there are other riders in the arena. This is when accidents can happen.

7. If you are coming into the arena and someone is having a lesson please be courteous and stay out of the area that they are having the lesson. If the rider is using up a good part of the arena, then communicate with the trainer to find out where the best area would be to ride.

Issues with lessons and trainers will depend on the size of your riding arena. If you have a smaller arena then you will really need to make sure that your clients and trainers communicate. With a larger arena the problems will not exist as much. Communication is key when it comes to riders, trainers and lessons. Once you get your boarders and trainers to communicate then most of your arena issues will disappear.

8. When using jump standards, ground poles and trail equipment, please set them up on one end of the arena so that others can ride around them and have room to ride on the other end of the arena. Remember to put everything back in the same place you found it when you are done. Some of the equipment may belong to other boarders so you need to have permission to use any equipment that is not yours PRIOR to use. All equipment needs to be put away when you are done using it.

You will have boarders that will bring all kinds of equipment to use at the stable. Having a place to store equipment will become important and you might need to limit what people bring. Equipment is great to have available but only as long as people understand that they can't dominate the arena with all their stuff and not leave room for others to ride. This can become a real problem if you have a small arena. Set some guidelines for your boarders and using equipment. It will save you stress and headaches if you set rules from the start. People can become impatient and irritated if they come to ride and equipment is all over the arena with not much room to ride. If this causes disruption then you will be the one that needs to solve the issues.

Having a large arena is an asset when it comes to using equipment.

9. Please be sure to communicate with each other. We are all equal in this arena and we are all here to help one another. If you are unsure about something, please ask each other or the barn manager.

This last rule is self-explanatory. Communication is a vital part in keeping the riding arena safe for all to use.

You will have many different clients throughout the years. Many of them will have never ridden in an arena before, or who come from other barns where the rules are much different, or there were no rules at all. There is always an adjustment period for each new boarder and if you take the time to explain things thoroughly in the beginning, it will reduce future issues.

You are going to learn a lot about barn management and leadership just through the on the job training you will get each day with your clients and arena use. The good news is that the more you are in contact with your clients and doing problem solving, the easier it will become. Once you gain experience, you will find that the issues that at first seemed insurmountable are minor, and you will know how to effectively resolve most problems. You will also develop the ability to maintain satisfied clients even when enforcing rules.

Horse Barn Management- The Real Deal

~19~

Chores–Making It Easy And Efficient

Most people who love horses also love the idea of feeding horses and mucking out the stalls. Surprisingly, many people will say that cleaning stalls is therapeutic for them and the perfect way to start the day. I still clean stalls five days a week and love the exercise but I also don't want to be working in the barn all day. Owning and operating a large boarding facility includes daily chores, as well as many other jobs that need to be done daily. Learning to streamline the chores and making them fast and efficient is part of creating a well-run operation. Many barn owners that hire employees find themselves with a larger payroll than was anticipated because they don't know how to streamline the chores or their employees don't work as efficiently as they could. Maybe it is wasted time on the job or maybe the barn is not well designed for the chores that need to get done twice a day every day of the year. There are many reasons that the chores could be taking longer than they should and in this chapter we will discuss some ways to streamline the daily chores that are a constant expense when taking care of horses.

Many factors can affect operational decisions and chores such as whether the horses go outside for the day or stay in their stalls daily. Weather is another factor that impacts operations. During the seasons when it snows or rains and the paddocks become very muddy, your chores can take much longer. Having the right equipment for different seasons is also very important and can either help get the job done faster or make jobs much harder than they need to be.

Feeding Horses

Deciding what type of hay you will feed and how you want to feed it will be a significant part of horse management. Since horses eat hay as their main food source, you want to be knowledgeable when purchasing hay. Unless you grow your hay yourself, you will need a hay supplier and you will encounter many opinions about hay and the best way to feed horses. Hay decisions can become very complicated. Consider your feeding program and learn as much as you can, because it can make your chore time much harder if you are not smart about it.

You will need to decide if you are going to feed a straight grass hay or a grass/alfalfa mix that could include other legumes mixed into the bale. Where you live will also dictate the types of hay available and the prices of hay. Some parts of the country are definitely more expensive, especially if the hay needs to be irrigated. If you live in a state where hay is not grown near you, then you will be shipping it in and that will have an added cost. I encourage you to take your time in this area of your business and get well educated on hay quality and different types of hay available where you live. Find out where other barns are getting their hay and shop around. Find out what suppliers sell good quality hay and who to stay away from. Your life will turn into a nightmare if you buy a semi-load of hay and it turns out to be moldy or not the quality that was promised by the seller. Be prepared and make sure your supplier has a strong reputation for being honest and selling high quality hay.

Feeding hay is customized at every barn and there really is not a wrong way to feed hay as long as the horses are able to get plenty of good quality hay to meet their individual needs. You should always seek to save time and be efficient, so evaluate the pros and cons on how hay is fed. The number of horses you need to feed and the type of weather you have in your area will play major parts in your hay feeding program. If you have to contend with snow and a lot of rain, then there will be times when feeding hay is just plain hard work.

The Many Opinions Of How To Feed Hay

There are many opinions about how to feed hay and for most people it is based on the amount of labor involved. Many barns will feed hay in large round bales or large square bales outside so the horses can eat anytime and it is much less labor for the workers. Hay can be placed in large hay feeders or hay nets that are off the ground to reduce waste. Another option is feeding hay in separate piles for the number of horses in a herd.

Feeding large bales (free choice) versus small individual piles of hay can bring unique issues, so listing the pros and cons of feeding styles can help guide your decisions. For example, consider that when the bales are rained on, over time there may be a loss of nutrients. Not every horse will have good dinner manners and share nicely while eating and the competition for hay can become a problem. Consider that if the horses can't get to the hay due to dominant horses in the herd, they could start to lose weight or become stressed. Injuries can happen more frequently if there are not enough round bales for the horses and aggression can develop toward each other.

With a boarding barn you need to remember that there may be more frequent changes to the herds and that impacts herd dynamics. Every time a new horse comes into a herd the horses need to reconfigure the dominance structure of who is at the top all the way down to the bottom and that will produce stress, especially during feeding time.

We have always fed all the horses at our boarding facility by placing individual piles (enough for the number of horses in each paddock) in separate areas so that the horses can get away from each other as they move from pile to pile. It takes more time but we reduce hay waste and we have far fewer injuries from horses fighting over hay. We have always used a 4-wheeler and small hay wagon to feed the horses at our barn and it has worked well for us and our employees. With the proper equipment you can feed horses pretty quickly once you get a system in place that works for the layout of your paddocks.

When deciding how you want to manage chores, you will of course want to make it as easy and as fast as possible while still focusing on what is best for the horses. You don't want to get a call from an upset boarder because they are concerned that their horse is losing weight because they can't get enough hay to eat outside! It will also become more stressful if the horses are getting hurt often because of issues over the hay. Feeding separate piles of hay can cut down on many issues in your herds.

Feeding Grain

Feeding Grain to horses can either be easy, complicated or even difficult depending on how you set up your daily chores. You are going to encounter many opinions about grains and the best feed for each horse. If you are not an equine nutritionist I would encourage you to meet with a nutrition expert in your area and develop a feeding program that will meet your needs at your boarding stable.

You can offer several different grain plans as part of your program or if your clients would like to supply their horse's grain and a grain bin, you can feed their grain. We currently offer three types of grains at our barn and we feed many types of grain that many of our clients supply. This works very well and it gives my boarders the option to feed what they want. Some people don't want the added effort of buying their own grain while other people like to manage their feed. Both options work well at our facility.

Once you experience the sound of impatient horses (some will kick, some will paw and some grind or rub their teeth on the grills) you will appreciate the need for speed in putting grains and supplements together and getting them into the horses' feed bins.

Setting up your feed area and organizing it for efficiency is important because you can fill the buckets quickly and get this part of the chores done fast and efficiently when things are in their place.

The Numbering System

I use a stall numbering system at our boarding barn and it has proved to make this part of our chores fast, efficient and less room for error. The numbers on the stalls and buckets will always stay the same even though horses will come and go. Many people will put the names of the horses on the grain buckets. The problem you run into is that you could have two horses with the same name, owners that change the name of their horse or new horses come in and now you are changing names on the bucket again. You will also have horses that switch stalls and that can also lead to confusion. In all these situations mistakes can happen, especially with different employees working different shifts. I have each stall numbered and it matches the grain buckets so there is no confusion. If I have two horses named Jack then we don't have an issue with who gets what because we are going by the stall and bucket number only. Of course, you are going to look at each horse to make sure you are feeding the right grain to the right horse but if you have a new person feeding for the first time then it should be very easy for them to follow this system.

Having a numbering system in place for feeding horses is a smart way to make sure each horse gets their specialized grain mixture and fewer mistakes are made.

I have always used a large dry erase board for keeping track of each horse and the grains and supplements they get each day. It is easy to read and can be changed when a client changes something in their horses feeding program. The one thing for sure is that you will have changes and some clients will change their grains and supplements often. Keeping this part of the job organized and simplified is important and it is smart to have a dry erase board with individualized instructions right where you fill the grain buckets.

Remember that you are not running a feed store and you will be doing this every day of the year twice a day, so KEEP IT SIMPLE. If you allow your clients to bring in what they choose if it is different than what you offer, then it's a win/win for everyone. Feeding many horses' individualized programs can become extremely complicated, so you need to do what works best for you and your employees.

There is nothing better or easier than dry erase boards to help keep things organized. The grains and supplements may change often with certain clients and the dry erase board makes it easy to make those changes for all employees to see.

Getting Organized With Grain Bins

When you board a large number of horses, organization is a top priority. The area for grains and supplements should have enough room for all the grain bins and containers that you and your boarders will use. I have always had the boarders who supply their own grain to also provide a specified type of grain bin (garbage bin) that fits well in the space I have. I keep everything the same and it makes our feeding program very efficient.

Feeding Multiple Supplements

When we were in the planning stages of how our barn would run, I decided that if a boarder had two or three supplements, then they would need to put them into baggies or containers for each day. Each container or baggie would consist of all of the supplements they wanted fed. It is very common to have a boarder pre-bag or container multiple supplements so you don't have to open two or three containers. It makes the job much easier, organized, and you don't have a bunch of large supplement containers all over the place taking up a lot of space. It also makes it much easier when you are working with gloves and temperatures are extremely cold. Everything you do at your barn will be motivated by time and necessity is the mother of invention. Once you start doing the chores and see how everything really works, you will start to come up with new and more efficient ways to cut down on the time it takes to feed grain and supplements and ultimately save you money, especially if you have employees.

Containers for multiple supplements will help make the job much easier.

Plastic baggies are another easy way to feed horses multiple supplements.

Different Forms Of Supplements

Supplements come in many different forms from pellets and powder to oils and paste. Once you start putting together grains and supplements for each horse, you start to realize what is easy to feed and what is not. When we opened our barn, I was willing to feed any kind of supplement that was on the market. I quickly realized that some of the mixtures created much more work for me and some were extremely messy and sticky.

You will get requests to add oils to the grain mixture and I found out very fast that oils are not only messy but leaves the bucket messy and it also attracts flies in the summer. Some oils can be squeezed right out of the bottle and that works well until the temperatures drop. Oils solidify when the temperatures drop down and it makes it very hard to get thick oil out of any kind of container. There are so many great fat and joint supplements on the market nowadays that you really don't need to use oils if you don't want to. Remember that everything is easy with only a few horses but if you are going to manage a large scale boarding facility, then all these little things can become big headaches if you are not equipped to manage them.

I don't believe you will lose a boarder over something so little as not feeding oils or certain supplements at your barn. There are so many comparable alternatives to replacing certain types of supplements and they come in many easy to feed forms. It has never been an easier time to keep your horse healthy.

Daily Turnout For Horses

When deciding how you want daily turnout to be done, there are a few things to think about. You will need to decide if you will turn horses outside all day or just a few hours a day. Will you offer night turnout with the horses being brought back in the next morning? Will you need to turn out horses in shifts or will you have enough paddocks available to put all horses out at the same time? Will you have private turnout only, herd turnout or both? Depending on how you set up this part of your program will dictate the number of hours you need someone working. If you are putting horses outside in split shifts, then you will either be working more hours during the day or will need to hire an employee to bring horses back in and let out others. It can become complicated, very time-consuming and not cost effective if you are not careful. I encourage you to start out simple and see what you can offer for turnout. You can expand to more alternatives for boarders once you have a good idea about the amount of time and money that will be needed for special turnout options.

Handling Horses And Turnout Routine

I have been to barns where they open the stall doors and let the horses walk, trot or run to their paddocks and pastures. The same is true for bringing them back inside for the evening. This practice generally includes people assuring that the horses go into the correct stalls. I am not here to say there is only one way to turn horses out for the day but there are some safety considerations involved with letting horses run from the barn to their outdoor designated place or back inside for the evening.

I have always been a fan of leading each horse to their paddocks. Having your paddocks close to the barn reduces the time turnout takes and reduces the risk of horses getting hurt.

As the barn owner, you are responsible for everything that happens at your place and that includes handling horses, by you and all your employees. How you choose to turn horses outside is a decision that all barn owners and managers need to make and sometimes a choice is motivated by trying to get the horses outside as fast as possible. When horses are excited to go outside and equally excited to come back in for the evening they will not be careful. They are not going to stop and think about safety as they come running full speed back into the barn. It may seem like an easy way to get the horses back into their stalls but all it takes is one horse that gets hurt and you will have problems. As you know, there is no guarantee that a horse won't get hurt but if you take appropriate precautions you will have fewer issues and your boarders will appreciate it.

If you want your barn to stand out as a place where safety is a top priority, then take the extra time and effort and hand walk the horses outside for the day, as well as bringing them back in.

Not only is it safer but you can evaluate each horse as they are being led out to make sure there are no new cuts, injuries or lameness issues and the same will be true for bringing them back inside for the evening. It is definitely worth the little bit of extra time it takes.

Safety And Handling Horses

It is important to set up a safety protocol regarding how you want your employees to handle the horses at your boarding barn. If they are going to be leading them outside daily and bringing them back in later, you need to make sure the employees understand the proper way to lead a horse and also how to release a horse, so that there are no accidents as the horses run off bucking and kicking.

There can be no exceptions to "Safety First" when it comes to doing chores and handling horses. I had a situation where an employee was in a hurry trying to get the job done and not paying attention to the horse in hand and the horse got away from her. Thankfully, we were able to catch the horse after a few minutes, but the situation occurred because the handler was in a hurry and not paying attention to how the halter was put on the horse.

Employees should never be texting or using their phone while handling horses. It is a major safety issue when they are not attending to the horse and not aware of what the horse is doing as they are leading them. Remember that this is a job with many risks, so the people working for you need to follow the safety guidelines you establish.

Be Clear On Turnout Protocols For Weather

One of the most challenging parts of the daily barn chores will be the weather. If you live in an area where you have all four seasons and also experience sudden weather changes, you are in for some additional work at times. I always tell people that running a boarding barn is easy when the sun is shining and the temperature is seventy-five degrees. When the rains arrive and the temperatures drop, things will start to become challenging. If you have snow during the winter, your job will become more difficult daily and you will find yourself checking the weather frequently so you are prepared for the worst.

I am lucky because my husband loves to watch the local weather and he will check it several times a day, especially when the weather looks like it could turn bad. We are very watchful of the weather because you need to plan for inclement weather when you manage horses. Trying to bring twenty-seven horses inside when a storm is hitting is not fun and can be dangerous, so we try to stay ahead of the storms. The horses can get agitated when the weather changes and becomes stormy, so it makes it that much more difficult to walk them safely back into the barn.

Boarders will also watch weather changes and they may have questions and concerns about how you handle the safety of their horses, especially if they are new to your barn. Much of their fear will be reflective of negative past boarding experiences, so you might spend some extra time during the first year explaining how you care for the horses when experiencing adverse weather conditions. The best thing you can do is to be very clear on what the protocol is for turnout under various weather conditions. You might be leaving them in because the temperatures are too cold, or the wind has created sub-zero wind-chills. You might leave them in because it is going to rain and the temperatures are below fifty degrees. You might turn out horses even if it is raining because the temperature will be in the eighties for the day. You might do turnout early in the morning on exceptionally hot and humid days but bring the horses in by midday to get them out of the hot sun and heat and into cooler conditions. As the weather changes from season to season so will your decision making for turnout.

Ice and Horses

As you already know, ice and horses are a deadly combination and if you are caring for horses in a climate that gets snow, then you will at some time experience the perils of ice and horses. It can make the job so much harder, especially if you can't get the horses outside due to the rain and above freezing temperatures that overnight froze to an ice skating rink on areas of your paddocks. This can be even more challenging if you have outside boarded horses and no place to bring them in to. It happens often in many parts of the country and finding solutions to correct the situation can be frustrating if you are not prepared.

If your paddocks have low areas and you find yourself in a situation where you have ice in many areas, then you can take some of your warm manure from your pile and spread it over the ice in a thin layer and let the warm manure melt the top of the ice. Once it cools and the ice freezes back up, the footing will be much better and rough enough that the horses can go outside on it. It is a messy job but it keeps the horses safe and they are not stuck in stalls for weeks on end because of the ice in the paddocks.

Adding hot manure on top of ice will create safe conditions once the manure has cooled and is now stuck to the ice. It is highly recommended to allow manure to sit on the ice overnight before turning horses back out into the paddocks. It is also important to walk the paddocks to make sure the footing is safe and the manure is firmly stuck into the ice before turning horses outside.

When using manure to cover the ice in your paddocks, you need to be aware that it will take longer for them to dry out in the springtime in some areas until you can scrape off all the manure you applied earlier in the season. The manure will keep the paddocks from drying out as quickly at times and can create more mud in some areas.

These paddocks have been covered with manure where ice was the day before.

You will need to do what works best for the layout of your paddocks, but we have found it is far better to be able to get our horses safely outside then to stand in their stalls until we get a good snow fall or the ice melts. You could possibly be waiting a long time and even then the ground conditions still might not be safe for horses. Adding manure is a quick and inexpensive fix when you need to correct an ice problem that has suddenly appeared due to the weather. It happens often in areas that experience below freezing temperatures.

Cleaning Stalls

There is no right way or wrong way to clean a stall as long as it is clean when you are done. That means all the urine is taken out as well as all the manure! Every barn will do stall cleaning differently. The type of bedding and amount of bedding used will be a determining factor in how you do stall cleaning. If you have deep bedding then it will take longer to clean. If you have a small number of stalls then it is not a big deal, but the added work and labor costs when cleaning a large number of stalls can be significant. You will need to decide the type and quantity of bedding you want to have in each stall and what your cleaning schedule will be. We have always cleaned our stalls early in the morning by starting after the horses have been turned outside for the day. Cleaning certainly goes faster when the stalls are unoccupied. There are advantages to early morning cleaning such as; working before the barn is open so you can work without obstacles and distractions, having the barn clean and orderly throughout the day, reducing urine and manure odors, more effective fly control, and having the stalls ready for whenever the horses need to be brought in. There are many ways to clean stalls that range from completely stripping the bedding and replacing with new bedding (obviously the most costly method) to picking the stall for urine soaked bedding and manure while leaving the remaining bedding and top dressing with new bedding.

Deciding how much bedding to put in each stall will take some time to figure out and cost and labor will need to be factored into the decisions you make with bedding your stalls.

The choice of bedding and packaging is a decision point that has cost and preference considerations. We use bulk wood shavings that we buy by the truck load from a local company. This bedding has worked well for us and has been very cost effective. You may choose to use bagged products such as wood shavings or compressed wood pellets, but each type of bedding should be evaluated for effectiveness as well as cost. This analysis is very important because bedding costs are one of your largest annual operation expenses.

Bedding many stalls with bulk shavings and a large wheelbarrow can prove to be much less labor intensive.

Cleaning Paddocks And Run-Ins

You may want to clean your paddocks and run-ins daily, but the weather will dictate how often you can clean them. It may seem like something you can do by hand at first, but you will quickly find out how time consuming it is and if the ground is muddy or snow covered then it is nearly impossible to clean by hand. We have found that cleaning our paddocks and run-ins works best with a skid-loader which is maneuverable and can easily scrape off all the manure and waste and then dispose of it. You will need to find ways to streamline this part of your chores and make it cost effective. Remember that you will have many jobs that need to get done, so making your daily chores as easy and efficient as possible should be a high priority. Once you have a reliable system in place, you will find that you have more time to attend to the others things on your work list.

Keep It Consistent

The one bit of advice that I feel is so important is to keep your chore routine consistent every day. Establish a daily work schedule that includes a morning and afternoon chore time. Create a start time just like any other job for you and your employees. When you do little things like this for the morning and afternoon shifts, it will make a difference in how your chores are done every day. Consistency in work routines will naturally produce speed and efficiency in completing tasks. That in turn will breed a job done well.

One of the best compliments that a boarder can give me is when they tell us that they can set their clocks by how we do chores. We are that consistent. I have had many people come to our barn for a tour over the years and a common complaint that they have is the lack of consistency at their current barn. One day the horses are fed at 7am and another day they are fed at 9am! It is very frustrating for the boarder and for many horses it can be very stressful. Part of creating a great reputation for your business is how you do daily chores in all types of weather. People share information and opinions, especially in the horse world. If you want to earn a great reputation and have a waiting list then create consistent morning and evening chores and it will say a lot about your business and your commitment to good horse management.

Keep It Organized!

Organization is a vital part of creating efficiency in barn chores. I have walked into barns that are confusing and not practical for doing chores. They don't have logic in how they feed grain and supplements so it takes them much longer than it needs to. The same would be true for feeding hay and cleaning stalls. A job that only should take twenty minutes to complete, takes forty-five minutes due to disorganization. Disorganization causes wasted time and higher operational costs for the barn owner. At our highest occupancy we were taking care of forty-two horses on our property and we were able to get everything done in a very reasonable time. We were not breaking our backs but we were taking care of the chores diligently and in a highly organized manner. We treated it like a regular job. Organization and consistency has always played a significant part in making our barn run as efficiently as it does.

The more efficient you make your boarding stable, the easier it will be for everyone involved in the chores. An efficient barn means less burnout and less turnover in employees. It is a very physical job and when the weather is bad or very cold it will become harder. If you make the jobs efficient and easier for the people doing the work, you will find that you will save money in the long run. You may have greater success retaining employees if the job is reasonable when it comes to the daily routines.

If you are not sure how to start streamlining your chores, then I encourage you to tour other barns and see how they do their chores. You will learn something new from every operation and you may be able to use ideas from all of them. After all these years I still discover new things that I think are useful ideas that I want to try at my barn. Never stop learning, improving your organization and streamlining chores.

Disposing Of Horse Manure

You are going to want to think about what you will do with the horse manure. Manure piles up fast and if you don't have a plan for disposal, it will become a problem. If you live in a rural or farming community, you might be able to spread the manure on the farm fields but that is not always an option. There are companies that will truck it away for a fee so you are rid of it. You can also compost it and sell it, which I have done for years. Horse manure makes good compost and the nutrients it provides is very beneficial. If you have an area to set aside for storing and composting small mounds of manure, you can turn it monthly as it breaks down. After about six months to a year depending on moisture levels, it will turn into black gold.

It's A Working Farm

The one thing that a few of your clients will not understand is that your boarding business is a "working farm or stable." That means that the chores need to get done, the manure needs to be hauled away, the snow needs to be moved and equipment will be used. There is grass that needs to be cut and weeds trimmed. The arenas will need to be watered and dragged. The hay will need to be baled and stacked. All of these kinds of jobs can require equipment that is large and can be loud. Activity and noise are part of your daily operation throughout all four seasons. You might have clients that are not comfortable with these activities while riding their horse. You might have a client that doesn't want you to plow snow or use large equipment while they are riding in the indoor arena because the noise might spook their horse. Boarders need to understand that you need to make hay when it is ready and you need to plow snow quickly after it has snowed so it doesn't become hard. You can't do these types of jobs in the dark and you shouldn't have to!

A stable is a working farm and certain jobs are a priority over the boarders' activities. If someone becomes upset or leaves your barn because they don't like the fact that you have to do all these other jobs during daylight hours, then perhaps they are not the right person for your stable. Educating your boarders about the realities of farming and all that goes into the care and boarding of horses might help you avoid conflict, but if a boarder has unrealistic expectations that cannot be met, they are unlikely to be happy at your facility. In those rare cases, they might leave your stable and it is far better to let them go and bring in a new client that will respect the fact that you have jobs that need to get done throughout the year.

~20~

Fees For Extra Services

Setting up a price list for optional services at your boarding facility might prove to be very challenging. When starting your business you might think you can do it all. In the beginning you will have lots of energy and putting on blankets or leg wraps may not seem like a big deal, but over time it will be exhausting as you become busy and the days get long. You will find yourself in the barn more than you anticipated and if you compute your hourly pay rate, you will find that you are making a lot less money than you expected. In business, time is money and there is nothing wrong with charging a reasonable fee for the extra services you offer.

Will Your Board Rate Reflect Extra Services?

You can set up your service rates in a few different ways. One model is to charge a base rate for boarding and additional charges based on the use of optional services. This is a very common model that requires a price list detailing the cost of services offered. Monthly charges are computed by adding all charges for optional services provided to the base boarding rate.

The second model is to include all services as part of the board rate, regardless of services used. Obviously, this will present more work and greater risk for the business owner. You will need to make sure that your boarding rates are sufficient to cover the services you will provide and the costs associated with them. In the early stages it is common to underestimate the amount of services that will be used and consequently underestimate the time and resources needed to provide services. Obviously, this all converts to operating costs! The problem with including the extra services in the board rate is that you might need to raise your rate to cover the cost of providing those services but not everyone will need or want those services. There is a chance that the monthly rate will become too expensive for some of your clients. You might have difficulty filling the stalls if the rates are too high for current boarders or even potential boarders due to pricing that includes many services they don't utilize for their horse.

A Third Option

You can offer a third option as part of your boarding business. I have seen barns that give the boarder a choice between two types of monthly board rates when they first arrive. They can choose to pay a lower board rate and then if they need a service that is not included, they just pay for that service as an add-on.

They can also choose to have a "Full Service" type of boarding where blanketing and holding for veterinarian and farrier are some of the services included when they pay a higher monthly rate. You can definitely offer this option for the busy client who wants you to automatically take care of everything and not have to worry about it. When setting up this type of boarding for a client, make sure you have figured into it the time and costs of services like blanketing, holding fee and private turnout which will be the most common services you will do on a daily and monthly basis.

Time Is Money

Giving clients a choice of services with a price list is beneficial for both them and the barn owner. This gives them the choice of whether they want to pay to have blanketing done for them, have their horse held for the farrier or use other services. In many cases they will find someone else to help them if they don't want to pay for services and it works for everyone. You might feel you are losing money if they ask someone else to help but I can guarantee that after a few months of very long hours you will appreciate the help. Once you grasp all that there is to do as daily maintenance to keep your business running well, you will understand why time is money and sometimes the extra services are not worth the money you are paid for them. You will need to find a balance in what you can and cannot offer at your barn so you don't get burned out. Balance is an important part of managing a successful boarding business.

I have created a list of extra services that you might want to think about as you are setting up your business. You may decide to include some of these in your board rate and some you will want to provide as optional for an extra fee. You can design your business anyway you want, and you can choose what you want to offer along with the cost structure for care. This list will get you thinking.

Extra Fees For Services Performed

- **Private turnout**-Individual or private turnout may not seem like a big deal but it takes more of your time each day. When offering private turnout you want to think about the labor cost of feeding hay and managing water for the horse. If you have the financial resources to put automatic waterers in each private paddock, then that will save you a lot of time. However, the initial cost for installing the water line, purchasing the automatic waterer and installing and maintaining the system is very substantial. Charging for private turnout is fair and necessary because you will incur added horse management costs year round. Remember that if you live in an area that has very cold winters then you will need to use heating elements which in turn will create higher electric bills. If you don't have an automatic water system but are using a water tank, it will be much more time consuming and your labor costs will be high because you will be dealing with hoses and freezing conditions. Labor, equipment and replacement cost for heating elements all add up and should be considered when figuring out a fee for private turnout.

- **Boots (on/off daily)**–There is a good chance you will have some clients that will want you to put boots on their horses daily. It may seem like an easy thing to do for a few horses but it can be a real burden if you are managing boots for many horses. The condition of your paddocks is significant when dealing with boots for horses. If the conditions are muddy, especially during the fall and spring rainy seasons, the boots will likely be covered in mud and difficult to remove. More time will be needed to clean the boots so they can be secured when they are put on the next day. It is appropriate to charge for this service because it is time consuming under adverse conditions and you need to be compensated for the extra time it takes. That is simply good business practice.

- **Blanketing (On/Off)**-Some clients will want blankets, turnout sheets, fly sheets etc. put on and taken off daily. This is part of the business and it can be extremely time consuming if you are changing many blankets frequently. Some barn owners have included blanketing in their board rate but have experienced the blanketing requiring more time than they expected. Dealing with wet, muddy and ill-fitting blankets will be part of the job. If your barn is heated, you will be changing blankets much more often due to the extreme temperature change from outside to inside the barn. Many clients don't mind paying for blanketing and some would rather do a buddy system with friends to take care of each other's horses and blanketing.

The size of your barn and the number of horses in your care will impact your blanketing options. If you are blanketing a couple of horses daily, then it is not a big deal, but if you could be blanketing ten horses or more it will consume your time and it is a lot of work. You will need to determine if you will be doing all the work or if you can afford to have employees help with blanketing. A lot will depend on your finances available for the business. Either way, you will be paying out more money when it comes to labor and time.

- **Extra bedding for the stall**-You can walk through different barns and they will all bed their stalls a little differently. Once you decide on how much bedding you want in the stalls daily then you will need to decide how you want to handle the situation when a client wants more bedding than you normally allow. You will have horses that are lame and need extra bedding and then will you have clients that want extra bedding just because. If you decide to allow a boarder to have extra bedding you want to remember that it is now costing you more money in shavings, time and labor and you should charge accordingly. Bedding will be your second highest expense next to hay in most cases and it adds up quickly.

- **Holding fee**–If you are going to hold a client's horse for a veterinarian or farrier then it is recommended that you charge a holding fee for your time. This service can be very time consuming and inconvenient. Incorporating this service into your board rate versus having it as an add-on is something to think about. I have always had a surcharge for holding a horse for the veterinarian or farrier and I put it on my clients invoice at the end of the month.

- **Simple medicating (veterinarian prescribed)**-At our facility I will give medications during the morning chores and evening chores at no extra charge. I do charge for any kind of medicating I need to do midday. You need to think about the fact that you will be working long days and split shifts of morning chores and evening chores. Your personal free time will be in the middle of the day so you will have limited time to attend to personal things. Having to stop what you are doing to medicate a horse will take time and it may not seem like a big deal at first but after several days you might look at it much differently. It is recommended to have a midday medication administering fee on your "Services and Fees" price sheet so clients can make informed decisions about this service.

- **Walking fee**–There is a good chance that you will be walking a horse a time or two during your career with horses. It comes with the territory and when they are colicky, and the owner is away you are next in line to take over. My husband and I have both walked horses for several hours a couple times over the years and we did it because we care about the horse, but it still took up a lot of our time and other things didn't get done. Emotions will run high for everyone involved when a horse gets sick and the health of the horse is a top priority, but you are still running a business and if you must hire someone to do chores while you walk a horse, then you are losing money. You will find a balance for what works for your business, but this is something to really think about.

- **Hosing fee**-This is another job that usually involves some sort of injury and will take some of your time if the owner is not available or if the horse will not stand still and the owner needs help.

- **Bandaging fee**-The type and severity of the injury and the amount of time it takes to bandage is something that may determine your fee. Some bandaging only takes a few minutes and then there are the serious injuries that take a long time to pull the old bandages and wraps, clean the wound and put new bandages and wraps on. The horse's behavior during this process can also be a factor in the time this takes.

- **Miscellaneous fee**–It is always good to have a miscellaneous fee because you never know what is going to come up and you want to be covered. With horses anything is possible.

- **Material/Medication fee**–When sickness or injury happens most people are not prepared. If you end up using your own supplies then you should be compensated for it.

Everything Is Easier with Only Two Or Three

The one thing I want you to think about when setting up your "Extra Services" price sheet is that everything is always much easier with a smaller number of horses. Blanketing is easy if you are only going to blanket a couple of horses but if you are blanketing ten horses it will start to take a lot of time. Putting on bell boots or leg wraps daily is easy with only one horse but if you need to put on five pairs of bell boots or leg wraps, you might start to rethink this service and being compensated for it. Think about the size of your boarding stable and factor it into all of your decisions about how you operate your business.

~21~

Special Requests

The special requests you will receive from your clients may surprise you as a new barn owner. I was completely caught off guard by all the special requests we received when we first opened. To this day I am still taken by surprise occasionally. I am just better equipped to handle it now because of years of experience.

What Is A Reasonable Request?

Once you open your barn you are going to need to determine what a reasonable request is and what is not. The only way to really figure this out is by experience and of course, trial and error. You will receive many requests that seem easy enough until you start doing them daily and then you realize it is taking up much more of your time then you expected. I had to learn what I could say yes to and what I had to say no to and it took me several years to get a clear understanding of how I wanted to handle this part of barn management.

I have compiled a list of some of the special requests that you may get so you can think ahead and be more prepared when presented with questions about services. This is NOT an exhaustive list, after all, anything is possible and that is especially true with horse people.

Some examples of special requests:

- Can you please turn my horse outside for the night and then bring back inside for the day? When a client only wants night turnout are you prepared for this request?
- Can I have special lighting in my stall for my horse's coat?
- Can you feed certain types of hay?
- Can I bring in my own hay?
- Can you wet the hay?
- Can you soak the grain to make a mash?
- Non-prescribed medicines will be often requested.

- Can you put on salves, ointments and sunscreen?
- Can you extend the barn hours in the morning or evening?
- Can you bed the stall a certain way?
- Can you take care of snow removal and other barn chores after the barn closes at night?
- Can you please put my horse in the same paddock as my friend's horse because we trail ride together?
- Can you please turn off the radio because my horse wants to sleep?
- Can you please not allow any carts in the arena while I am riding?
- Can you please go get my horse because I don't want to get my shoes dirty?
- Can you leave my horse in for the day because I don't want them to get muddy?
- Can I place a carpet in my horse's stall?
- Can I move my saddles to a new spot?
- Can I bring in an extra saddle stand for another saddle I have just purchased?
- Can I change stalls again?...for the third time!
- Can I have a special parking spot for my horse trailer?
- Can I move my horse to a quieter paddock?
- Can I move my horse to a more playful paddock?
- Can we put special lighting in my horses stall because he has moon-blindness?
- Can I keep a few six-packs of beer in the refrigerator?

Many of the requests you receive will be normal and reasonable but some of them will not be. Some of the requests you receive will have you shaking your head. I have been very happy to say yes to many requests, but only when they fit within the scope of activities and chores at our barn. The design of your barn and paddocks will also determine what you can provide at your barn including special requests.

There have been situations over the years where I have said yes to a request only to find out quickly that it wasn't going to work out. That is when I had to talk to the boarder and tell them that I had changed my mind. It usually didn't go over very well when I had to talk to my client. Those were the times I learned a lot about running my barn and evaluating special requests before agreeing to them.

If you find yourself in this kind of situation, the best thing you can do is talk to the boarder immediately and be honest with them about the reasons you can no longer honor the request. You can't control how they will respond but you can control how you handle it while staying professional and honest. The client may not like your decision but they are likely to appreciate your efforts, explanations and honesty. All your client interactions help to build a trusting relationship.

One thing you need to remember is that many of your clients will have come from other boarding stables where things were allowed that you might not allow at your barn. It will be an adjustment time for a new boarder and you need to be understanding of this.

When A Boarder Chooses To Leave

When you tell a client that you cannot provide a special service there is always a chance that they will find another boarding stable that will agree to their request. Having a boarder decide to leave your barn is part of the business that you will need to accept. This is a business that may not be suitable for some people. It is not possible to meet the expectations and special requests of every boarder without potentially compromising your business and your family life. A special request could affect the other horses, boarders and even how you do chores, so it calls for thoughtful consideration prior to approval. Sometimes a special request just won't work out, so you need to tell your boarder that you can't comply with their request. Saying "NO" to a client at times is very important for a healthy business.

An important consideration when discussing special requests is that when you say yes to one person, there is a very good chance someone else will notice and want the same thing. Are you prepared to provide special services to ten other boarders simultaneously? You can't say yes to one and then say no to the others unless there are circumstances or conditions that justify an exception. If you want your barn to run without drama, then be prepared to provide explanations for your exceptions. You always need to think about your decisions and how they affect the entire business and all your clients. Looking at the big picture is important.

Once You Become Established

You will find that the longer you run your boarding barn the fewer special requests you will receive. Part of this is because you will start to develop a reputation for what you will allow and not allow at your barn. People will discuss the things that transpire at barns and you will start to become known for your standards. For example, if you don't allow lights in your stalls for the horses' coats, then show people will become aware of that rule and make boarding decisions accordingly. If all the horses go outside for daily turnout no matter what their discipline and breed, then you will become known for that. If you don't allow alcohol or drinking in the barn or while riding outside on the property, then you will become known for that. Once you develop the standards that support your business model you will find that special requests will be minimal. But be prepared because just when you think things have finally settled down someone will come to you with a request that will leave you surprised. I still get surprised every now and then.

~22~

Employees

If you are going to hire employees to work at your boarding stable, then you need to have a very good idea of how long each job will take before they start working for you. One of the fastest ways to lose money is through the money you will pay out to your employees for hours spent doing basic chores that should have taken much less time. It is usually not the employees fault but instead it is the lack of knowing how to make the chores efficient and very streamlined so that they are done in a much quicker timeframe. Often the barn owner has never done the chores themselves so they don't have a good idea of what it really takes to get the job done and how much physical work it is.

Prior to hiring employees for your boarding stable you will need to create job descriptions that include estimates of the time each job will take. Take note of how much time the chores will take under various conditions so that you can monitor the efficiency and competency of each employee.

Give Good Instruction

Once you have a good routine for chores as well as a consistent feeding and turnout program, it is time to get your employees on board and teach them how you want things done at your barn. I have found that doing the chores with my employees for a day or two will help them understand how I want things done and how I want the horses handled. You need to remember that many of your employees will have worked at other barns and stables where they may have done chores much differently, so you need to start from scratch and be as clear as possible about your expectations.

Your employees will try to do things the way you want them done but it may take some time for them to get used to the routine, so it is important to be patient. It is no different than any other job that takes adjustment, but this job includes getting to know the horses and all their unique behaviors.

Provide a detailed list of chores with the order that they are to be done, along with a list of the horses and their vices so that the employees can refer to it when they are on their own. Until the new employees get comfortable with the chore routine and the horses, it might take them longer to get the job done than it would an experienced worker. They will become faster with time and experience, just as you did when you first started doing chores at your barn.

Expectations For Employees

When we first started hiring employees to help with barn chores I didn't know what my expectations should be for my employees. I had never had employees before, so I was about to learn a lot about this part of my business. Having employees is much different than volunteers but sometimes we treat them both the same without realizing it. The other part of the equation is that many of your employees will also be your boarders. This can make things a little complicated and even uncomfortable if you need to talk with them about something like being late to work or if the stalls weren't cleaned well. A person might be on the phone while cleaning stalls and it is not a big deal…until you pay them at the end of the month and it turns out to be a lot more than you expected!

It doesn't matter if your employees are also your boarders or friends. You need to be very clear about how much time is allotted for each job and what is acceptable behavior while working. If they are getting paid then you need to have job guidelines and manage all of them the same. If you are not diligent in monitoring chore times you may lose money and risk your financial health. You need to remember that this is a business and you are the person responsible for employees and cost management.

Establish a work schedule for each employee with a daily start time. If employees are late, you need to address it. If they are on their phone while working, you need to talk to them about it and tell them that calls need to wait until break time. If the job normally takes two hours and they put down four hours, then you need to talk to them and ask them why it took them so long. These things are not easy to confront but they are an important part of managing a business.

It is your responsibility as the barn manager to know how long each job should take. That means you might need to clean stalls for a week or two to get personal experience of what is involved and the time it takes. Every job that is part of the basic chores including feeding hay, grain and supplements in the morning and afternoon, should also be done by the barn owner and barn manager because only then will you have an accurate estimate of all tasks and the time that they take.

Disenchantment With The Job

One of the biggest challenges a barn manager will have with employees is setting the expectation that this is a "real job" with specific responsibilities that help the business maintain financial stability and build a strong reputation for excellence. All employees need to feel a part of the business success and reputation.

The idea of working at a horse farm sounds fun and exciting to many people but often once they have done it for a few days they realize it is a lot of mucking stalls and cleaning the barn and very little horse interaction. Some people have this vision of working with horses all day long and that simply is not the case. In fact, most of the daily chores have very little to do with handling horses. Some people might become disenchanted after a week or so because it is not what they envisioned it would be.

When interviewing people to work at your stable, be as clear as possible when describing the job responsibilities. In many cases it is even a good idea to have them help with chores for a day so they will get a better idea of what they will be doing. Once you get a good team of employees that know the job and still love it, then you are off to a great start.

Being Dependable Is A Must!

Having dependable employees is essential when you are taking care of animals. When someone doesn't show up for work and you are left doing the chores that were supposed to be done by your employee, it will become frustrating. The job of running a barn is already hard enough without the added stress of unreliable employees. Working with animals is not the kind of job that you can close on Sundays and holidays or when you are sick. The animals still need to be fed and watered plus everything else that needs to be done for their daily care. If you have employees that don't show up or call in sick often, then you need to make changes quickly or you will find yourself working seven days a week. This is how barn owners burn themselves out.

It is also important that your employees fully understand that they need to come to work even if the weather is bad. The job is always fun when the sun is shining and the weather is warm, but they need to be at work when it is raining and cold and they would have rather stayed in bed. It is important to talk about your expectations and your business will run much smoother with a committed team of workers.

Creating A Team

One of the signs of a well-run boarding barn is a good team of employees that efficiently takes care of the horses and the chores that need to be done. When I had surgery this last summer, I knew I wouldn't be able to do anything for about six weeks, so we hired full-time employees while I was recuperating. It was something we had never had to do in all the years we have been open, so of course I was nervous to leave the barn in the hands of other people. My surgery was scheduled for mid-July, so I spent the month of June teaching the people who would work for me exactly how I wanted things done. I showed them how I wanted each horse handled and shared any issues that might arise from certain horses.

I reviewed how I wanted hay and grain fed and made sure they felt comfortable with the process. Before I had surgery, I let them work independently for a few days while I just watched and soon I faded out of the picture to let them have complete control. After my surgery, I was in the hospital for six days and they took over and before I knew it they were running the barn and doing an excellent job. We had very few issues come up and the team was able to problem solve most of them, so I couldn't have been more pleased. The three people who worked for me became a team and took care of my barn just like it was their barn. Creating a team spirit is important because you want your employees to feel like they are part of something very special. That may mean spending some extra time helping them learn your system and conveying how you value their work and their commitment to the success of the stable.

Part of building a successful barn is building a strong team of employees. If you have a team that cares about your barn and takes pride in what they do, let them know. Tell them how much you appreciate them and the hard work they are doing daily. Make them feel important and valued and you will retain employees because they enjoy working for you-maybe not as much as they enjoy the horses but they are still happy to work for you.

~23~

Trainers At Your Barn

The business relationship between the trainer and the barn owner and manager can be a perilous matter if not set up properly. Boarding barns all handle trainer relationships and the business relationship differently. Some will have multiple trainers come to their barn while others will have just one home based trainer that everyone uses. It is up to the barn owner to decide how they want to manage the trainer business relationships, so this chapter is written to help guide you through some scenarios and options for trainers working out of your boarding barn.

Trainers And Your Business

If you are a barn owner but not a horse trainer, then it is in your best interest to find some good trainers to give lessons and work with clients at your barn. The services provided by horse trainers will help make your job easier by providing riding instruction and developing strategies for managing issues with horses and their owners. For horse owners of all levels, a trainer can be an integral part of developing horsemanship skills, confidence handling horses and an awareness of safety issues. Having access to skilled trainers is an asset for a boarding stable, especially when promoting a range of services offered.

Trainers can prove to be an asset or liability for your boarding barn. They will either help your business or they will hurt it. Having trainers work out of your barn is a smart thing to do if you are not a trainer yourself, but you need to be very knowledgeable about the relationships and set some guidelines that every trainer needs to follow.

I have listed some points that I feel are important when evaluating for trainers to work out of your barn.

- **All trainers need to carry their own liability insurance.** If a person is calling themselves a professional horse trainer or riding instructor, then they should carry the proper insurance. If they don't have trainers insurance or that you should be carrying the insurance for them, then they should not work out of your facility. It is their responsibility to carry the insurance unless they work for you.

It is important that you understand that you are at significant risk if the trainer does something wrong and a horse or person is hurt in the process. You will be liable for the accident and if the client sues the trainer, it will trickle down to you as well. The buck always stops with the owner of the barn or stable. As the barn owner, you carry all the responsibility for everything that transpires at your barn including horse trainers.

- **You need to have rules for trainers running their business out of your barn.** It is important that you establish rules for the trainers at your barn. This is not their barn and they need to first follow all the barn rules. Second, they need to follow the rules you have established for when they are working with horses and giving lessons out of your barn. I often hear from people at other boarding barns that they can't get arena time because the trainer won't allow them access at certain times to ride. Another problem is that some boarders will feel uncomfortable riding when there are lessons going on, especially if the arena has size limitations.

You need to sit down and talk with new trainers coming into your barn and give them a list of guidelines for how lessons should be conducted and also how they should handle themselves around other boarders that want to ride. Setting your expectations is important right from the start. Keep the communication open.

- **You and the trainer need to have the same ideas and beliefs about training horses.** It can take years of experience to be able to discern the differences in trainers' styles and underlying philosophies of horse management. It is your responsibility as the stable owner to select the trainers for your facility that support your beliefs about horse management and standards of excellence with clients and horses. It is vitally important that you have a very good understanding of the methods a trainer practices in order to maintain consistency when it comes to the handling and care of the horses at your stable.

Everything a horse trainer does out of your barn is reflective of the type of establishment you are operating. It is reflective of you. Your reputation and your business can be damaged by a trainer that is hard on horses and allowed to continue training at your barn. If things are being done that are upsetting to watch, then you need to correct the situation lest it appear that you are promoting that kind of treatment as a barn owner. There are trainers out there that should not be training horses and they could end up at your barn if you are not careful.

- **Setting up lesson and training fees and commissions.** There are many ways to handle financial relationships with trainers. Many barn owners receive a percentage of all income received by the trainer for all lessons and training. Some barn owners charge a flat rate each month to keep things simple. You can decide not to charge a percentage or flat rate at all except for haul-ins. You can set this up any way you would like to, but you need to remember that the trainer is using your facility and all the amenities without the risk, financial overhead or the responsibility.

- **Will the trainers have training stalls in your stable and will they pay full price for the stall or have a discount?** Many trainers will own lesson horses as part of their program and if they are working out of your barn, then there is a good chance they will ask for a stall or two for their horses. I have talked with many barn owners that will give a trainer the stalls for free or a discounted price. I personally don't agree with this type of arrangement because the barn owner still needs to cover the cost of boarding and care for the horse. In most cases the barn owner will lose money on those stalls if they are discounted and definitely if they are free. The trainer might argue that they are bringing business to your barn but that is not accountable. The trainer is running a business out of your barn with very low costs and risks. You are not responsible for supporting the trainer's business nor carrying their cost of horse ownership.

I have always believed that the best way to run this part of my business is to charge full rate to any trainers that contract for a stall at my barn. Training stalls or stalls for lesson horses are charged full price board.

You need to remember more than anything else that you are the one that has taken the financial risk, not the trainers. They may lose a little money if lessons or training horses are not coming in as much as they had planned but you will be losing much more and have a lot more on the line if you start giving away stalls. Your cost and overhead will always be much greater than the trainers.

Asking A Trainer To Leave

What do you do when the relationship between the trainer and the barn owner has turned sour? What do you do when things are not working out as planned and you know it is time for a change? How do you ask a trainer to leave when you know it will impact many of your boarders? These are questions that I hope you never have to answer but the reality is trainer conflicts happen more often than you would expect. There are many reasons why the relationship between a trainer and the barn owner might deteriorate to the point that something needs to be done.

Asking a trainer to leave your barn will come with risks that you must be willing to accept because you know it will make your barn better in the long run. It is YOUR business and you need to protect your business even when hard decisions need to be made that affect your boarders. Your clients may be oblivious to escalating issues with a trainer because they are only focused on their lessons or horse training. If they are happy with their lesson program or the training of their horse, that is all that matters to them.

If you are in a situation where you know it is time to ask a trainer to leave your stable, then I encourage you to make every effort to work out any differences you have and see if the business relationship can be salvaged. Only after exhausting all avenues and finding no common ground, that it is time to move forward with change. Every barn owner may experience this once in their career but hopefully not more than that. It is an incredibly stressful situation to manage and it has financial implications that will add to the stress.

When you have boarders that are attached to their trainer, you could easily lose their business when their trainer leaves your barn. It happens and you need to prepare yourself for empty stalls and reduced income. I have always believed that there are many capable trainers, so don't panic but work diligently to find the right ones for your boarders and their horses. Once the word is out that you are interviewing trainers, you are likely to find that your reputation precedes you and many trainers are interested in the opportunities at your stable. You may go through some ups and downs during this transition, but once you get new trainers and new clients in your barn you will realize how strong your business is and that new perspectives and approaches can be uplifting and beneficial. This is a time to embrace change!

The Risks That Come With A One-Trainer Barn

I believe there are some risks involved with a one-trainer barn. If your barn is a general boarding barn but you only allow one trainer to work out of it, then you are creating a "training barn" atmosphere and you may be hurting your business in many ways. If you only allow one trainer to work out of your facility and you have clients that would like to use a different trainer, then there is a good chance you will lose boarders who will go where they can choose their trainer. This doesn't mean you have to say yes to every trainer that wants to work out of your barn. Remember, there are some trainers that you will not want to work out of your barn and it is okay to say no. Giving your boarders many options for training and riding instruction is a good thing for your business. It's like the old saying *don't put all your eggs in one basket*, the same is true for your business and trainers.

I have always believed that having trainers with different ways of teaching and training will open peoples' minds to different ways of doing things and advance in their horsemanship. It is a good thing to get different opinions because not every training method will work with every horse and rider. Variety is a good thing.

The Training Barn VS. The Boarding Barn

I wanted to explain some of the differences between a training barn and boarding barn and even though this list is not exhaustive, it will give you a good perspective on both worlds. There is nothing wrong with either type of barn, but it can be difficult to have both types of businesses out of the same facility.

The Boarding Barn-In many cases the boarding barn will be a multi-discipline barn with many different breeds, styles of riding and ages of clients. You will have people who show and people who trail ride and the barn generally will have a much more relaxed atmosphere only because not all the horses are in training and people can do pretty much whatever they like in accordance with the rules of the barn. You might have boarders that don't come out much to see their horse and even have retired horses that are living out their retirement with no demands on them. The people who do show out of a boarding barn may be very serious about showing but they are not usually following the dictates of a trainer that is working with the horse in preparation for show season. If the boarding barn is well-run, then there will be low turnover with consequent herd stability.

The Training Barn-The training barn is exactly what is says it is. It is a barn where horses are in training primarily for showing and competition. You will often find young horses that need to be broke in a training barn and they will stay until they reach the goals of the trainer and owner. Most training barns are headed by a lead trainer with some assistants and the training program is often the same for most of the horses. For example, a trainer that trains and gives lessons for western pleasure riders will strive to excel at this discipline and that is all he will do. You will not find a saddle seat rider boarding at this type of barn because the trainer will not usually be skilled or interested in training a saddle seat rider. Most trainers that have training barns have a discipline of choice that they train and that is what attracts students and horse owners. At training barns you will see more turnover as training horses leave and new ones arrive, because most horses are in training for a limited amount of time. Once they are done with their training, they return home to their owners unless the owner wants to keep the lessons and training program for the horse and rider as a permanent arrangement.

If you ask people that have boarded at both a training barn and a boarding barn they will tell you that there is a difference and at times a training barn will be perfect for what they are trying to accomplish with their horse, while at other times a boarding barn is the best option for their situation.

Both operations are important to the horse industry and both help promote education and training for horse owners. You will want to learn more about this topic when deciding the type of operation you want as well as structuring business relationships with trainers.

Expect Honesty And Integrity

Once you have dealt with a few trainers at your stable and the outcome wasn't positive, you will appreciate and cherish the trainer that runs their business with honesty, integrity and a positive mindset. They will become an asset to your business and they are out there, you just need to find them. You need to define what you want when looking for a trainer and don't settle for less. Remember that, even though they are independent, they are seen as representing your barn and business and may be the first person many of your boarders and the public meet when they come to the barn.

~24~

Veterinarians

You are going to have many other equine professionals coming to your barn, but veterinarians and farriers will be the ones you see most often. When setting up your business, you will want to make a few decisions about how this part of your boarding business will be handled. Veterinarians and farriers will play a huge part in the health and well-being of all the horses on your property and having a good relationship with them will not only benefit you as the barn manager, but it will benefit them as well. The one thing that many people forget is that we are all working together for the good of the horse and it should be a team effort. It doesn't mean it always works that way but that is what the goal should be.

Good communication between you and the veterinarians and farriers that come to your barn is vital and will make your job easier in many ways. You are also very important to the veterinarians and farriers because you will know the horses better than they do and that will include their vices, quirks and issues. Your communication with the care providers about a horse's issues and behavior in advance of treatment can be beneficial, as it can help save time and minimize risk for the veterinarians, farriers and others providing care.

If you are running a barn for the first time, you will quickly learn that your relationship with other equine professionals will change. You are now an equine professional and you need to start thinking of yourself as one. You all have a distinct perspective and when you interact well it can make a difference in the atmosphere and enhance the care of the horses.

Veterinarians And Your Business

When setting up your business you will want to decide if you have an open door for all veterinarians in your area or will prefer to use just one vet clinic. I have seen it done both ways and I personally feel it is much better to allow the boarders to choose the veterinarian they would like to have for their horse. The one thing you want to consider is that not every vet clinic does twenty-four hour service. If something happens on a Sunday you might have a hard time contacting a veterinarian if they don't work on weekends or holidays. It is very important to have a relationship with a vet clinic that can be at your barn any day or time of the year.

The veterinarian will not necessarily know the horses and may depend on you to let them know if there are any safety concerns they should be aware of. As the barn manager, your knowledge of the horses is vital in keeping the doctors safe under very stressful circumstances when a horse is hard to handle or unpredictable. Some horses will rear and strike out at the sight of needles and it can compromise everyone's safety. If you know the horse has a tendency to panic, then sharing this with the doctor is the best thing you can do. There is a good chance that you will also know some of the horses better than their owners, especially if they are new horse owners. They might come out to hold the horse for the veterinarian but if the horse starts to panic the owner might not know how to handle the horse and might aggravate the situation. Giving this kind of knowledge to the vet ahead of time will help keep everyone safe.

Professional To Professional

Your relationship with the veterinarians has now become equine professional to equine professional and with that there may be some unique dynamics. Your conversations will at times concern special situations at your barn and how to best address them. It could be a sickness that is going through the barn or a special circumstance with one horse. You might need to call and get their perspective on a situation and ask for their professional opinion. The same will be true for your role and how you might help them in certain situations with clients. You are a team now and your role is equally important to having a positive outcome.

Their Professional Opinion Can Affect Your Job

When a veterinarian comes to your barn for a sick or injured horse, the main goal is to get the horse back to complete health. Depending on the horse's problem, there may be a discussion between the doctor and the owner in which some advice is given regarding how you are to manage that horse. You might need to move the horse from the herd it is in or the horse might need to stay in private turnout or placed in isolation. You might need to change the feeding program if the horse now has special dietary needs. This often happens with older horses and horses with digestive issues. You might have a horse on stall rest for several months and only limited turnout in a very small area. You might need to add more bedding to keep the horse comfortable while they rehabilitate. You could have to quarantine your barn under the most severe and serious cases of illness and that would affect everyone.

These situations happen so you need to be prepared. The veterinarians are not out to make your job more difficult but you need to understand that special cases will dictate changes to your normal program.

Having A Second Choice

If your new boarder has a preferred veterinarian but that doctor and clinic doesn't do emergency service on weekends, late nights or holidays, then I would recommend talking with your client and having a back-up with a clinic that does twenty-four hour/seven day a week coverage. I would also get this in writing from your boarder and have it on the stall card with the clinic phone numbers included. It would great if all sickness and accidents happened between the hours of 9am and 5pm but that is not reality and you want to make sure you are prepared if you need a veterinarian in a hurry.

Giving Medications-Is It Worth the Risk?

When managing a boarding facility you are going to need to decide how you want to deal with medications and the horses in your care. You will see many different types of medications and some of them will NOT be veterinarian prescribed. It is one thing if the owner of the horse wants to administer their own medications, but if they ask you to administer medications you need to understand the risks you are taking and how to protect yourself if something should go wrong.

When we started our boarding business, I was not prepared for this part of barn management and I was asked to give medications I was unfamiliar with. I will be honest and tell you that I didn't understand the risk I was taking giving some of those medications. I quickly had to change how I was handling this part of my business to protect the business.

If you give any medication that is not veterinarian prescribed to a horse in your care and something goes wrong, you can be held responsible. It is as simple as that. If a horse dies in your care and it was the direct result of a medication you administered that was not prescribed, you could be at risk of a lawsuit for loss of the horse. It doesn't matter if they asked you to give the medication or not. The client is assuming you know what you are doing as a barn manager and that will include knowledge of drugs. When emotions run high, things can get out of hand very quickly. You need to protect yourself as the owner of the business.

Ask Your Veterinarian

I want you to understand that if you choose to say no to a boarder about giving a certain drug there is a chance they will become irritated at your decision. I had a boarder leave our barn because I refused to give the medications they wanted me to give for an extended amount of time. The medications were not prescribed and they wanted me to give it over a very long period of time and I knew some of the side effects of this drug. I decided it was best for me to call my own veterinarian and ask their opinion on this situation. After my discussion with them regarding the drug, it reinforced my decision not to administer the medication at all.

It is okay to call your veterinarian and ask their opinion and ask them to educate you on the drug that you are being asked to administer. It can stay confidential for all parties involved but it will educate you about what you are giving and help you make a much more knowledgeable decision.

I also want to stress the importance of having written approval from the veterinarian that is ordering the medication. It is very easy for someone to say they have a "doctor prescribed medication" when in reality they don't. We always want to think the best of people but you need to protect yourself because, unfortunately, there are those that will not be honest with you.

The longer you are working in the horse industry the more familiar you will become with the standard medications that are being given in your area. If something comes along that you have never seen before and there is no written prescription, then call your veterinarian and find out what it is. You don't want to take chances with the horses in your care or your business. You don't want to risk losing it all because you couldn't say no. It is **never** worth the risk.

When A Boarder Refuses To Call The Veterinarian

What do you do when you have a boarder that refuses to call the veterinarian for a sick or injured horse? If you are boarding horses then there is a chance you will run into this kind of situation a time or two during your career. You would never think this would be a part of your job, but it can happen and you will need to decide how you want to handle the owner and the horse.

There are a few reasons why an owner won't call the veterinarian when their horse needs help but the most common reason is money. They may not want to spend the money or they just don't have it. We all know that a vet call is going to be expensive, so often a client will wait to see if the health problem goes away or the injury can be treated without a veterinarian. You may face a situation where the boarder doesn't truly understand how serious the injury is and you will need to educate them. This will become a real balancing act for you as the barn manager. You are going to learn a lot about people and horses in this type of situation.

As the barn manager, you might need to insist on having a veterinarian come out for a sick or injured horse. This situation is not good, as the boarder may become angry that you have insisted on care for their horse. No one likes to be told what to do, but if you are put into this situation you need to stand strong in your decision. Each situation will be unique and you can expect a different response from each client. I am not trying to scare you, but I want you to fully understand your role as a barn manager includes making decisions from time to time that do not please some of your clients.

The bottom line is providing quality care for the horse. If the owner of the horse won't do anything then you will need to step in and make sure the horse gets the care it needs. There is also a possibility that a boarder will leave your barn after a situation like this happens. In that case, you need to let them go and move forward. You don't want to have a client at your stable that is not going to take care of their horse when they need it most.

Check Your Boarding Contract

It is important that your boarding contract provides protection under these types of situations. When they happen, you want to be prepared and also protected. Make sure you have a paragraph in your boarding contract about veterinary care and your rights as the barn owner and manager to require veterinary care when needed. As with any boarding contract, make sure you have your attorney review it to make sure it is legal for the state that you are doing business in.

~25~

Farriers

I can't express enough how important a good farrier is to your horse. You depend on your farrier to make sure your horse is sound and moving well. When you become the barn owner or manager you will start to experience a whole new side to the farrier/client relationship and it can be very good and it can also be very maddening. I don't know how else to put it but there are some farriers out there that should not be trimming and shoeing horses.

Before you became a business owner you probably were only familiar with a few farriers that happen to come to the place you boarded. You probably didn't pay attention to the other farriers that were there because it didn't involve you and your horse. That is exactly how I was when we opened our barn to the public. All of a sudden, I had many farriers coming to work on horses. My eyes were opened to all the different schools of thought about hooves, trimming and shoeing. I also began to get a good understanding of the damage a bad farrier can inflict on a horse and once that happened, I quickly realized that I would need to be involved through my role at the barn.

Creating a safe place for farriers to do their job is important. Having a grooming bay for the farriers to work on horses will make their job much easier.

Will You Allow Multiple Farriers?

Another decision point...When you start to set up your boarding business you will need to decide if you will allow your boarders to choose who they would like for a farrier or just have one "barn farrier." I have seen it done both ways and I have always looked at this part of our business through the eyes of my boarders, since I was a boarder myself for many years.

I have always allowed my boarders to choose their farrier. It is their horse and they should be able to choose who they want for a farrier. When asked, I have recommended the farriers that I believed were very skilled and professional. Giving your clients the choice of who they want to use for a farrier can be good for everyone, as it gives control and responsibility back to the horse owner. Making decisions for their horse helps owners grow in the process, especially when they are new horse owners.

The Risks With Just One Farrier

There are some risks involved with only allowing one farrier to come to your barn, especially if it is a large facility. Each farrier has their specialties and if you have a multi-discipline barn you would be asking a farrier to be good at every kind of shoeing and trimming for every breed and style of riding. I don't believe that is possible. You will have some farriers that are fantastic at putting on show shoes for Saddlebreds and other farriers that are not schooled in that type of work. Some farriers study natural trimming and that is all they do. Each farrier will have opinions, preferences and skills for the type of shoeing they do. The same is often true of owners' preferences. It can be frustrating for your boarders and the farrier if they can't come to agreement. You could even lose a boarder over this.

Another risk with only allowing one farrier to come to your barn is the risk that the farrier will get sick, injured or too busy to keep appointments. Unexpected things can happen, so you need to have a back-up farrier when you rely on one farrier to service all of your horses. I have had horses lose a shoe the day before a big show and the farrier was not able to make it to my barn to get the shoe back on. That is when having several options is a huge advantage.

You will have horses that pull shoes and need a farrier as soon as possible because you have nails sticking out of the hoof or the shoe is half on. You will have horses that look like they are abscessing and you need a farrier's opinion and care. Having one farrier could mean you need to wait a long time for them to arrive at your barn if they are busy.

Before deciding if you will use one farrier or many in your business, you should look at the big picture and your responsibilities at your facility. If you are choosing the farrier for your barn, then the responsibility falls back on you if they do an unsatisfactory job or cause lameness in a horse. Not only will the boarder be angry with the farrier but they will be upset with you. At that point, if you don't allow the owner to choose another farrier there is a good chance you will lose a boarder. I truly believe it is bad for business when you micromanage these types of decisions for your boarders.

The Pros And Cons Of Free Choice Farriers

There are many positive aspects of your boarders choosing the farrier of their choice. I believe giving your clients the freedom to choose their farrier helps them grow in their knowledge about horse care. When a person makes an educated decision about the type of care they want for their horse it involves some homework on their part and that is an important part of learning and growing in horsemanship. They may seek your opinion and that of others, but the final selection is their choice and responsibility.

Not every farrier is the perfect choice for every horse and if you have a barn with many breeds and styles of riding, then having different farriers with their own specialty is a huge benefit. Farriers generally aren't knowledgeable and skilled with all types of shoeing and some farriers prefer certain breeds and types of shoes to work on.

Having several farriers practice at a stable is a benefit because you can always get a second opinion if needed. As the barn owner, you will see many different types of farrier work and learn from all of it. You will even start to learn a farriers' preferences based on the shoes a horse is wearing. There are definitely differences amongst farriers' practices.

One issue that can be a huge headache for you as the barn owner is when a farrier causes lameness in a horse due to poor farrier work. I hope you never will experience this but it happens. Throughout the years we have had a small number of situations where a farrier has come to our barn to work on a client's horse and when they left, the horse was lame and you could easily see the feet were poorly trimmed. I have been contacted by a boarder who was upset to the point of crying and asking for my farrier's number to have them come out for her horse. In one situation, a horse was trimmed so short that it needed shoes and pads just to get comfortable. In another case, the veterinarian had to be called out for pain medication, along with a different farrier. That is when it gets really bad for the horse and everyone involved.

If something like this happens it could make more work for you involving aftercare and you will find yourself consoling the client and feeling horrible for the horse. Overall, allowing your boarders to choose who they want for a farrier is a good strategy for your business.

As a side note, if a farrier botches up a horse's feet badly, the word spreads and you usually don't see the farrier back at your barn again. People talk and sometimes that is a good thing.

Setting Up Appointments And Holding Fees

As the barn owner you will need to decide if you want to be in control of farrier appointments or not. If you only have a couple of horses then it is easy to manage, but if you have a large barn you may find yourself very busy making appointments for everyone and holding their horse as well. You need to decide if you want to offer this service as part of the board fee or have it as separate charge.

We have always had this as an optional service with a separate charge and if a client wants me to hold their horse, then I add an extra service fee to their invoice. It doesn't happen often but if I am asked, then I am paid for my time. You need to realize that when you are setting up appointments and holding horses you will be in the barn for many hours and it may become difficult, especially if you are doing chores in the morning and afternoon and trying to get everything else done in the hours between. Your days will become very, very long. I encourage you to think about offering this as a separate service and then you can be selective and will get paid for your time. After a couple of years, you are likely to find that you will be glad you set it up this way because you will understand how valuable your time is when you are running the rest of the business.

~26~

Barn Hours

I want to start off this chapter by saying that if you are running a boarding barn, then barn hours are not only healthy for the business but even more important for your personal life and family. Not everyone will agree with this but I would venture to say that if they don't, then they probably haven't had their own business on the same property where they live.

When we first opened our barn, words cannot express how excited I was. I had an unbelievable amount of energy and barn hours didn't seem important at the time. When we first set up our barn hours we decided to stay open until 10pm every night. It was summertime when the first horses arrived and here in Wisconsin it stays light until about 9pm so staying open another hour wasn't a big deal in the beginning. Soon we were into the daily grind of doing chores seven days a week and being in charge of everything. As the summer faded away and the weather became cooler, the days also became shorter. We would go out to do an evening check and top off the waters and by the time we got back in the house it would be close to 10:30pm. Soon we would be getting up to do it all over again. Another part of the picture that was unfolding in front of my eyes was that I soon found out that if the barn was open until 10pm every night, then there was a very good chance you would get phone calls or text messages all the way up to that closing time. We were becoming exhausted and one day blended into another with the late hours and early mornings. We didn't have employees to do evening chores and couldn't afford to hire employees, so it was incumbent on us to do all of the work. We realized we had to make changes to our barn hours.

What Works Best For You?

I cannot stress enough how important it is to set up your barn hours for what works best for you and your family. It doesn't matter if the boarding stable down the road is open later than you at night or before you in the morning. The majority of people looking for a good boarding stable will make the hours work for them if they want to be at your facility. Barn hours are not the number one reason a person chooses a boarding barn. To some it might be important but it is usually not the deciding factor.

Many barns are going to have different hours depending on the climate and weather. If you live in an area where the weather is extremely hot then you might have late evening hours to allow riding in the coolest part of the day. If you live in a state that has extremely cold temperatures then closing your barn earlier in the winter is normal, especially if no one comes out in the evening hours. Finding what works best for your barn is a completely individual choice. It may be possible to accommodate late closing hours if you have employees that can be responsible for closing down the barn in a reliable manner. If you are running the business yourself and doing all the work, then your barn hours might shorten a bit in the wintertime.

Your Barn Hours Will Fit Their Schedule

Late barn hours will be important to some people but I believe once you set your barn hours, the right people will find you and your hours will work for them. Your barn hours will never be perfect for everyone unless you are open twenty-four hours a day. Don't be disappointed or start to worry if someone chooses to go somewhere else because your barn hours don't work for them. That will be a unique situation. If your horse care is consistently good and you are reliable, then most people will organize their schedule so that they can board at your barn.

A Huge Reason For Burn-Out

I have had the privilege of talking with many barn owners over the last few years and I found that one of the main reasons for burn-out is barn hours. They have lost some of their privacy and it seems like they get calls at all hours of the evening because something has happened to someone's horse late at night or someone has fallen off and is hurt. It can be very frustrating and exhausting when you are ready for bed and the phone rings. I have talked to barn owners that will share their frustration at having people at their barn at 6am in the morning because when they go out to do chores they need to also deal with people. I am going to be very candid here and tell you that although you may love talking with people and enjoy their company, it will get tiresome when you are doing chores at 6am in the morning.

Finding balance is very important in this part of barn management, especially if you don't have employees to take over some of the chores. I always tell people that if you don't want a call at midnight then don't keep your barn open until midnight. It is as straight forward as that.

Setting Barn Hours Is Healthy For Your Business

Many new businesses will go through changes over the first couple of years and yours will be no exception. As a new business owner, you will feel like you can do it all at first and most new businesses can't afford to hire much help in the beginning. If you have established your barn hours and later you are starting to feel stressed, it may be time to reevaluate your barn hours and make the necessary changes to provide personal time.

Setting reasonable barn hours is an important part of running a boarding barn. It is not only good for you as a business owner but good for the horses in your care. It doesn't matter what other barns are doing so don't get caught up in the pressure to follow the crowd. If you find yourself in a situation where you are going to change your barn hours, I suggest writing a letter to your boarders with the reasons for change. Give a month's notice so they have time to adjust and if someone leaves because the new hours don't work for them, accept their decision. You need to do what is best for you and your family, and your clients need to do what is best for them.

I have been to many barns and they all have different hours. Some will close early on Sundays and holidays and I have talked to a couple barn owners that close their barn one day a week for maintenance. You can design your barn and how it operates anyway you want and how it starts out in the beginning will probably change over time. If you are feeling overwhelmed in certain areas of your business, then take a look at your barn hours, because that may be why other areas of your business and even personal life are having issues. Everything in your barn and stable is connected in some way and it all needs to work together to maintain a respectable operation and barn hours are part of it.

~27~

The Challenges Of Outdoor Board

Many boarding stables will offer "Outdoor or Rough Board" as part of their boarding package. What this means is that the horse will live outside year-round with food, water and a shelter to protect them from the elements. Some outdoor boarding is much rougher than others and you will see many different types of conditions for outdoor board. Having boarded horses in Southern California when I was younger was much different than taking care of horses in Wisconsin, with the weather being the main reason. I also know that most healthy horses prefer to be outside and do just fine outside as long as they have enough hay, fresh (not frozen) water and shelter to get out of the wind and bad weather.

If you are going to board horses and offer outdoor boarding, you need to understand what is involved so you are prepared when issues arise. Outdoor boarding may be easy and better for the horse in most cases but it can be very hard on the owner of the horse when the weather is severe. Outdoor board always looks wonderful when the sun is shining and the weather is warm but once the temperatures drop and the snow arrives you will start to get special requests for the horses on outdoor board. The requests may catch you off guard and could create much more work for you at times.

There are many styles and sizes of run-in shelters. The most important element is to make sure the shelters are not overcrowded.

Planning Your Outdoor Boarding

When we were setting up our business we decided to have some outdoor boarded horses and we built some run-ins and put up the fencing. We planned to have a maximum of three horses in each paddock so that they could have plenty of room in the shelter. It seemed like a manageable number for chores and would be easy to feed grain to only three horses at a time. In the beginning we felt outdoor board would be very easy work and easy money as well. Outdoor board required very little daily upkeep and no stall cleaning! Our learning curve went through the roof when it came to the horses, herd management and the clients who chose outdoor board for their horse. We had issues with horses that didn't get along and it seemed one horse was always left out of the shelter because the others wouldn't let him in. This was very difficult for us to manage and upsetting to the boarder as well. We had to deal with clients that wanted their horses brought into stalls even though the weather didn't warrant it and they didn't fully understand the term "Outdoor board." Graining became more difficult than we had expected and when the weather was bad, it was very hard standing outside waiting for a slow eater to finish their grain. These are a few of the issues that were new to us and problem solving became a daily part of the job.

Most horses do very well on outdoor board as long as they can get into the shelter during inclement weather.

When you are planning your outdoor boarding program for your stable you need to think about the variables that could become issues. The more prepared you are the less stress you will have down the road.

I have compiled a list of issues that you might experience with outdoor boarded horses and their owners. I want you to have a realistic view of outdoor boarded horses and all that it entails. You may never have an issue but you should be prepared, especially when one of your clients is upset.

Things To Think About With Outdoor Board

- **The herd size compared to the shelter size**-Many people will build a shelter and then put too many horses in the paddocks for the size of the shelter. The chances of every horse standing quietly in the shelter together will become less likely, especially if they are crowded. Your new clients may not even notice this or see it as a problem until they come out one day and the weather is bad and their horse is the one standing out in the rain, soaked to the bone.

  As the barn manager, you will be getting the call and you will need to decide how to handle this situation. I have always believed that as a barn owner and manager, my job is to make sure every horse in my care is safe, healthy and happy. If a horse is shivering because he cannot get into the shelter, then I am not doing my job as the caretaker. If you are in the business to take care of the horses at your barn, then keep a close eye on your outdoor boarded horses and make sure they can get into the shelter if they need to. I know some horses will stand out in the rain by choice, but you need to know the difference because the horse's wellbeing may be in jeopardy.

- **When the horses don't get along**-When you have horses on outdoor board it is of the utmost importance that they get along. They don't get a reprieve from each other at night in their own stalls. They are with each other twenty-four hours a day and it can become very stressful for a horse if he can't get into the shelter or is constantly being chased. When this kind of situation happens it will lead to other problems like weight loss. A stressed horse may stop eating normally and will lose weight. Your boarder may notice weight loss, but if they don't it is your responsibility to check for wellness and correct the situation. If you are putting the care of the horses first, then resolving issues like this will be a part of the job.

- **Feeding program for outdoor boarded horses**-Deciding how you want to feed the horses on outdoor board is important. You can choose to feed large round or square bales or small individual piles or even using an off the ground feeder. They all may seem like viable choices at first. Horses have a hierarchy in each herd and the top horse will make the bottom horses move. If you only have one round bale for a number of horses and some are not allowed to eat (in some cases until hours later), then you have a problem. Some very dominant horses will never leave the round bale and I have even heard of horses laying down on the bale as it spreads and eating like they are the king! It may look cute, but it won't be funny for the boarder who has the horse that can't get enough food. In some cases, the dominant horse will eat too much and start gaining weight while another will lose weight.

  Feeding round bales is an easy and less labor intensive way to feed horses but you need to make sure that you have enough round bales in the paddocks so every horse can eat enough, especially if the weather is extremely cold. One of the draw backs of feeding round bales is that the rain and weather can breakdown the nutrients of the hay if it is in consistently wet conditions. Putting a shelter over the round bale is a good idea that your boarders will appreciate.

  I have always been a fan of feeding individual piles of hay for each horse that is in the outdoor paddocks. It might be more work daily, but it helps me track how much the horses are eating and reduces stress in the herds. This kind of feeding method helps ensure that each horse has a pile of food and can eat enough to maintain weight. Even if they are being moved off of one pile, they can move to another available pile and keep eating. I have found fewer problems with this type of feeding program and it makes for much happier horses and clients.

- **Grain and supplements**-You will need to decide if you are going to feed grain and supplements as part of your program and how often. Feeding outdoor horses their grain and supplements can be challenging, especially if you don't have a stall to put them in while they eat. Keeping them from moving to each other's grain will have you at times frustrated, especially if you have one horse that inhales his grain while another is a very slow eater. Another issue that can create more work is when you have a client that wants their horse to have a large amount of grain while the others in the herd only get a small amount. It is no fun standing by a horse for fifteen minutes while he eats his grain no matter what type of weather you are having. How are you going to set this part of your feeding program up? If you have stalls you can use while a few horses eat their grain, then it will really make your job easier. If you don't have available stalls, then you really need to think about what you can and cannot offer with this part of your program.

Another decision you will need to make is whether you will feed grain and supplements twice a day. We have chosen to feed our outdoor horses, grain and supplements in the morning only and then our boarders have the choice if they want to come out and feed evening grain. This will not suit everyone and you need to understand that. It will be very important for some people to have their horse fed grain twice a day and if you don't provide it you could lose a client and you need to accept that. I believe there are many people that will be fine having you feed grain one time daily, as many of them enjoy coming out and feeding grain to their horses as part of caring for their horse.

These scenarios are intended to get you thinking about the possible issues and extra work involved in outdoor board. However you decide to manage this part of your outdoor feeding program, you are likely to encounter some surprises.

- **Blanketing**-If you have decided to offer outdoor board and live in a colder climate then you will have boarders that blanket their horses during the cold weather. In most cases this will not be problematic, but it can become an issue if you have a client that doesn't understand blanketing. You will want to make sure that the owner of an outdoor boarded horse uses the correct blankets at all times. Changes in weather and rain that comes with the seasons require that your clients have waterproof blankets if they are going to blanket. A boarder that buys a blanket not knowing what kind to buy could leave you to find out that it isn't waterproof at all. I have gone out to a paddock after the owner has left and been in shock with what I see for outerwear. I have had an owner put a full show sleazy on their horse and not think anything about it. I have had turnout sheets and coolers left on horses that were only meant to be worn inside. In both cases, I had to call the clients and explain the problem with what they put on their horse and they needed to come change the blanket. You will want to pay close attention to what the owner puts on their horse if they are outdoor boarded so that the horse doesn't get caught in bad weather and become chilled and possibly sick due to a soaked blanket.

- **Harsh weather**-When someone comes to board at your barn in outdoor board, they might say they are fine with how you do things at your place, but when the weather becomes harsh you could receive a call. I have had clients call me when thunderstorms are coming during the summer and when blizzards are expected in the winter. If the temperatures drop to below zero there is a good chance I will receive a call from a worried client. You really want to think about how you want to set up your outdoor board throughout all four seasons and all weather conditions and you need to make this very clear to your clients. At our barn we have inside stalls to bring in horses if a blizzard is coming or if the air temperatures have plummeted to dangerously low temperatures. We offer inclement weather stalls as part of our outdoor board. If you don't have stalls to bring the horses into, then you need to be clear that they will be staying outside no matter the weather and make sure the owner is comfortable with that. Some barns will put all the outdoor boarded horses into an indoor arena during bad weather and you could be asked if you will do that for the horses at your stable. Outdoor board is not for everyone even though most healthy horses do just fine with proper shelter, enough food and fresh water. It is often harder on the owner than the horse.

- **Injured or sick horses**-What are you going to do if a horse becomes seriously sick or injured and all you have is one paddock with other horses living in it? It is important that you have a place to keep a sick or injured horse so they can get the proper medical attention and recover from their injuries or illness.

- **Special requests**-You will get special requests with outdoor board and over time you will determine what you can and cannot do for your clients. I have had requests over the years that range from asking to change the fencing to bringing in horses during times of bad weather because the owner was concerned. With each request you will learn what you can accommodate at your stable.

- **The senior horse**-When a person comes for a tour of your stable and is thinking of bringing their horse to your place, it is a good idea to find out some details about their horse before you offer them a spot in outdoor board. Over the years I have learned that the horses that have the hardest time on outdoor board are the very senior horses. As they grow old they not only slow down, but they also start to have health problems and that could include eating and digestion. Living in an area that has extremely cold weather can be very hard on the older horse and many times they will lose weight during the cold spells if they cannot get enough proper nutrition. If you board a horse with special health and dietary needs it will take more work for you as the caretaker.

Many senior horses are very slow eaters and they can become stressed easily if they are in a herd where they can't get enough food because the others horses have eaten most of it or forced them away. There have been a couple of times throughout the years when I have declined a new client and horse because I knew the horse would not be a good fit for the herds that were established due to his old age and the care he needed. That is when I recommend stall board as a better alternative.

When Outdoor Board Is Not A Good Fit

If you have a horse that is struggling with outdoor board due to age or health issues, it is critical to be honest with the owner. If you have stall board then you can offer indoor board as a better choice but if you don't have an opening for indoor board, recommend a stable that can take better care of the horse that has the special needs. If you try to keep every client because of the income, then you are not doing what is in the best interest of the horse. Not every horse or owner is well suited for outdoor board.

The other scenario to think about is the mix of herds. If you have a group of horses living together then you need to make sure they are compatible. This may be challenging when you are new to the business, but as you get to know the horses and their personalities you will be much more prepared for the arrival of a new horse. Once I talk with a prospective boarder and ask them about their horse, I can usually tell if the horse will be a good match for the horses that are already established in the outdoor board herds. There are periodic surprises but if you know your horses then it does become easier. For example, if you have a couple of geldings and you know that one doesn't get along with mares, then don't put a mare in the mix. Could it cost you a possible client if there is no other place to put the mare? Of course, but it is much better to refuse a client than to have problems later with injured horses and fences torn down. It happens more frequently than you know.

Outdoor Board Guidelines

When you are setting up your outdoor board amenities, write down exactly what comes with outdoor board and how you do things. This is very important for your clients to have. Explain how you will feed the horses with both hay and grain. Explain how you manage water, especially in the winter. Be very clear about how you manage the horses during times of inclement weather. If you are going to bring horses inside during blizzards or extremely cold temperatures, then be as specific as possible. Explain the factors that play a part in deciding when to bring the horses inside. That could include the wind, wind chill and blizzard conditions that come with cold weather. The more specific you are with your outdoor board the easier your job will be in the long run.

Once your clients have been with you through the change of seasons and with their horse doing well, they will start to relax and trust that you will take good care of their horse. It can take time to gain the owner's trust, especially if they have boarded at other places where the care was less than desired.

This Is Important!

You need to remember that your idea of bad weather might be much different than your boarders. There will be times when you think the weather is fine and they will be wondering or even ask if you are going to bring the horses inside. If you don't have the option to bring the horse in when the weather is bad, then your job will be easier because your clients will already know there are no stalls available. If you do have indoor stalls available, then you could be asked more often about when you will bring the horses in. This can be challenging because outdoor board usually doesn't come with a stall as part of the board rate. If you are going to offer stalls, then make sure you are clear about who is going to bed and clean them. Once you bring the outdoor horses inside, then your labor has just increased. Besides filling the water buckets (which could be heater buckets and are expensive to run) the stalls will need to be cleaned. Are you going to have your boarders provide the bedding and do the clean up or will you offer the shavings and stall cleaning for an added fee? I have seen it done both ways and you will want to figure out this part of it before you start taking in boarders.

Remember that if you live in a place that gets dangerously cold temperatures and the weather has been severe, then you could possibly have outdoor horses inside for quite a few days and that is a lot of manure that needs to be cleaned. If you take responsibility for cleaning the stalls, then you have just added more time and labor to your already busy day and if you hire employees to clean the extra stalls, you will now be losing money unless you add a charge for the extra service. You need to be very clear with your clients about how you do things during very bad weather.

One more thought-you will see their horse much more than the owner will and you will become very familiar with all their habits including eating, pooping and sleeping. You will be the first one to see if there are problems and recognize if the horse is becoming stressed for any number of reasons. If you notice an issue, then it is best to talk to the owner about your concerns. Sometimes things get resolved, but once in a while they don't and that is when it is time to think about another living arrangement for the horse. Put the health and well-being of the horse first and your clients will greatly appreciate it. Not only is it good for the horse but it shows the honesty and integrity you have as a barn manager and that is great for your reputation and your boarding stable.

~28~

Herd Management

Herd management will be one of the most important parts of your job as a barn manager/owner and even if you worked at many barns as an employee and have experience, it will take on a whole new dimension when you are the barn owner and all the responsibility falls on you. There are many variables to consider when matching horses for the purpose of creating a herd and despite your best efforts, horses will be horses and you will almost always have some challenges with behaviors in the herds.

If a horse gets hurt in a herd setting, the owners of the horse will often times bypass the barn manager and go directly to the barn owner. Herd management is extremely important and can be challenging, so in this chapter we will take a look at many scenarios along with ways to avoid problems or resolve them. As the barn owner/manager you are likely to be exposed to many opinions on herd management and there will be times when the opinions feel like an assault on your knowledge and competency.

After all these years, I have to say that this is one of the areas of barn management where I learned the most about horses and how they communicate with each other in both good and not so good ways. No one likes to come see their horse and find a new bite mark or cut from another horse or even worse, lame due to a kick. You can read many books on herd management and behavior, but when you have to do it yourself and study the horses and decide where to put each of them, there is no better classroom.

Mares And Geldings

There are many varying opinions regarding how to match horses for compatibility in a paddock. Every boarding facility will address herd management differently depending on their paddock design and composition of horses. How much land you can allocate for paddocks and how many paddocks can you maintain will be two important questions to answer. You will need to build enough paddocks to provide safe spaces for the horses in your care. If you have sufficient paddocks to enclose a small number of horses per paddock you will have more flexibility in herd creation and fewer issues with horse behavior and injuries.

Some boarding facilities will put all their geldings in one herd and all the mares in another. Others will mix them. Many people believe that you should never put mares and geldings together, while others believe it solely depends on the horses and their personalities. I agree with the later opinion and I have had both separate herds of mares and geldings as well as mixed herds, and they both do fine as long as I am aware of how they interact when they are together. The more time you spend in the care of horses, the faster you will learn about the nuances of their personalities and interactions and the more success you will have at creating compatible herds.

At our boarding facility I have a couple of mixed herds that work well not by chance, but because I study the horses and know their behavior. I really need to know the horses I am putting together and if a gelding acts "Studdish" then he is not put in with any mares on our farm. The same is true for mares. If a mare acts "Marish" all the time and has a hard time being around geldings, then I need to find a paddock with all mares for her. I have had a few situations over the years where the personality of a very quiet gelding has changed because he was put in with a mare and the same would be true for a quiet mare that goes crazy once she is with a gelding. To avoid horse conflicts you will need to learn how to read the horses in your care. If you are going to combine geldings and mares in paddocks, then you will need to understand the signs that there is impending trouble and take action.

You are not going to have much of a choice of which sex of horses come to your barn to board unless you specifically say only geldings or only mares allowed, which would not be a practical business decision. Many geldings love to play and often will look like a bunch of young boys having a good time without regard for safety. Mares are quieter and can be moody and rarely touch each other, except to smell each other or scratch each other's withers. I have found both sexes to be easy to read and, except for the occasional horse that doesn't fit the mold, once you figure out their personality and if their dominant, it becomes much easier to place them in a suitable herd.

Introducing A New Horse Into A Herd

I have always believed it is far better to introduce a new horse by placing him in his new paddock alone for a time so he can smell everything and get used to the new surroundings including the fencing. Next I will introduce him to one horse at a time. The goal is to find a herd buddy or pasture mate so they can bond and the new horse won't feel so isolated. I feel it is very stressful to throw a horse into a herd that is already in the paddocks. The new horse may become overwhelmed by horses charging around, bucking and nipping and for some horses this will be too stressful. If you introduce the horse to the other horses slowly and allow the new horse to adjust to the paddock, things will usually settle down much quicker. Take your time in the beginning and you will never regret it when it comes to introducing horses.

There Are No Guarantees In Herd Management

I know that having more paddocks never guarantees that horses will always get along, but it can help. You can have two horses together and have all kinds of problems. The best way to make the job of herd management easier and cut down on problems is to have enough paddocks to be flexible if you must move a horse. You will always have scuffles with horses, but if you can reduce conflict by having more flexibility to move a horse when it needs to be moved, it will make a significant difference in your job.

The best thing for your business is to fence sufficient paddocks to assure flexibility. I can promise you that you will have horses that don't get along and they do get injured. I have been there and it is not fun. Many people go into the boarding business and after they are open they realize pretty early on that they need more paddocks. Herd management can be easy if you plan ahead in this very important area. You can never be certain what kinds of dynamics you will have until you put horses together in a herd and see how they get along. Are you prepared to make changes if needed? Herd management will be one of the most important parts of your job and you want to make sure you are prepared for most outcomes.

I have learned a great deal throughout the years about herd management and I have had my share of mistakes when it comes to reading a horse's personality. I am always learning and new situations are always on the horizon. That is what makes these beautiful animals so amazing. They each have their own personality and if you watch them long enough, you will be amazed at how easy they are to read.

Introducing a new horse to a herd can be challenging enough, but when it is a boarder's horse, the pressure to have the horses all get along will amplify during those first few hours or days. Herd management will be one of the most challenging parts of your boarding business for the simple reason that we really don't know what horses will do until we put them together and then we cross our fingers and hope our initial guess is correct.

It is great to be able decide how you want your boarding business to operate under normal conditions, but it is equally important to your success to have an alternative plan for those unexpected circumstances. It is vital for success in herd management. When working with horses you will have the unexpected more often than you ever dreamed. It comes with the job. Take the time to learn from those unexpected occurrences and each time they will become easier to handle.

Red Flags And How To Spot Them In A Herd

I have had many years of experience with herd management and I learned on the job with each new horse that has come to our barn. There were trials and errors along the way, as it will be for anyone that is running a barn and dealing with herds daily. All it takes is one new horse to change the herd dynamics and learning to recognize the signs that things are not going well in a herd takes time. Sure, you might know the basics of horse behavior so you can see when a horse is angry, content or even stressed, but I guarantee you are going to learn so much more about horses and how they bond, play, fight and communicate with each other. You will start to see which horses are insecure and quiet, which ones are loud and obnoxious, etc. If more people would take the time to really study how horses communicate in a herd, they would learn so much more about their own horse just by watching them be a horse.

I have compiled a list of what I call "Red flags" that I have seen in different situations in the herds at our facility and what I have done to correct the situation. This is not an exhaustive list because anything can happen, and just when you think you have seen it all, a horse will do something that will totally surprise you. When I start to see a red flag issue in a herd, I know that I need to make changes to preempt conflicts and help the horse in need.

I also want you to know that issues with horses may take a few days to work themselves out, but if things don't settle down, then you need to watch all the horses and see what the problem is. It might be what you least expect and a simple change is all that it takes to create harmony in the herd again. This is why having enough paddocks is so important in herd management and maintaining herd harmony.

Red Flags In A Herd:

- **Pacing the fence constantly**-I understand that when it's time to bring a horse in for dinner some will pace the fence in anticipation, but when they pace the fence all day long every day that is a red flag that something is not right. That is when I will watch the new horse to see if they are not fitting in with the herd or if there is another problem. In one situation, we had a new horse pace the fence for several days. The horse was not bonding with any of the other horses so I moved the horse to a different paddock with a different herd. He settled down as he buddied up with one particular horse and the entire personality of the new horse changed and within the week he stopped pacing. A move can be very hard on a horse, especially if they had been at the same place for a long time and were bonded with the horses. Sometimes all it takes is one horse to help a new horse fit in and find his place.

- **Constant aggressive behavior towards a new horse**-It is normal for horses to establish a herd hierarchy, so every time you introduce a new horse you disrupt their pecking order. The horses will protect their position in the herd order and, in the process some will assert themselves to the point of aggression. Once the new horse has figured out where he fits in the hierarchy, things settle down very quickly. It is a red flag when you have an established dominant horse that continues to harass the new horse despite the new horse conceding to his dominance. Horses are generally fair, so this doesn't happen often, but when it does you will need to think of alternative placements for the new horse. For reasons unknown to us, a horse will sometimes show incredible aggression towards a new horse and in this case you may need to move the horse fast to avoid injuries or stress. These cases are unusual, but they do happen.

- **When two horses just don't get along**-Once in a while you will get two horses that are equally dominant, aggressive and they both refuse to back down and accept a lower position in the herd. These are the times when horses can get hurt. No matter how much you want things to settle down and have horses get along, it is not likely to happen so you need to have an alternative plan for moving one of the horses. Not everyone will agree with this statement and some barn owners believe that horses need to fight it out to settle down. If you are committed to providing a healthy environment for the horses you board, you will need to provide a second herd option at times to avoid catastrophic injuries.

- **The "Gang up"**-Horses can be bullies. They can effectively work together to harass another horse, corner them and proceed to assault them with teeth and hooves. It is hard to say why this happens with a few horses, but in any case you are going to need to take action immediately to avert a very dangerous situation.

You may witness two horses in a herd actually work together very strategically to run down and corner a new horse. If you watch this behavior you will see how calculated both horses can be at placing themselves on each side of the new horse and cornering them so they can kick or bite the horse. It is both amazing and terrifying to watch. Depending on personalities you can have two scenarios: take the established dominant horse out of the paddock for a few days and allow time for the new horse to adjust within the herd. In this situation, the second top horse usually won't do much without his ally by his side. When the new horse seems acclimated, has regained his confidence and perhaps a pasture mate, put the top horse back in with the herd. This seems to work well in many situations. The second option is to move the new horse to a paddock that is more accepting of a new horse. Both solutions can work but require paddock options to be successful.

- **The very young horse**-You are going to board horses of different ages at your barn and that can be a major factor when doing herd placement. If you board very young horses (yearlings), then you will want to be very selective on where you place them. Putting very young horses in with a herd of adult horses can be traumatizing because in many cases the older horses will be very hard on the young horse. I would recommend placement in a paddock with just a few horses that are a good match for the youngster until he can grow up a little. Mares and geldings can both be good role models and teachers for the young horse and it may work best when another young horse is not available for a herd mate. If no other young horse is available for a pasture mate, then be very selective on which adult horse you choose to put in with a yearling.

- **The very senior horse**-An older horse can be intolerant of a large herd and the antics of other horses and in some cases can get stressed out. He can't move like he used to and it takes him much longer to eat. At times you may need to take a very senior horse out of a herd and create a new herd with him and just one other horse so that he can live out his days in peace and quiet. It is much better for the senior horse as there is nothing worse than watching a horse struggle as he loses his place in the hierarchy of a herd as he ages.

Helping a horse live to old age can be challenging and heart-breaking and that is why I believe you are going to need special accommodations for the requirements of the senior horse. Recognizing the signs that it is time to move a senior horse to a different paddock is important for you as the barn manager and equally important for the owner. A senior horse can be vulnerable to illness, bullying and weight loss, so it is necessary to become educated, understand how you can keep an aging horse healthy, sound and happy and make plans for care management changes. Not all stables are equipped to board old horses or very young horses.

I have given you a few examples of what I feel are red flags and good indicators that it is time to move a horse. No two situations will ever be the same and you will have to take it one situation at a time. Your job will include problem solving herd issues. The good news is the longer you are running your barn and watching horses in the herds, the better you will be at understanding horse body language and herd dynamics. It does get much easier. There will be times when you can anticipate activities because you know the horses very well. In fact, at times you will know the horses better than the owner when it comes to their personality, quirks and vices and how they interact with other horses.

A Little Time-Out Can Go A Long Way

I want to share a tip on something I do if I am having an issue with introducing a new horse into an established herd where the dominant horse won't let up. In the perfect world it would be wonderful if all the horses would just be nice to each other, but that is not the case. The first twenty-four to forty-eight hours are the most crucial in making sure the new horse is settling in well. Many of your horses will do just fine adjusting to a new herd, but I can promise that you will get horses that will have a very difficult time, and the more you can do to make the transition easy the better it will be for the new horse.

I have found over the years that if a horse comes to my barn and is a very nervous and insecure horse, the transition will most likely be a more challenging. One of the things I will do is to watch the herd closely after I have introduced the new horse and if there is one horse that is not easing off and is creating more stress to the new horse, I will pull that dominant horse out of the herd for a day to two.

Once a new horse feels more comfortable, then they can start to figure out the herd and where they are in the hierarchy of the herd. When the dominant horse is placed back in the herd a few days later, the new horse is ready to deal with the situation and many times has gained enough confidence to let the top horse know to leave him alone. This has happened many times over the years and in each situation the herd settles down much faster.

There is no guarantee when placing horses together that they will always get along, but this little tip of pulling the dominant horse out for a day or two can make a huge difference in many cases. Is it more work? Of course it is, but if you do the work in the beginning when there is an issue it can save you much stress in the long run.

Not Enough Paddocks

One of the biggest issues I see at many barns is that there are not enough paddocks. I have toured stables where they have fifteen horses in one large paddock and if a horse is not doing well in that herd, the barn owner has no other place to move them. I have talked to many concerned boarders over the years that boarded at places where their horse couldn't get to the hay or was being chased constantly and there were no other herd and paddock options to move their horse.

A barn manager can become very frustrated because they are losing boarders and they don't know why. They don't realize it is because of their herd management and the lack of flexibility to move a horse when there is a serious situation. I am NOT suggesting that you should move a horse every time a horse gets a bite or kick mark or a client asks you to move their horse because, if that were the case, you would be moving horses quite often. What I am saying is that good herd management means being prepared for the horse that does need to be moved and thinking ahead about your paddock set up and design. If there is one thing I can promise you about boarding horses, it is that you will board horses that don't get along well with others and at times herd adjustments will need to be done. It may not happen often, but it will happen.

A large boarding facility is going to have changes in the herds more often than a small private stable, and you never know if the next new horse will be a mare or gelding until you talk with the new boarder. That is when you start re-evaluating the herds to help figure out which herd is best suited for each horse. Your time observing the herds and getting to know all the horses will enable you to build your herds effectively and reposition horses whenever necessary.

Gaining The Trust From A New Boarder

One of the biggest hurdles you will come across as the barn manager is earning the trust of a new boarder that has had a bad experience with their horse in herds. There is a chance that they were at a facility that didn't group the horses properly and their horse was harassed by the other horses. Some managers will not modify herds under any circumstances, even dangerous ones. It could be that they don't know how to make good herds or that they don't have enough paddocks to be flexible. They might even believe that the horses need to work it out.

Boarders will bring their horses and their boarding baggage and fears with them to the new stable and this will present special challenges for the barn manager. I believe it is your job as the barn manager to educate and reassure a new boarder and you will gradually earn their trust. Sometimes specific situations will create a rapid bond of trust quickly but in most cases gaining trust usually takes time with consistency and good horse care.

There are always going to be different views on herd management and I really believe there is so much more to consider than just the sex of the horse. You have to do what is best for your boarding program, but I encourage you to be vigilant and watch for personality changes that might lead to problems. If your client's horse gets hurt in a situation that could have been avoided or corrected, you will be the one responsible and you might lose a horse, a boarder and jeopardize your reputation and business.

Private Turnout

Your boarding operation will not be complete without a private turnout area. It is actually best to have several private turnouts and you will use them. Horses in rehab may need private turnout so that once they can go back outside, they can progress slowly according to veterinarian orders. Some horses will have an injury that could take months to heal and private turnout is needed.

The one reason that some people don't put their horse in private turnout is because many boarding barns charge an extra fee for private turnout. Sometimes you will need to strongly advise an owner to put their horse in private turnout, because they don't realize how quickly the horse can reinjure themselves. This type of client needs to understand that it is far better to pay for private turnout then to have more vet bills after the horse reinjures his self again. Re-injuries are very common in herd paddocks and they are upsetting, frustrating and expensive for the owner and terrible for the horse, but equally frustrating for the barn manager.

Using private turnout to allow a new horse to settle into his new surroundings for a few days is very effective. Adjusting to a new stable can be stressful for any horse, so having private turnout for new horses is something that will be useful. Private turnout availability will be an important asset for your operation and standards of care.

Once in a while you will come across a horse that doesn't do well in private turnout. The owner may be nervous to put him in with a herd for fear that he will get hurt, but you may start to see some new negative behaviors if he is stressed due to being alone. If you are going to set up some private turnouts at your barn, then I would suggest having them near other horses so that the horse can be comforted by the presence of other horses.

Educating Will Be Part Of Your Job

The decisions you make for the horses and their herd placement will by watched by boarders and if something isn't going well (or they think it's not going well) it will be your job to help them to understand the dynamics of the herds. If you take the time to explain the horses' behavior in a herd, it will help educate your concerned boarders and you will have fewer questions and issues in the future because they will trust you.

As a boarding operation you will have many different clients and a lot of them will be first time horse owners that don't know much about horses and how they communicate. You will have some boarders that don't know the difference between horses playing and horses fighting. They won't realize that a thousand pound animal can play pretty rough and using their teeth and body are all part of it. You will have boarders that worry because they see a horse not eating and they don't realize that he is resting and has had enough to eat at that moment.

Many people have this idea that all horses will continually eat until every blade of hay is gone, but that simply is not true for all of them. If the horses are getting plenty to eat then you will have many horses that will stop for a while and rest or play.

Of course, you will always have at least one horse that never stops eating and barely comes up from his hay to breathe. Some horses prioritize play over food and they will start playing before they even take a bite to eat. We have had many horses over the years that will be put out in the morning with fresh hay and focus on playing rather than feasting. That is a sign that they are content and are not worried about having enough food to eat. It tells me that they trust they can get hay at any time without another horse forcing them away.

You will have situations every now and then where someone witnesses horses with what looks like ears pinned and hooves flying in an apparent dispute. It can be frightening and unsettling until you realize that the horses are just playing! You might even get a call about the concern and you will find yourself in a great place to help your boarder learn what is actually going on. Horses have days where they are grumpy, moody and even quiet. They also have days when they play enthusiastically. When the mares come into heat it can change the herd dynamics for a while and a quiet mare can become unusually dominant for a short time. This is also true for some geldings that sense a mare is in heat.

The wind can blow a different direction and the horses act like they have lost their brain and will do things that they normally don't do. Sometimes they feel bold and will try to move up the ladder in the herd and it can result in some confrontation from the horses that are higher up. It doesn't mean you need to move a horse, it just means you should keep an eye on them until things settle down. This happens often when a new horse is introduced, and suddenly everyone is trying to figure out their place in the herd.

You will have boarders that don't understand the hierarchy of a horse herd and how dominance works. It is important to help them understand this part of horses' lives, especially with respect to their horse's herd position and their safety when going out to the paddocks to bring their horse back into the barn. Some boarders are oblivious of horses' body language and the cues they impart. Educating owners about body language and cues will be very helpful when trying to keep them safe as they enter a paddock to get their horse.

I believe watching a group of horses interact is the best classroom a barn manager can have and it is constantly changing with the weather, seasons and horses coming and going. You will come to appreciate the nuances of their behavior and you will never stop learning with each horse that comes to your barn.

~29~

Is Your Barn Set Up For The Horse With Special Needs?

We have had so many wonderful horses stay at our facility over the years. We have had horses as young as four months all the way through thirty-four years old. Each horse holds a special place in my heart and each one came with their own personality, quirks and vices. Most of the horses have been very easy to take care of, but we have also had our fair share of horses with special needs for many different reasons.

Special needs horses may require extra work, care and accommodations. If you are not prepared for how you want to handle a senior horse, a very young horse or a horse with health issues and dietary needs, you might find yourself becoming stressed because of the extra work that you hadn't considered. You need to make sure your boarding stable can accommodate this type of horse care before you say yes to the person who wants to board at your facility. If you are going to run a boarding business, then you need to think about the horse with special needs.

Many senior horses will have special needs from special feeding programs to special paddocks with fewer horses.

Modifying Your Program For The Special Needs Horse

There have been some challenging situations where we needed to modify our program to fit the horse that had special needs. We have had some very senior horses that needed to be in a special paddock with only one other horse that we felt would be a great fit. We have had to soak the hay and grain for a few senior horses where eating became difficult. We have had some very young horses come that were too young to put out in the regular herds and special accommodations were needed. We have had horses with moon blindness that needed special lighting in their stall at night. We have had horses that have been through major surgery and needed special accommodations to rest and heal. Many horses that come to your barn will have dietary issues and you will be surprised how each one will differ in their feeding program. No two are ever the same!

The very young horses will have special needs as far as diet and even the horses they will live with until they become a little older.

Even horses coming off the show circuit or racetrack will have their own set of special needs if they are not used to going outside with other horses. There can be a prolonged adjustment period for some of these horses and they need to be handled with care and patience while they adjust to their new life.

I encourage you to take a look at your business and employees to determine if you are ready to handle the horse with special needs. You will have many different horses come to your barn and you should have a good understanding of what each horse requires for care and more importantly you need to know if you can accommodate these special needs. It is so much better to be honest with the owner if you can't provide the care needed in certain circumstances. Please don't try to fit the horse with special needs into your way of doing things at your barn. That usually doesn't work. If you want to care for the horse with special needs, then you need to be open to modifying your program to accommodate these types of horses for it to be a success for you and the horses in your care.

I encourage you to talk with others in the boarding business if you are just starting out and find out how they handle horses with special needs. The more you educate and prepare yourself, the more ready you will be to handle these horses that come to live at your barn. For many of them it will be the last place they live. Wouldn't it be great if their last years were their best years?

If you choose to accommodate the horse with special needs, then learn from each situation what you can and cannot offer at your stable. It will definitely be a learning experience with each horse and it will prepare you better for the next horse that comes that needs special accommodations.

~30~

When A Horse Doesn't Fit Your Program

The one thing I want you to learn from this chapter is that not every horse will fit the boarding program that you offer. Not every horse will be a good fit for your outdoor program and that could be true in some situations for your stall board as well.

One of the mistakes I have seen a few new horse owners make is when they choose a boarding arrangement for a newly purchased horse, without regard for how the horse will be affected. So much depends on the living environment that the horse experienced before it was welcomed into a new family. For example, a horse that has lived his entire life in a stall and never experienced herd turnout or outside turnout will have a major adjustment ahead. Putting him outside on outdoor board could be very stressful and could lead to other problems including sickness. Another great example is when a new owner purchases a thin skinned horse like a Thoroughbred from a warm climate and this horse has known only stall board and warm weather. I have had people want outdoor board in the middle of winter and the horse is coming from Florida. Talk about a shock to the system! In certain cases, I have said I didn't think it was a good fit and have offered a stall instead, but have explained the reasons for my answer. At that point, it will either work for the new clients or they will seek boarding elsewhere and you need to be okay with that because the well-being of the horse takes priority. Most new horse owners do not realize that horses need an adjustment period when being moved, but some horses will struggle more due to their history. Each scenario will be different.

The Barn Manager's Responsibility

It will be the responsibility of the barn manager to inform the client if their horse is having a hard time adjusting to his new surroundings. In many cases the owner is not present at the barn sufficiently to see the signs that their horse is depressed or stressed. It is not easy to tell a client that their horse is having some adjustment issues, but it is important and will help them learn about horse behavior and decisions about the best care possible for their new equine. As the barn manager, you will be the voice of the horses at your barn. In most cases, the transition to your stable will go smoothly but eventually you will experience a horse or two that has a very difficult time adjusting and sometimes you know it isn't a good fit at all.

If your barn insists that all horses have daily turnout and you have a new client that wants their horse to stay inside twenty-four hours a day, except for when it is worked, then you will have some problems. We had a horse board with us when we first opened and this horse was accustomed to living outside all of his life. He had never been in a stall except on rare occasion. The new owners wanted to turn this horse into a show horse, but the horse was having difficulty adjusting to being in a stall twenty-four hours a day. He starting chewing, other vices started to appear and he wasn't eating well. I talked with the owners and described the behavior and we watched a little longer to see if the horse would settle down. He never did settle in, so after a time I had to insist that the horse go outside daily with all the others. The clients were not happy with my decision and they ended up moving the horse. From that day forward, I made it very clear to boarders and prospective boarders that all horses go outside daily for turnout to avoid that problem from happening again.

When There Are No More Options

The worst thing you can do is try to make a horse fit into your program because of the money. If you try to board a horse that is not well-suited for your stable, you will likely find that the cost of care is high and will consume your profits. The horse may not thrive and it could also cost you your reputation. It is not about the money because you need to put the care of the horse first or you shouldn't be boarding horses. It is important to know exactly what you can offer for horses at your barn and some of that will come from trial and error experiences. If you have a horse that doesn't fit into your program, be very honest with the owner and even help them find a stable that will work better for what they want to do or what the horse needs. Putting the horse first is the right thing to do and it will demonstrate your professionalism and your ethics.

Not Every Person Is A Good Fit

While running a stable you will interact with many people with one shared interest—the love of horses. They may have very different personalities, backgrounds, and knowledge of equine activities. The one thing most of them will have is opinions! It is important to realize that not every person that comes to your barn will be a good fit. Sometimes a boarder will come with high expectations that they didn't share with you in the beginning and quickly you will find out that they are very demanding or expecting things done that you don't offer at your barn. If you have tried everything you can and it still isn't working out with a particular client, then it is time to talk with them and tell them that they might need to find a barn that better suits their needs.

There are plenty of barns and stables that board horses and each one has something different to offer. People need to take the time to evaluate the area boarding facilities for compatibility with their needs and to get exactly what they want for their horse. In the long run, it will be much less stressful for you as the barn manager and it will be better for your business if an unsatisfied boarder moves on.

Most horses will do just fine in a new setting, given a slow adjustment with good care and patience. Keep your eyes open for red flags and signs of stress in the horse. Also, keep the communication open with the client and work together to assure a good outcome. The more you communicate with the owner, the more they will be willing to trust you and the decisions you are making for their horse.

If you are running a multi-discipline barn with many breeds, then you might have some issues depending on the breed and climate you live in. Horses are being moved across the country for relocation with greater frequency and that presents unique concerns that you may need to contend with. Remember, that a Thoroughbred may not handle the cold Midwest winters on outside board as well as a draft horse. When talking to prospective clients, I want you to think about possible issues for the breed coming to your barn. It could make a difference on the preparations and outcome for a prospective horse, client and your facility.

~31~

When A Horse Needs To Be Euthanized

There are so many wonderful things about working in the horse industry. If you are crazy about horses, then making a living working with them is a dream come true for many of us. There are also some very difficult areas that come with boarding horses for a living. One of the most challenging and even heartbreaking parts of your role as a barn manager will come when a horse needs to be euthanized. When you experience the end of the life for a horse that has been in your care you share the pain of loss with their owners. Your support and empathy will help the owner work through the needed arrangements as well as the emotional assault they will experience.

The Different Reasons A Horse Is Euthanized

If you have never experienced watching a veterinarian put down a horse, then you are in for an emotional roller coaster, especially if it was a long time in coming. As a barn manager you will see the exceptional bond of horses and people. You may think that most horses are put down due to old age but that simply is not true. As a barn owner, I learned very quickly that I would witness horses being down for many reasons besides old age. Some of those reasons will leave you heartbroken and even confused, especially in the early years of your career.

I have experienced the pain and heartache of watching a horse try to stand with a broken leg and there is absolutely nothing anyone can do but watch and wait for the veterinarian to come. I have had horses put down due to colic after watching them endure pain and struggle through treatment to the point where there is nothing that can be done except that last act of kindness. I have had horses become completely blind and it was time to say good-bye. There have been horses that have succumbed to illnesses that would leave the horse so sick that the owner decided it was time to euthanize the horse. I have watched owners put down a horse that had minor lameness issues but they didn't want to rehome the horse. I have watched horses put down because of neurological issues and the horse was in pain and no longer acting "normal." And I have watched as a senior horse had lived out his days and it was time to put him at rest and say good-bye.

You always hope that this will not become part of your job, but the reality is that at one time or another a horse will need to be put down at your barn and you may need to make the arrangements and manage the respectful disposition of the body. This is a very emotionally taxing part of barn management and your strength and professionalism will help the owner face the decision and accept the loss knowing that it is their final gift to their companion.

The Barn Manager's Role

You will determine what your role is when a horse is put down at your stable and with each client it will be different. You will have some clients that want to be a part of the process all the way to the very end, and others that can't handle the pain and will stay away. You will have some that want you close by at all times, and others that will give you signs that they want you to stand back so they can have some privacy. As a barn manager you are going to be dealing with an emotionally charged situation and the best thing you can do is offer gentle guidance and let the client decide how much support they want from you. Some people will want you to handle everything from holding the horse while the veterinarian gives the injection through the disposal of the body or cremation. In almost every situation the owner will not know who to call to pick up the body and will rely on you to make the arrangements. You will want to know the services in your area and the costs involved. Most people will not stay to watch the removal process so that will be part of your job. You can get everything arranged and get a check for payment so after the owners say good-bye to their horse you can take care of the rest of the business that needs to be done.

As the barn manager it is very important for you to support your clients. You may want to fall apart but you need to be strong for them and control your emotions for that moment. You will have time later to grieve in the privacy of your home.

Grieving

Horse owners all grieve differently and you need to understand this without judgement. You might be one that sheds tears while some of your clients will hold it in until they are alone. Some will stay away from the barn while others will be looking for a new horse the next day. Each person and situation will be different and their way of grieving will be part of that. You never know what the person is feeling and as the professional, you need to keep your opinions to yourself and not share them with anyone else at the barn.

The Other Boarders And Their Opinions

The one thing that came as a shock to me were all the different opinions that were expressed in certain situations when a horse needed to be put down at my barn. How the owner of the horse deals with death and how the other people react WHEN IT IS NOT THEIR HORSE can be very surprising. I have watched boarders offer kind support to the owner and I have also witnessed the opposite when someone was angered by how things were handled and judgmental of the owner's decisions. Whether you agree with the boarder who chooses to put down a horse or not, it is your responsibility to make sure things go smoothly and people keep their opinions to themselves.

We live in a world where everyone has a different view of the responsibilities of animal ownership. Some horse owners will delay a decision to euthanize even though their horse may be suffering, because they are hurting and can't face the finality of loss. The opposite is also true where owners are quick to put an animal down without making every effort to resolve the health issues. In many cases, money will be the deciding factor as medical treatment can be very expensive and many people don't have the extra money for colic surgery or other expensive treatments. It is easy for people to be quick to judge and you may need to make sure others at the barn keep their opinions to themselves so they don't hurt the person that just lost their horse.

There is no easy way to manage attitudes, but as you develop people skills through experience you will become more effective and learn to preempt situations before they create drama. I encourage you to be there for the client that is facing a very difficult decision for their horse. They will be looking to you, the knowledgeable barn manager, for guidance, advice and reassurance. Your boarders will appreciate the support and kindness you show the owner as well as your dedication to the comfort and care of the horse.

~32~

Barn Owner/Barn Manager

There are differences in the roles of the barn manager and barn owner. If you have been performing both roles as owner/manager and have recently hired a full-time barn manager to oversee your boarding business, then it will likely create some new dynamics in the barn and the business. Sometimes friction and confusion can come into play if each person doesn't have a clear understanding of their roles and responsibilities. It is important to respect both roles and determine how to work together effectively while pursuing common goals.

Boarding businesses can start to have significant problems due to conflict between the barn owner and barn manager because roles and responsibilities were not clearly defined and there is confusion over who is in charge. For example; if the barn manager is the last to find out when the barn owner is changing things at the barn, and in the process oversteps the barn manager's decisions, there are bound to be problems. Sometimes these issues are the result of inexperience, but they could also be caused by the owner's resistance to giving up total control of the business.

I have talked with barn owners that do not know how to share responsibilities with their barn manager and get upset because their manager is doing things that they didn't want done. I have also talked with barn managers who recognize a way to make things run more smoothly and efficiently, but the barn owner won't let them change anything. This can be frustrating for both parties and it affects the business in many ways. If these problems are occurring in your barn then your boarders will feel the conflict and drama.

Having A Common Goal And Vision

Most of the time when a business is having issues it is a direct result of a difference in vision and goals along with a lack of communication. Having the same vision is one of the most important parts of any business and it will be true for your boarding barn.

I have talked with barn owners that are frustrated because the barn manager they hired didn't have the same vision for the business. The barn manger might be very good at taking care of the needs of the horses and clients but in other areas of the business there seems to be a tug-o-war going on for who is in charge. This same complaint has also come from barn managers who thought they were hired to take the barn in one direction and then the barn owner decided to change the direction of the business. This is stressful for everyone involved and can lead to other issues. Usually the problem is poor communication and a lack of appreciation for the pressure each one feels when changes are happening. If you can formulate a common vision for client relations, horse care and boarding, then you will have a good foundation to build on, but it will take respectful communication from all involved in management to sustain success. Having a common vision is vital in keeping a business healthy, strong and running smoothly.

Important points that need common goals and vision:

- **The type of boarding barn**-It is very important for the barn owner and manager to have a common vision on the type of boarding barn they are providing. If the barn owner wants a hunter/jumper facility and the barn manager feels that the barn should be a multi-discipline barn, you could run into conflicts over arena time and space due to jump courses using the entire arena. Turnout practices can also create conflicts between manager and owner. If the barn owner wants the horses turned out daily and the barn manager chooses to keep horses inside because of their client's riding discipline, there will be frustration for both parties. Ultimately, the barn owner makes all final decisions but the barn manager needs to be in agreement to maintain a good working relationship.

- **Handling horses**-If you watch ten people handle horses you will notice that they all handle horses differently. Some people will have confidence in handling even the most unruly horse and correct them with fairness. Others will over-correct, become upset and will not let it go. If you are going to hire a barn manager you need to make sure they handle your client's horses the way you want. Handling includes management and correction, when needed. I have had employees that over-corrected difficult horses when leading them and I would have to explain to them how I wanted it to be done. Consistency in handling is good for the horses and the clients.

- **The daily care**-The barn manager needs to have complete agreement with the barn owner about the daily care of the horses which will include everything from daily turnout and feeding program to herd management and medical care.

- **Job description, job duties and chores**-As the barn owner you need to be very clear about the job description for the barn manager. The barn manager needs to have a complete understanding of the job, including all responsibilities that could range from cleaning stalls to managing other employees. Some barn managers may not want to clean stalls or do both morning and evening chores, and that needs to be discussed before the person is hired. There needs to be complete agreement on the job description, otherwise it can cause future issues if the barn owner thinks the manager is not fulfilling their responsibilities.

- **Understanding about money**-When a barn manager is ordering supplies and scheduling employees they are spending the barn owner's money. They need to be very careful to get maximum value for the money spent. Make sure the barn manager understands the budget and how much money can be spent monthly, as well as how it is to be spent.

- **Hours to be put in throughout the week**-Everything always looks good on paper and a job will sound great when reading an ad. The barn owner needs to be very specific about the amount of time the barn manager will be required to work each week and what days they will have off. You will need to make sure that the barn manager does not get burned out because they don't take their time off due to the demands at the barn. It happens more than you know in this type of industry.

- **Talking with boarders and how to resolve issues**-The barn manager you employ must be good with horses but they need to have good people skills also. Get to know them before you hire them and ask them about their experience dealing with issues in barns and talking to clients when problems arise. You need to agree on how you want the clients treated under the most difficult situations including asking a boarder to leave and giving a thirty-day notice.

- **Medical care**-When hiring a barn manager you want to make sure they are knowledgeable about equine medical care and good at maintaining their composure in stressful conditions. They should be able to tell if a horse is not feeling well and determine when to call a veterinarian. You need to make sure they can handle an emergency (such as a horse that is seriously injured) by evaluating the situation and taking appropriate action without overreacting, especially in the presence of the owner.

- **Upkeep and maintenance of the barn**-If you want a clean barn and your barn manager is a slob then you are going to have problems! The barn manager needs to attend to those things that you consider important in running a barn or you will not be satisfied. If something gets broken then you want a barn manager who gets it fixed right away, NOT two weeks later. Remember that what your barn manager does will reflect on you as the barn owner and your business. Define your expectations and demand adherence to your standards.

- **Trainers**-Make sure you and your barn manager discuss the types of trainers and techniques acceptable at your facility. A good trainer can help a boarding business if they partner well, provide education, improve horsemanship and reinforce a positive atmosphere. A trainer that does not share a common training philosophy can disrupt your barn operations and cause drama by negatively influencing your boarders and undermining the trust between owner and boarders. This type of trainer is not beneficial to the owners, riders or the stable. As the barn owner, make sure you discuss what the trainers are allowed and NOT allowed to do and make sure your barn manager is in agreement with your rules. Carefully evaluate trainers for professional experience and suitability before authorizing use of your barn and monitor their activity periodically. It is important that the barn manager understands and agrees with what you expect from trainers.

- **Same vision for the future of the barn**-It is critically important to be in agreement with the vision for the barn as it grows and changes. Over time a boarding barn will change, especially during the first couple of years, and the barn owner and barn manager need to be in agreement when introducing changes that the barn owner plans. This could include types of disciplines, events and horse shows, breeding and the care of babies and much more.

- **Boundaries**-Having a good understanding of boundaries is vital for a barn owner and barn manager and they need mutual respect and trust when discussing important and private issues. Both parties need to have a clear understanding of what can be said or shared with boarders. Without proper boundaries the business will have many problems including turnover in clients.

When looking for a barn manager, treat the search process like any other business and do a thorough evaluation through resumes, reference checks and job interviews with the applicants. If possible, have them work with you at your barn for a week to see if they have the necessary skills and attitudes to make a good team leader.

The Barn Owner

The barn owner will be the one that carries the liability, risks and financial responsibility for the business. This is the most important difference between the two positions. If something goes wrong and a horse gets hurt due to poor judgment by the barn manager, it will be the responsibility of the barn owner. It is the way business works. That is why it is so important that you and your barn manager agree on the care and handling of horses at your stable as well as client relations. Many barn owners want to review all changes before the barn manager institutes any changes in order to manage risks and also to maintain consistency of care.

The barn owner is the one who pays all the bills including the barn manager's wage. The barn owner carries responsibility for everything that happens on the property and will incur the financial loss if a client leaves or there is an injury caused by negligence. The barn manager will still get paid the same regardless of occupancy rate. Many barn owners will have a job outside the barn and hire a full-time barn manager to run their facility to help ensure that everything is running smoothly.

The Bottom Line Is the Financials

Each barn owner will have different goals and desires for his barn but the one common thing every barn owner has are the financials. They do not want to lose money! The barn owner will always look at his business as an investment. That will include hay, shavings and daily chores. It will include employees, paying clients and their horses. It will include repairs and the monthly electric and gas bills and all utilities to keep things going. It is a business first and it is about more than just the horses. The business management needs to come first to assure profitability or there will be no horses.

I am a barn owner and my passion is horses, but I have learned to treat my boarding barn as a business first. Every time a horse pulls down a fence or kicks and breaks a corner feeder in their stall, someone needs to fix it and there is an associated cost. The barn manager won't feel the frustration and financial pressure that comes with this part of the business because they do not pay the bills and balance the books. They might empathize and care about the business but they won't feel the pressure or stress that can come with ownership.

When Finances Lead To A Different Direction

The barn owner and barn manager might have some different goals and ideas for a barn but the finances will ultimately dictate most decisions. The barn manager will not usually be allowed to make financial decisions unless owner and manager alike have a concrete understanding about how the boarding business needs to run to be sustainable and meet the owner's business objectives. The barn owner doesn't have the luxury of making poor decisions, so expenditures need to be based on sound financial decisions. Turning any financial responsibilities over to the barn manager requires a great deal of trust.

Barn Owners Are Often Misjudged

Before I became a barn owner I was guilty of driving past a beautiful boarding facility and assuming that the people that owned the business were very well off. At the time I didn't have an understanding of the costs that go into a boarding facility to keep it going, including a large business mortgage. I have had many people over the years count the number of horses we board at our barn and then ask what our boarding rates are. You can see that they are adding numbers up in their head and that is when they blurt out, "You guys must be making a ton of money!" If you board horses, then you probably have experienced this misconception and are smiling as you read this. Most people don't know how much it costs to feed a large number of horses and that is just the beginning of the costs. With more horses you will have higher costs for hay, bedding, labor, employees and wear and tear on everything. Your insurance will be higher along with workers' compensation for employees. The more horses you board, the more expenses you will have each month and if hay prices happen to go up due to a poor growing season, then that needs to be accounted for.

If you take the time to share some of the financials with your barn manager it will help them gain an understanding of your business and appreciate the decisions you make for your boarding business. Ultimately, it is the barn owner's responsibility to keep a close check on everything that transpires in the business and a routine monthly meeting with the barn manager is a sound way to do that.

The Barn Manager

The job duties of a barn manager can vary depending on the type and size of the boarding facility. I believe a barn manger that is very knowledgeable in their field will be a huge asset to any horse business and if you are in a financial position to hire a barn manager even part-time, then you should. They will help take some of the burden off of the barn owner especially since this type of career is a seven day a week/365 days a year job.

One of the problems that occur in a barn owner/barn manager relationship is that often the barn manager doesn't have a clear definition of what their job duties are and, even worse, they get mixed signals on what they can and cannot do. This can be very frustrating for the barn manager if his hands are tied in certain areas of barn management, so when there are problems in the barn, he can't manage them in an effective way. This can happen if the barn owner doesn't have a good understanding about barn management and the work that goes into creating a healthy and sound boarding business.

Most barn managers understand that many of their job duties will include helping and overseeing daily chores and the health and well-being of the horses. They will most likely have authorization to make decisions regarding nutrition for horses with special needs and changing specifics that are requested from the owner of the horse. They will oversee herd management and all that is included in that part of the job. Barn managers can be caught between a rock and a hard place trying to please the boarders and getting approval from the barn owner for changes and improvements. Most barn managers will not know how much authority they will have running the barn until they do it for a while and prove themselves as a knowledgeable equine professional.

I have compiled a list of some of the barn management duties that are common in many boarding barns. This list is not exhaustive and will depend on what the barn owner is looking for in a manager. For example, a barn that is structured for race horses and the high turnover of horses coming and going would have its own set of job requirements and you would not be doing some of your normal barn management services at this type of barn. Some of the barn management duties I have listed are optional depending on the type of boarding barn you would be working at. A smaller stable would have less responsibility and some jobs would not be necessary where a large facility would have a more expansive job description.

Barn Management Job Duties

- **They need to be skilled in horsemanship**-A barn manager needs to have good horsemanship skills and capable of handling any horse on the property. They need to be able to recognize and understand vices and dangerous behaviors and know how to handle them and the special issues a particular horse may have. They need to have experience in the safe and proper use of different equipment that might be needed on a horse for the safe handling such as walking, standing for farrier and veterinarian visits and any emergency that could arise.
- **They will oversee the health, living conditions and well-being of the horses boarded**-The barn manager should have good knowledge of horse care and understand how to maintain a healthy environment for the well-being of the horse. They should be able to pick out when a horse is stressed or not adjusting well and be able to problem solve in order to make the living conditions better for the horse.
- **Daily chores both in the morning and afternoon**-They should be very familiar with daily chores and know how to feed horses hay, grains and supplements in the proper amount. They should have experience in cleaning stalls and daily chores and be willing to work these types of jobs if their help is needed. It is important that a barn manager be able to look into the future and make sure the stable is prepared for holidays, weather and unforeseen

circumstances that could come up. This would mean making sure the stable is stocked with plenty of hay, grain and bedding for employees to feed and use in the stalls when the barn manager is off of work.

- **Wellness checks on all horses at the start of the day and at the end of the day**-They need to have knowledge and recognize the signs to look for if a horse is acting sick, lame or has an injury and know what procedures should be taken to address the issue.

- **Good communication and problem solving skills**-It is important for the barn manager to have good communication skills with the boarders. That means returning text messages and phone calls in a timely manner. It also means informing the clients of any changes at the stable or events that are going to take place. This skill is very important because without good communication skills many other problems will occur. Problem solving will be a part of the barn manager's job with horses and with people. The barn manager doesn't need to have an answer for every situation that comes up (that would be impossible), but they need to have some idea of what steps need to be taken or who to contact to resolve the situation. They also need to know when to tell the client that they will think about it and get back to them after they can have time to assess the situation. Problem solving and good communication is something that most of us learn on the job and often through trial and error. The important point is that a barn manager needs to be willing to learn how to keep the lines of communication open, to try to do things better the next time and learn from mistakes.

- **Scheduling employees**-Part of a barn manager's job might include scheduling employees if it is a larger facility. Keeping things organized and making sure employees show up to work could be part of the job, and hiring and firing might be part of the job as well.

- **Scheduling Trainers**-If the barn is larger with several trainers coming and going, then part of the job could include communication between the barn manager and the trainers and creating a schedule for the facility.

- **Scheduling Farriers and Veterinarians**-Many larger barns will have the barn manager schedule the standard farrier and veterinarian appointments and make sure the horses are ready for their appointment. Holding horses for appointments when the owner is not able to be there is often part of the job.

- **Medical care and basic medical treatments; leg wrapping, giving medications, walking horses etc.**-The barn manager should have basic knowledge of first-aid for horses. They should be able to take their temperature, pulse, capillary refill and be able to interpret some of the signs that would indicate a horse is sick. They should know how to wrap a horse's leg and how to administer basic first-aid for minor cuts and scrapes.

- **Giving tours to prospective clients**-The barn manger's role might include giving tours to prospective boarders and filling stalls that have been vacated.

- **Updating information for clients and horses**-Book keeping and paperwork could be part of the job description. Making sure clients emergency and contact information is up to date, as well as any important information such as immunization records, deworming protocols and compliance, etc. is often part of a barn manager's job, especially at a larger stable.

- **Handling emergency situations**-Emergency protocol for horse or human should be discussed with all employees and the barn manager should oversee how things need to be handled if a serious problem arises. There will always be the unexpected occurrence to manage and no person will know how to handle everything, but having a response plan is a good first step in trying to cover most situations.

- **Herd management and good equine behavioral management techniques**-The barn manager needs to have good herd management skills and understand horse behavior in a herd setting. The barn manager might be responsible for grouping horses into herds and placing new horses into herds.

- **Transporting horses**-In some larger barns the barn manager might be asked to transport horses to other facilities, horse shows or clinics as part of the job description.

- **Organizing events such as clinics, horse shows and workshops**-At a larger facility there might be many clinics, shows and workshops throughout the year and scheduling events might be part of the barn manager's job.

A good barn manager needs to have an even temperament, positive perspective, understanding of their strengths and weaknesses and their role as an equine professional. Their knowledge of horse care is vital but equally important is a strong work ethic, honesty and good people skills. If you are looking for a barn manager to run your operation, remember that they might not be experienced in all areas of the job but as long as they are honest, willing to learn and have a positive approach in handling the daily routine, you can cultivate them into an incredible barn manager. Every barn manager has to start somewhere and the ones that go far are the people who are willing to learn along the way.

Poor People Skills

What do you do if the barn owner or barn manager is great with horses but terrible with people? Sadly, this happens because some people do not have good communication or people skills and they are not willing to learn. Trying to run a boarding barn without good communication skills can hurt a business if you are not careful. This doesn't mean you need to be everyone's friend, but you need to keep the lines of communication open so that the boarders feel comfortable coming to you when they have questions, concerns or frustrations.

Many people will leave a boarding barn if the barn owner or manager has made the barn unwelcome or overly restrictive. If that is happening at your barn, then you need to reevaluate how you are doing things and how you communicate. Remember that every horse you lose becomes additional work for you to fill the stall and recoup the money you have lost. The other thing you need to think about is that people talk and if you want to keep a good reputation, then make sure you have a good balance in all areas of your business including interpersonal relations.

When You Are Both The Barn Owner And Barn Manager

I believe that most people who start a boarding business will fall into this category. I am definitely one of them and I love doing both parts of the business, but it does become very demanding at times. My husband and I knew we wanted to make boarding horses our full-time career and we work it as a team. It can be challenging when the work schedule is seven days a week and you also have family and a life to live. Finding a balance between work and personal time is key and it takes time to figure out priorities and have the discipline to maintain balance. I often tell people to give themselves two full years to get a good grasp on running their barn and everything else that comes with it.

You will become both the financial wizard and the stall cleaner much of the time. You will learn to pull money out of nowhere to fix the things that need to be fixed and at the same time host clinics and workshops for your boarders. You will work side by side with your employees and your relationships with your clients will grow and strengthen. You will bring different value to different people and you will learn and grow with each experience both good and bad.

Are You A Conservative Barn Manager?

This is not a political question-I am simply asking if you are a risk taker when it comes to the horses in your care? When people come for a tour at my barn, I will often tell them that I am very conservative in decisions made for the horses at our stable. I often hear horror stories about horses that were turned out on ice, broke a leg and needed to be put down or mud so deep it compromised the tendons on a horse. As a barn manager, you will be the one to make some important decisions about the well-being and safety of the horses at your barn. If you live in an area where temperatures are warm one day then plummet to below freezing with a mix of icy rain the next, your decision whether to put the horses out for the day will be difficult. Is the footing good and drainage of water sufficient to move the water off the paddocks before it freezes into a lake of ice? If you live in the Midwest, then you can probably relate to this picture as we deal with this every year to some degree, especially if the temperatures are warmer than normal. It can be frustrating when clients are becoming impatient because they can't get their horse outside due to inclement weather and you might even feel pressure to put the horses out when the footing is not safe. I encourage you to maintain your position and the clients will need to accept your decision as being in their horses' best interest. I want you to remember that the first time a horse pulls a tendon in deep, thick mud or breaks a leg on the ice, it will be considered your responsibility and you will forever regret the decision you made.

Are you conservative in what is allowed and not allowed at your facility? Do you allow riders to do things that are unsafe? Are you willing to intervene if you see unsafe practices at your barn? As a barn manager, you will be making decisions every day that have a direct impact on the horses in your care. Whether it is about the weather and turnout or a trainer that is doing something that is hurting a horse, it is up to you to take action and stand by your decision. It may not always be easy, but it is part of the job and it will reflect on the barn and on you as a barn manager. A good barn manager is willing to make tough decisions and stand by them even when the clients don't agree. Always remember that it is the care and well-being of the horses that matters the most.

Find A Support System

If you are going to operate a boarding barn, then I encourage you to find a support system outside the barn. Having a mentor outside the barn that will listen to you and help you through the tough situations and hard days is the best thing you can do for yourself. You are going to experience many issues that you never imagined and having someone who has been there and done that as support will be not only good for you, but also for your family. Your family is part of this business by association, whether they want to be or not, and they will be exposed to the emotional and financial roller coaster.

The position of barn owner/manager can have its downside, with long days that seem lonely even though you have many people in your barn. It can be hard because you don't want to unload your problems onto your clients and few will understand how you are feeling except another business owner. If you find yourself in conflict and becoming overwhelmed, you need to find someone you trust and they can help you work through it.

Many businesses have management consultants to help make sure the business is focused, healthy and financially sound. In the horse industry you usually don't hear of this type of practice and surely not in boarding barns. It is vital to have someone who can evaluate your business with a business perspective and expertise to help you identify the issues that persist, the opportunities for improvement and the financial concerns.

What most people need to realize is that you don't need to be a huge boarding barn to have problems. They can happen in very small stables just as often as large ones. The size difference has more to do with the financials. The larger the barn and stable the more risk that is involved, especially if you have a large building with many amenities and a large business mortgage attached. No matter the size of your stable, take the time to meet with someone periodically to get an outside analysis of what is happening in your barn and business.

To this day, I love being the barn owner and barn manager and through many trials and errors, it has become much easier over the years. Just remember that no one can do it all themselves and it truly does take a team (no matter the size) to make your boarding barn successful.

~33~

The Many Hats You Will Wear

I talk often about the many hats you will wear as a barn owner or manager, because I truly believe most new equine professionals are not prepared to handle the different roles that come with running a horse boarding business. When we opened our barn many years ago, I didn't give any thought to the different roles I would have in my business. Simply put, I mainly thought about managing the horses and their daily health care needs and I figured the clients wouldn't need me for much. I was going to learn so much about myself and people. I now have a completely different perspective on barn management and what the role of a manager entails. It involves much more than the horses.

As you develop as a barn manager, you will slowly be introduced to many different roles and each role has a "hat" to put on, as I like to call it. Your first priority will always be the health and well-being of the horses in your care. I have listed the many roles that a well-balanced barn manager will play at some time in their career. Some of the roles will require daily activity and others only periodic or random activity. You will find some of your roles very difficult to embrace at first, but the longer you do them the easier they will become.

The Caretaker Hat

Once you become a barn owner and manager you not only will grow in your knowledge of good and sound horse care, but you will start to learn what works and doesn't work at your place. The one thing you will find out quickly is that what looks good on paper doesn't always work in real life when it comes to horses. You will watch the horses closely in their stalls and out in the paddocks and pastures and you will change little things, especially during the first couple of years. You will wear the caretaker hat daily as you do your job and all that it entails for the well-being of the horses at your stable.

You will begin to learn each horse as if they were your own and you will know their personality, quirks and vices even better than many of their owners. You will learn their eating habits and notice right away if they didn't eat their hay or drink much water when they are normally a vigorous eater. You will be able to walk by their stall and if it looks unusually messy, you will think to yourself that maybe that particular horse didn't sleep well the night before and you will make a mental note of it or note it in a log book.

You will watch them in the paddocks and will quickly know if one of your playful horses is unusually quiet and even lying down more than normal. You will look for any signs of stress or lameness daily and if a horse isn't feeling good, you will be the first one to notice it.

You will be giving medications and taking care of cuts and wounds. You are going to learn every day and your education will not stop advancing. This will be the part of barn management that you absolutely love and the reason you got into the business to begin with. It also will be the easiest hat to wear and you will wear it all the time. The caretaker hat really never comes off.

The Teacher Hat

As a previous boarder myself, I never gave any thought to the roles of the barn manager and "teacher" was definitely not part of it. I was about to learn a lot about this part of barn management and the teacher hat.

As a barn manager, you will have many different kinds of horse owners at your barn. Some of them will be very knowledgeable, but many of them will be inexperienced horse owners that will need guidance at times, especially in the beginning. You will learn to offer advice when you see someone struggling with their horse in a certain situation and you will help educate when appropriate or when asked. You will guide and educate when it comes to feeding and nutrition and offer advice about grains and supplements. You will help owners if they have questions about tack and grooming. If you notice they are having a problem with some behavioral issues, you will step in to help them correct the behavior and help them gain confidence. You will educate on safety and help when you see an accident about to happen.

The teacher hat can be uncomfortable to wear if you have never worn it before, and it takes time to find a balance on when to put it on and when to leave it off. Not all your clients will want instruction or advice and you will need to stand back and sometimes not say a word and that is okay. The only time that your clients don't get a choice is when it becomes a safety issue and you need to step in quickly.

Having the heart of a teacher is wonderful and when you help someone who is learning something about their horse, you are educating them and giving them the confidence to move forward and grow in their horsemanship.

The Rule Enforcer Hat

Out of all the hats you will wear as the barn manager the "rule enforcer" will probably be the most difficult one. No one likes to be the one who enforces the rules, but as the barn manager it will be your responsibility. Safety is the number one reason you need to wear this hat. It is the barn manager's job to be watchful and aware of the activities at the barn that could develop into safety issues. To prevent accidents, you will need to intervene when you see something that is not allowed or presents a danger to boarders or others at the barn. You will also find yourself reminding clients to clean up after themselves and their horses at times. People may need to be reminded to turn off the lights and close the doors that are left open. You will remind people to put away their tack and arena toys from time to time. You might need to remind people not to add so much bedding to their stalls if they clean it themselves or feed so much hay.

When you have your barn rules established, you will find yourself reminding people about each of the rules at different times throughout the year. You will set the guidelines for what is allowed and not allowed at your barn and you will need to enforce them. It just comes with the territory of horse boarding. To this day, this hat can be challenging for me to put on, but it is part of running a strong and healthy boarding business. Once you start to grasp the idea that it is a business first, you will become more comfortable with enforcing the rules.

The Medical Hat

Even though you may not be a veterinarian, you will find yourself wearing the medical hat more often then you expected. This means you may be the first to recognize signs of illnesses or lameness and contact the horse's owner to help assure evaluation and treatment is managed in a timely and effective manner. Your experience and common sense will play an important part in helping your clients with possible illness and lameness issues.

As the barn manager, you will be asked to look at many cuts and abrasions and a boarder will want your opinion if a veterinarian needs to be called. In many cases, you will be able to offer simple wound and dressing first-aid in order to help save veterinarian costs. There will also be times where it is much better to tell the client that you are not sure how serious it is and advise them to get a second opinion or call the veterinarian. Your experience will be invaluable when determining when the veterinarian needs to be called.

You may be asked to watch a horse move and give your opinion on possible lameness issues. You will be the person commanding action and calming support when you are waiting for the veterinarian to arrive because something serious has happened and it has become an emergency situation.

Another part of your responsibility will be to provide guidance and support when a horse needs to be euthanized. As the barn manager, you might need to explain the process to your client and answer their questions. If you are running a large facility, then you may experience this part of the job more often then you thought you would.

The Student Hat

As a barn manager, you will be learning on the job about horses, people and yourself. You are going to be a student and a subject expert all within the same day, so you should never stop learning. You will never have all the answers, so if you humble yourself and ask for help from others that have more knowledge, then you will gain the knowledge and experience to be an effective barn manager, leader and business owner.

I believe you will learn more from your mistakes then you will ever learn from never having made a mistake-which we all know is impossible. If you are willing to learn each day then you are only going to become better at what you do. Growth as a barn manager and leader comes from being teachable and that will mainly come from the experience you will get on the job daily. Be ready to learn as a student when a teachable moment happens and watch your leadership skills and confidence dynamically expand.

The Weatherman Hat

The weatherman hat will be the hat you wear that sets the tone for your barn. You will be the one to create an atmosphere of harmony and positive attitudes. When you walk into your barn as the barn owner/ manager your boarders will notice what kind of mood you are in. If you are a moody person, then you will probably have your clients walking on eggs shells at times and that is not good for any business.

You have the power to create a relaxed, welcoming atmosphere or a place where people wished you stayed in the house until they went home. You will need to be aware of your moods and the influence you have on your clients. It might take a while for you to realize you are making people uncomfortable at times.

As the barn manager, you might be having a bad day, but as the professional you need to keep it together and not take it out on your clients. You can be honest with them if your day has been stressful, but don't leave them wondering if they did something wrong. I want you to remember that your boarders pay a lot of money to board at your place and part of the reason they are there is the atmosphere you have created. They come out to relax and enjoy their horse and they should not be subjected to your temper or bad mood. Be as professional as possible and apologize if your attitude disturbs the peace. Learn from those times because it is your responsibility to set the tone of the barn. Make it a positive and inviting place to be.

Behind every successful boarding business is a barn manager who is willing to educate, comfort, enforce and learn along with the boarders when appropriate. It does get easier the more you do it.

~34~

Yearly Health Care

Having a program for yearly health care checks for the horses at your barn is important. Boarding stables will do this differently depending on the regional practices and who they use for a veterinarian. Setting up a health care plan for your facility is easy and you can call your veterinarian to have them help you develop one that fits your boarding business.

The most common type of health care program for boarding stables occurs twice a year with spring and fall vaccinations. If you have a small stable, then taking care of spring and fall shots and everything else that needs to be done is relatively quick, but if you are a large facility it might be an all-day event. Deciding how to make this day run efficiently for the vets and boarders might be up to you as the barn owner and establishing a plan and schedule will be essential.

We have a large facility with almost forty horses, so I had to learn over the years how to make this day run efficiently for the veterinarians, boarders and myself. If you have a larger barn then there is a chance the clinic might send two vets and vet assistants. I have also had the opposite happen where we had two doctors working on the horses and then one was called out on an emergency and that day ended up taking much longer than originally scheduled. You and your boarders will need to adapt to schedule changes throughout the day because some visits will take longer or shorter than anticipated, resulting in the need to advise clients of changes.

Veterinarians-Giving Your Boarders A Choice

Some boarding stables do not give the boarders a choice on the equine vet clinic they use for spring and fall shots and other health care concerns. They have a "barn vet" that boarders are required to use. It is your choice as a barn owner whether to designate the selection of veterinarians or give your boarders the ability to choose the clinic and veterinarian they would like to use. If you have more than one vet clinic in your area, then allowing your clients to select the veterinarian of their choice is a smart decision. As long as the horses are getting the recommended shots and care that adheres to best practices of care, I believe the owners should have the choice of veterinarians to provide care.

Try not to micromanage your clients when it comes to veterinary care. You can cautiously and professionally share your opinions, but recognize that their choices and decisions need to be respected. It may be helpful in some situations, to make the client aware of the vets and specialists that are available to provide care both in and out of the area. Sometimes a second opinion from a different doctor and different clinic can help with decisions when developing a care plan for the horse. Don't miss the opportunity to learn something different from each veterinarian that comes to your barn!

Establishing A Yearly Health Care Plan

When a potential client comes to your barn for a tour, you will want to be very explicit about what you require for shots and health care if they choose to move their horse to your stable. There are many different opinions about spring and fall shots and yearly health care and you will find out that some people don't vaccinate. If you come across a person that doesn't do shots or the recommended health care protocol that you require, then you should ***not*** board their horse UNLESS they are willing to change. You can't compromise the health and wellbeing of the horses due to exposure of an unvaccinated horse that gets sick and spreads disease to the other horses. You bear the responsibility to maintain standards of care that protect the horses. If you don't strictly enforce your policy, not only will you have many angry boarders, but you will probably lose many of them and expose yourself to legal liability.

Horses may have exposure to disease by going to horse shows, trail rides and many other events outside your barn, so their protection through immunization needs to be diligently managed and documented to prevent a potential disease outbreak at your boarding facility. Horses will come and go with clinics and events at your barn, so you may need to extend your requirements of immunization records to any horse brought on site for such events. It is much different than having a couple of horses in your backyard with no contact with the outside world. Every time a horse travels and comes back to your barn they could have brought something with them. Be conscientious about this part of your business and you will preserve your reputation for quality horse care and enhance your relationship with veterinarians responsible for disease prevention and containment.

Deworming And Record Keeping

Having a deworming program at your boarding stable is essential. This is another part of horse health care where you are going to have many different opinions. As a barn owner you have the final decision on deworming for the horses in your care, not the boarders. However, collaboration with boarders and veterinarians is important to assure the best deworming protocols and compliance for each horse.

Deworming protocols have changed over the years, so it is advisable to contact veterinarians to determine the most effective protocol for your boarding barn.

It is now scientifically accepted that a horse that is confirmed to be a low shedder by a fecal check requires deworming only twice a year. However, it is up to each stable to determine the deworming protocols for your barn.

At our facility, I give our boarders two options. If they do a fecal count and their horse is a low shedder, then they only need to deworm twice a year in the fall and early spring. If owners choose not to do a fecal count, then they need to deworm their horse four times a year. It is a system that works.

You should provide a deworming log for your boarders and you to document when a horse was dewormed and the type of dewormer used. You should also document the horse's fecal count and shedder classification. It will be up to the barn owner to modify the deworming protocols as veterinary researches advances. Compliance is the most important component of any deworming protocol, so enforcement is critical.

Who Will Administer Dewormer At Your Barn?

When setting up your deworming protocol for your stable you will need to decide if you are going to select and administer deworming medication to all the horses in your care, or if you will require your boarders to manage this. You can give your clients a choice so that if someone is nervous about administering medication to their horse, you can do it for them. The most important thing is to make sure every horse is being dewormed according to protocols used.

Some barns deworm horses as part of the boarding fee and other places will charge an extra fee. If you choose to purchase and administer dewormer for the horses at your stable, make sure you know the per dose cost so that you charge appropriately and don't lose money. To control costs you can order bulk dewormers at a reduced price and when they are on sale the prices are even lower. It is very easy to lose money when deworming is included in the regular board rate and cost adjustments are not made when the prices go up. Consider an "a la cart" kind of system where you itemize the added cost of the dewormer and administration on the invoice, so boarders see what they are paying for and you never lose money as the business owner. This method does create more bookkeeping, but if you have a computerized accounting system for your business it is very easy to manage.

Deworming Issues

I wish I could tell you that everyone at your barn will deworm their horse when asked but they may not. It is up to you as the barn owner to make certain that all horses are dewormed. One method is to have all owners document deworming information into a log book and also provide the used medication container as evidence that dewormer was administered. Make sure the horses name is on the box and tube. Once you have verified the information, then you know they are in compliance.

Once in a while you will run into someone that doesn't want to deworm their horse and they will keep "forgetting." If you run into this situation, then you will need to deworm their horse for them and add it on to their invoice. Make sure you have this included in your boarding contract.

Make It Very Clear

You will want to explain your deworming protocol and get agreement from all new clients before they sign your boarding contract. I have had a few situations early in my career where new boarders refused to deworm their horses according to the recommendations of the veterinarians and the standards of our stable. This happened after the horses were moved to my barn, so I tried to resolve the dispute but was unsuccessful. In this situation the owners ultimately left the stable over this issue. You will come across many different opinions regarding health care for horses, so be as transparent and thorough as possible during discussions and tours so you avoid future misunderstandings.

~35~

Clinics

Clinics are a great way to showcase your boarding stable and your boarders will appreciate having clinicians at your facility for continuing education. It is a win/win for everyone. Clinics might bring in extra income but that is not always the case. Some clinics will be well-attended, while others struggle to get even a few auditors and you might find out they are not worth the work involved. Learning how to host a clinic takes some trial and error and you can reduce the work and risk by initially offering a small clinic for your boarders.

The first clinic we ever had at our barn was a little overwhelming. I was so excited when I agreed to host a two-day dressage clinic with an Olympic judge and the person who was promoting the event painted a rosy picture and promised to help with everything including the clean-up! Having never participated in managing a clinic, I didn't know how to organize for it nor what to charge for participation and auditing, so I didn't realize it could be a financially risky event. Riders from all over the state came to the clinic and needed to be stalled overnight. In retrospect, I believe I made two important mistakes; I didn't charge enough for overnight stalling and I charged too much for auditing which resulted in low attendance. The fees received didn't cover the cost of my time, services and wear and tear on my facility. When the clinic was completed, the participants left with their horses and didn't clean any of the stalls as they were supposed to. We had to clean every stall as well as the facility and property, and that consumed the remainder of our profits. I ended up losing money because I purchased extra insurance needed for the clinic along with spending on other unanticipated expenses. The clinic was not a total loss however, because I did learn a lot about what to do and what NOT to do when hosting clinics. That was an expensive lesson but a necessary one. That one lesson taught me how to plan a clinic, host it successfully and be profitable in the process.

Keep Your First Clinic Simple

Over the years I have had many different kinds of clinics and workshops and they have all been a learning experience from my perspective. Some are definitely more work than others, but they all bring something new and fresh to each barn that offers them. If you are thinking of putting on a clinic for the first time, I would recommend starting off small and keep it simple.

You can have a clinic with just your boarders so you can get a feel of how it will go. Remember that when you open clinics to the public and have horses hauled in, you may need to provide stalling and that entails extra time, paperwork, set-up and possible clean-up. There are many different types of clinics and even a simple workshop like nutrition or veterinary care is a great place to start.

I have compiled a list of clinics to give you an idea of what you might offer and encourage you to think outside the box from the normal riding clinics.

List Of Clinics

- Trailer Loading
- Nutrition Workshop
- Health Care Workshop
- First-Aid Clinic
- Saddle Fitting and Correct Tack
- Clipping
- Braiding
- Farrier and Learning About the Hoof
- Blanketing-Types Of Blankets and How To Blanket
- Trail Riding Clinic
- Jumping Clinic
- Driving Clinic
- Facing Your Fears Clinic
- Getting Your Horse In Shape
- Getting Your Horse Show Ready
- Breeding and Taking Care of a Foal
- Showmanship Clinic
- Western or English Riding Clinic
- Dressage Clinic
- Western Dressage Clinic
- Natural Horsemanship Clinic
- Teaching Your Horse Tricks Clinic
- Learning To Ride All Over Again-For Riders Over Fifty
- Reining Clinic
- Fun With Ground Poles Clinic
- Yoga and Your Horse

This is just a short list of the creative clinics you could offer and sometimes the most well-attended clinics are the ones that are new and different. I encourage you to think outside the traditional riding clinic and get ready to have some fun. Horse owners are always looking for new things to learn with their horse and even something like teaching your horse tricks is fun and can teach confidence to both the horse and participant.

What Do I Charge For A Clinic?

When setting up a clinic you want to make sure you are not losing money when the day is over. You won't get rich off of a clinic, but you definitely don't want to lose money. I have written down a few simple guidelines and things to consider when setting up a clinic.

The Clinic Check List:

- **Find out what the clinician's fee is**-Once you decide who you want to come and do a clinic, the first thing you need to do is find out what their total fee is for the day or days. Do they need a hotel? Are you providing meals? Do they get part of the auditing fee? Is there a sur-charge for extra travel and mileage? Are they bringing a horse and do you need to stable it?

- **How many riders/participants does the clinician require to do a clinic?** Does he have a minimum or maximum per day? This is an important part of the equation because once you know the number of participants you can start to decide what the cost will be for each one individually and what your break-even point is.

- **How much will extra insurance cost to host a clinic?** When hosting a clinic it is advisable to purchase extra insurance. The cost of event insurance will vary depending on the size of the clinic and number of days it runs. The location of your facility could also be a factor in determining cost. If you are planning to have many clinics throughout the year, have a discussion with your insurance company about an insurance add-on that will cover you throughout the year. Evaluate insurance needs ahead of time and determine the best coverage for the money and your situation.

- **What are you going to charge for a stall fee?** When booking stalls for a clinic, consider that it will be time consuming. There is work involved in getting the stalls ready and cleaning the stalls afterwards.

- **What do you charge the participants?** Once you know what your total fee will be for having the clinician, then you will add in all the other fees and start to figure out a price that will cover your costs to sponsor the clinic. A good method is to determine the total event cost for the clinic and then divide it by the number of riders/participants.

- **Are you going to offer food through-out the day?** Having food available for purchase at a clinic is a convenience for everyone, but it may not be a money maker. Having food and beverages takes work and you will probably be too busy to be taking care of all that. I have found it helpful to offer my lounge to the local 4-H clubs for a fundraiser and they always do a wonderful job. It helps them raise money and it is one less thing you need to think about.

- **Bathroom facilities**-If you don't have a bathroom at your barn you can still put on a clinic. Renting a portable toilet from a reputable company that provides sanitary services works well. Make sure you include this charge in your total cost.

- **Do you have a sound system?** If you are going to host a large clinic, then you will probably need a sound system so that the auditors can hear the clinician while they are talking to the riders. It can be very frustrating for the auditor who has paid money when they can't hear what the clinician is saying.

- **Does the clinician have the ground equipment or are they asking you to supply everything?** Some clinicians will bring their own equipment and others may expect you to supply them. For example—if you are having a jump clinic it would be much easier for the barn host to supply the jumps since they are difficult to transport, especially if the clinician is coming from a long distance. Some clinicians will need their own equipment because of the specific requirements of their program. This is something you will want to talk over with the clinician for certain types of clinics.

- **Charging the clinician a flat rate for use of your facility**-You can decide to charge a usage fee to the clinician for the use of your facility. I have known barn owners to charge a flat rate anytime a clinician comes to their facility for an event. You can modify how you want to implement this part of your business involving clinics as long as you are covered for the extra costs of insurance, time and labor to host the clinic. That will also include any other rentals or necessities that are needed to host the clinic.

Some clinics will be fabulous and some may not meet your expectations, but with each one you will figure out what works for your barn and the type of clientele you want to have. Clinics are a good way to provide new learning opportunities for everyone and support riding disciplines through exposure to new training methods.

~36~

Blanketing And How It Affects Your Job

Blanketing horses will depend largely on where you live and the type of weather you have. If you live in a climate where you have all four seasons, then there is a very good chance you will have boarders that blanket their horses in the cold months. Blanketing is not a big deal if you only have a small number of horses to contend with, but at a larger facility, blanketing the horses for the owners will be time consuming extra work. I didn't realize the amount of work blanketing would require until we built our barn and all of sudden we had twenty horses with blankets on. I wasn't expecting this workload nor was I prepared for this part of barn management including setting the fee schedule for blanketing when we first opened.

Do I Charge For Blanketing Or Not?

When you set up your boarding business including the board fees, you will need to decide if blanketing will be part of the board fee or not. I have seen barns do it both ways and they both work. The problem comes in if you are including it in your board rate and it is taking up much more of your time then you anticipated, and now other things are not getting done.

The one mistake that many barn owners make when including the blanketing as part of the board rate is the extra time it takes to blanket and change blankets for each horse. Whether you have employees doing the blanketing or you do the work yourself, you have labor costs for this service and they are coming directly out of your profits. If you are going to have this as part of the services included in the board, then I would suggest figuring out a price per blanket change and total that up for a monthly fee, and add that onto the board rate so you don't lose money. If you have a heated barn, then your blanketing time will increase significantly because you will be switching blankets as the horses go outside and again when they come in. Blanketing is very time consuming and you need to get a good grasp of costs otherwise you will lose money on each blanket change.

If you choose not to charge your boarders for blanketing, there is a very good chance you will come to regret that business decision. Blanketing will be easy at first, but it will start to wear you down after a month or so and the winter season becomes long. Blankets get muddy, straps break, fabric tears and you must make sure they stay safely on the horse day after day. Handling heavy, muddy and smelly blankets for many horses is not a joyful task. Remember that you are running a business and your time is valuable.

Blanketing As A Separate Fee

I have found that boarders appreciate optional blanketing services. If you have a blanketing service as a separate fee, your boarders will have a choice of whether they want to use the service or not. You need to remember that many of your boarders may not blanket and if you include it in the board rate, then they are paying for something that they are not using. For a few people that may be the difference on whether they come to your barn or not, especially if money is tight. You could be losing a great boarder because of the extra fee they have to pay for a service they don't use.

The Issues That Come With Blanketing

As the barn manager, you are going to see many different ways to blanket a horse and there are many possible issues that come with blanketing. You will have boarders that use multiple blankets and want them changed according to the air temperature. You will have boarders that will only put on a blanket when it is extremely cold. Some clients like to double up on their blankets, which is time consuming and usually comes with issues trying to get everything adjusted and fitting properly.

You will have some boarders that are very diligent in making sure their blankets fit the horse correctly and are the correct weight for the weather conditions. You will also have clients that have no idea what to use and in some cases a client may not care if the blanket is ill-fitting. The truth is that many of your clients will try to do things right but many of them won't be knowledgeable about blanketing and what to use for the breed and size of the horse, as well as weather conditions and temperatures. They may need your help as they learn about proper blanketing methods.

You will have blankets that are too small for the size of the horse and some that are way too large as well. You will have blankets on horses that are too warm for the air temperature or too light and the horse becomes cold as the temperatures drop. You will have blankets that have either broken or missing straps and the blanket is sliding to one side of the horse. You will see blankets that are torn so badly that the rain is soaking through the blanket and now the horse is wet underneath. You will have clients that do not understand the difference between a turnout sheet, show sheet and a water proof blanket. I have had clients completely pull their blanket when the temperatures become unseasonably warm, then the temperatures dip way down and the horse is found shivering. There will be clients that do not understand (and sometimes don't care) when the horse is becoming overheated because the weather has become too warm for the type of blanket that is on the horse. I have given you some real life examples and I want you to know that these scenarios will not be the norm for most of your clients. But all it takes is one person to make your job more stressful when it comes to blanketing and all that goes with it.

A Surcharge For Special Situations

Blanketing for an extra fee gives boarders a choice to use stable services or not, but some situations require action without owners approval for the charge. When there is a situation where a blanket is pulled because the horse is sweating underneath, then a fee is charged for pulling the blanket. If I need to pull a blanket because the straps are broken or missing and the blanket is starting to fall off, there is a surcharge. If the blanket it not water-proof and the horse becomes wet and I need to pull it, then I might add a surcharge depending on the situation. Sometimes a blanket will say "waterproof" but they were clearly not and the horse is soaked. In all these scenarios the client is not given an option as the action is in the horse's best interest. I encourage you to make this very clear to new clients when they come to your barn.

Educating Your Boarders On Blanketing

Everything your clients do will in some way affect your job and the tasks and time required. I have found it beneficial to educate new horse owners on blanketing and the use of different kinds of blankets, so that they purchase blankets that are constructed well and very functional for the type of horse and weather they have. It might take time in the beginning, but it will save time in the long run. Keep it simple and even printing out information on blankets so they can take it home to read is helpful. There is so much information about blanketing available, so giving them the name of a good website or blanket dealer will help them find the best blankets for their horse.

Your blanketing knowledge and experience will be invaluable to your boarders. Sharing information about blankets and suggesting which manufacturers make quality blankets and which ones are not worth buying, will save clients time and money. You are going to start to think you should have gone into the blanket business.

Once you deal with a shivering horse, a wet horse or a horse that is sweating under their blanket, you will start to become assertive as a barn manager about proper blanketing for breed and conditions. Having to call your client about improper blanketing or a shivering horse will be a necessary part of your job. When boarding horses, it is your job to make sure the horses in your care are safe and comfortable.

When Horses Destroy Each Other's Blanket

When a horse destroys another horse's blanket, who is to blame? I get asked this question often from other barn owners who are dealing with irate boarders over torn blankets. Blankets and horses are quite the combination. We go out and purchase these beautiful looking blankets in many colors and designs and within a day or two they are muddy, stained and some are even torn and duct tape has been added as part of the design. It happens when you have horses and it can be upsetting when the boarder needs to purchase a new blanket.

Horses have been known to pull on each other's blankets until one of them comes off! Then it begins-The game of Tug-O-War!

After years of dealing with herd dynamics, I have found that when you put even two horses together, you could have blanket issues, especially with young geldings who love to play. They somehow think the blanket is a new toy and the goal is to get the blanket off and then play with it even more. When you are setting up your herds and boarding program, you are going to want to have a good grasp on this issue, especially when a client comes to you and wants to move their horse, or worse, wants someone to pay for their torn blanket. It is a very real part of barn management and it happens occasionally.

I have learned over the years to make it VERY clear that when a blanket is torn in the paddock, no one is responsible to replace or repair the blanket due to horses being horses. It is part of herd dynamics. If they want their horse moved so that the blanket doesn't become more torn, you need to think about how you want to handle this. You can easily say yes, but now you are disrupting two herds and there is no guarantee that the same thing won't happen. Some horses never have a torn blanket and stay out of trouble, while others create the issue. You need to think about the horses involved and their personalities. I had a horse that wore a neck cover and he would play over the electric fence with another gelding and his neck cover kept coming off and was used as a toy in the next paddock. It may sound crazy but it happens!

Most of the time when a client is dealing with a torn blanket they will purchase a higher quality and higher denier blanket the next time, and then most of the issues disappear. There are some very well-made blankets that can handle even the mouthiest of horses and hold up pretty well. Your clients need to understand that you get what you pay for and they might need to spend more to get a better quality blanket.

Torn Blankets And Drama

As the barn manager, you are going to need to decide how you want to handle the boarder that wants to put the blame on another horse when a blanket is damaged. Believe it or not this one issue can cause drama and problems between boarders and you will need to be the one to defuse it. You will learn to be very direct about the situation and there will be clients that do not like your approach, but you have to put things in perspective.

If you start moving horses every time a blanket gets torn, then you will be doing it constantly and your work has increased but the problem is not resolved because most horses play. You also need to make it clear that the blaming needs to stop. Something as simple as blaming another horse for a torn blanket can quickly escalate and then there are hurt feelings between boarders. It is bad for the atmosphere in any barn.

If a client has willingly agreed to have his horse turned out with other horses, then they need to understand that these are some of the chances you take when dealing with groups of horses. Your client may not like it at the time, but they will either accept it or pay for private turnout.

The Horse That Destroys His Own Blanket!

Once in a while you will find a horse that pulls continually on his own blanket and straps like it is a toy. They will pull and pull until the front chest straps eventually break. Once a horse starts doing this behavior it can be very hard to stop it. You can suggest to the owner to buy some spray made for blankets to deter them from pulling with their teeth on the blanket, but it doesn't always work. In some cases, it is better not to blanket and you might need to suggest that. You will never have two situations that are the same and this part of barn management will truly keep you on your toes.

Storing Blankets

Have you thought about where you are going to put all the blankets that will be at your barn? They will take up a lot of room and can make your job more difficult working around them if you have no place to hang them. I suggest having a blanket bar on each stall for hanging one blanket and having a designated area for hanging extra blankets. Creating a designated area for blankets is great because as the blankets become dirty it gets them out of the way of the barn aisle. As a rule, we do not allow our clients to put dirty blankets in the tack rooms. If your boarders start putting dirty blankets in your tack rooms, you will not only have a very stinky tack room, but the hair and mud will soon be everywhere. Your tack room will become extremely dirty and congested.

I am very clear about blanket storage and even specify when they should be taken home after a long winter. Once the cold weather is gone and I know for sure the horses will not be wearing mid-weight and heavy-weight blankets, I will inform clients of a deadline for removal of all the fall and winter blankets. I have found that if I don't give a deadline, then the blankets will hang in the designated area all summer. It is so much easier to be direct and you will have fewer issues over all.

~37~

The Multi-Discipline Barn

If you are thinking about boarding horses as a business, then it would be safe to say that you have some knowledge of the many different riding disciplines even if you are not an expert on each of them. They each will bring something special to your barn, but each one will also change the dynamics of your stable in some ways.

Deciding what kind of riding disciplines you want to have at your barn is something you need to think about. When we were building our barn and looking for boarders I didn't give this any thought. I had been a boarder myself and the different stables I boarded at had many riding disciplines, so I never thought much about it. In fact, I embraced the idea of having a multi-discipline boarding barn and was looking forward to all the different breeds and different styles of riders that would come. I had always looked at boarding through the eyes of a boarder, but now I was the barn owner and I was going to see things in a whole new way and some of it was challenging.

I would like to get you thinking about some of the possible issues that will come with a multi-discipline barn. You can have a multi-discipline barn and have harmony, but it might take some work in the beginning to get everyone on the same page. You need to remember that different disciplines mean different usages of the arena and sometimes they can clash if there isn't good communication.

Let's Talk Different Riding Disciplines

Unless you have a huge facility, there is a good chance you will only have one indoor arena and one outside arena. That means if the weather is bad, most everyone will be using the indoor arena and that can cause some issues. I want to first talk about the different disciplines and how they each use the arena.

- **Hunter/Jumpers**-People that love to jump their horses use many jump standards. If your arena is large, then setting up jumps is not an issue because there is plenty of space for other riders. If your riding arena is small then you could have some issues with others trying to ride at the same time.

- **Dressage Riders**–Dressage riders will often practice dressage patterns and this can prove challenging for them if they are trying to work around equipment that is set up. They will use the entire arena and that will include lateral work.
- **Saddle Seat Riders**–Saddle seat riders are incredible to watch. They love high stepping horses that really move out. This can be intimidating to other riders if they are not familiar with this type of riding discipline.
- **Trail Riders and setting up a trail course**-Many trail riders and even other disciplines love to work on trail course obstacles. It is fun for all, but can be challenging vying for space if the obstacles are taking up a large part of the arena.
- **Cart Driving**–Cart driving is fun to watch, but I have had clients who would not go into the arena when a person was driving their horse. Carts can make some horses nervous and how the owner handles it could become something you need to deal with.
- **Playing with horses**-You will have some people that love to play with their horses on the ground using large balls and other equipment like tarps. This is something that might make another boarder nervous and you will need to think about how you want to deal with this if you get a complaint.
- **Western and English riders and pattern work**–If you have riders that show hunt seat or western, then you often see them working on patterns in the arena.
- **Barrel Racers and speed events practice**–This riding discipline needs very little explanation. They love to go fast and they use three barrels and most of the space in the arena. If they are running a course, it is very hard to ride around them and it could be dangerous.
- **Reining horses**–Watching a good reining horse is incredible and this type of discipline does work on patterns and at times speed is a part of it. Reining horses might require special footing materials and increased depths of footing for the arena sand.

I have listed a few (but not all) of the different disciplines you will find at a boarding barn and they are all wonderful. This list is to get you to start thinking about how your arena will be used and some of the possible issues that will come with it. Each one of these riding disciplines will use the arena in a different way and if your arena is very large, you still will have complaints now and then. Some issues can arise because some of your boarders will not understand what they are seeing and it may seem unsafe to them. Then you could have a few clients who will feel like there is not enough room with all the equipment that is set up in the arena and they feel squeezed out.

You will have nervous boarders who want a very calm and quiet riding arena and to them saddle seat riders may seem loud and out of control. You will have boarders that will not ride if someone is driving a cart and they will leave if they see the cart is pulled out to hook-up. You might even have a boarder that will become annoyed because they see someone playing with a tarp and doing ground work and they don't feel safe riding their horse while the tarp is on the ground. You might say to yourself, "well they need to get over it," and yes, that is true, but as the barn manager you can help the situation by talking to them about their concern. You won't be able to please everyone all of the time, but the more you keep the communications open the better it will be.

We have gone through many transitions throughout the years with our riding arenas and some things work and others don't. You will come to find out that maybe some riding disciplines won't work at your barn due to limited arena space. You will find that some clients won't be happy unless they are the only one in the arena. You won't be able to change them and there is a good chance they will leave if your barn is often a busy place.

Designated Riding Times

Sometimes it is easier to set up designated times for riders if you have a few that want to use a complete jump course. We have done that a few times over the years and it has worked well. Giving your clients plenty of time to know when the arena will be used for certain activities is great communication, and then they won't waste a trip out to the barn to find out they can't use the arena until later that day.

When A Riding Discipline Doesn't Work

I am going to be honest and tell you that unless you have a huge arena or a couple of riding arenas, there is a good chance that some riding disciplines won't work at your barn. It is okay to be honest with a potential client and tell them that your barn is geared more towards trail riders or is a hunter/jumper barn. Better to be honest at first then to deal with upset clients later because the arena is always tied up. Your barn won't be perfect for everyone, so don't try to be everything to everyone. Find out what riding disciplines work best for your barn and then you will find the right clientele.

Communication And Respect Is Vital!

If there is no communication and respect when using the arena, then you are in for trouble. The barn atmosphere will deteriorate quickly if there is no respect for each other's riding disciplines and different styles of doing things. If you have never experienced this at a barn then you are one of the lucky ones. As the barn owner you will be the one to set the tone for the atmosphere in your barn and that will include how boarders treat each other, along with respect for each other's riding discipline. The plain truth is that some people believe that their chosen riding discipline is the best and the others have inferior horsemanship skills. If that attitude comes into your barn, it could be opening the door to drama. It is important to make sure that negative or critical attitudes are not tolerated in your barn. Conceding to drama will only hurt your boarding business and your reputation as well.

It is bad for a barn's atmosphere when there is conspicuous lack of respect between two people who are using the arena at the same time. I have had a few situations throughout the years where someone has made another rider feel bad and then that person will not ride when the other person is riding. Sometimes they will not even come to the barn. If you have paying clients then they should NEVER feel uncomfortable coming to your barn. You may have to do some detective work to find out what is going on, but once you do, you need to correct it quickly. Be prepared because the high standards you create and expect from your client's may not be acceptable to a person who thinks their discipline is better than everyone else's. In some cases they may leave and you need to accept that. When you stand up for what is right, then eventually the word will get out and your stalls will stay full. Respect is huge and the lack of it can really hurt your barn and business if you are not careful.

During the first couple years running your business you will encounter many unexpected behaviors and part of it will have to do with the different disciplines and the dynamics between them at your barn. Embrace the challenge. If something isn't working, then try something different to help create a multi-discipline barn with harmony. A fun, peaceful environment can be sustained but it needs to be reinforced by strong leadership.

~38~

Has Your Tack Room Become Too Small?

It is amazing how much stuff one horse and owner can have. If you own a horse, then you know exactly what I mean. It is so easy to start collecting everything from tack to brushes and treats for our horses and we love every minute of it. If you are boarding horses and have many clients, you will need to limit the space that each boarder can occupy in the tack room. Tack rooms can never be big enough because boarders will never stop buying stuff for their horse and themselves!

I have walked into some gorgeous barns and the one thing I notice in some of them is how over-crowded the tack rooms are. In fact, some of them are so stuffed that you can barely get through to the other end. If you don't give your boarders a designated amount of space, their stuff will be spilling into another boarder's area and then new issues will arise.

When we first opened I was not prepared for the amount of stuff my new clients would bring. They brought huge tack trunks and one person even had a large armoire which, thankfully, didn't fit in our tack room. I didn't know how to enforce space limits or voice my concerns, so our large tack rooms became overcrowded quickly.

Giving Your Boarders A Designated Space

When you design your tack room I would recommend giving each boarder the same amount of space. You will need to specify what you will allow and not allow as far as tack trunks and more. If you don't keep it equal for all your boarders, then that will breed the start of other problems in your barn. I have talked with barn owners that are having drama problems in their barn and part of the issues are about the space in the tack room and how unfairly the space is divided. If they all pay a base rate and that includes tack room space, then the space needs to be equal. Your boarders want to be treated fairly without exception.

You will have many different personalities at your barn and some may be overbearing. They might even intimidate others at your barn and that can include use of the tack room area. Some people will move in like they own the place and if they spread to another person's space you might not hear about it if the other person is timid. It is up to you as the barn manager to monitor this. Not everyone will voice their complaints, but they could give their notice because they feel they have been pushed out. It may seem like they are overreacting, but to them leaving was the best option. It is bad for your business if the tack rooms are disorderly, dirty and cramped because of excess client storage and lack of respect for each other's space.

The Small Stable And Tack Room

If you are only planning to board a few horses, then many of these issues won't come up on such a significant level because you will be dealing with only a few people. I still recommend that if you are taking payment for board, even if it is for only two horses, to keep space allocation equal. If one person has three saddle racks, then make sure the other person can have three saddle racks if they choose. I am a believer that the size of your boarding stable doesn't matter and the issues can be the same for large and small alike.

Keeping The Tack Room Clean

I have compiled a list of tips for keeping your tack room clean and orderly. Your tack room will become a disaster zone fast if you don't have some kind of rules for keeping everything in its place. Without rules, one day you will walk in and find disarray, dirt, and potentially something smelling terrible and you might be surprised at what you find!

Keeping the tack room clean and in order:

- **Give everyone an equal area for saddles and bridles**. Figure out how many saddle racks and bridle hooks each boarder will have, then figure out the space allotted for each.

- **Give each space (including saddle racks and bridles hooks) a designated number that corresponds with the stalls for identification.** We have twenty-seven stalls in our large barn and each stall has a stall number and that corresponds to the saddle racks and bridle hooks. There is no confusing boarders' space when boarders' numbers are displayed. It is easy and very clear. Mark each saddle rack with the number along with the bridle hooks. If you don't mark the saddle racks and hooks, I can guarantee one day you will walk in and someone will be using the unmarked spaces. It happens all the time. YOU HAVE TO BE VERY CLEAR.

- **Make it very clear how much space is allowed for tack trunks.** When you are showing your new boarder the tack room and their space, you need to be clear on what you allow and don't allow and that will include the size of their tack trunk. If you don't, then you might be surprised at what they bring in. I have had to tell someone they couldn't use the storage unit they just bought, because it was too big and would crowd into another person's space. This was after they had spent an hour putting it together. That was a tough one and I learned from that experience.

- **Keep all fly sprays, shampoos and liquids in a bucket or container so that they don't tip over and spill.** There have been quite a few times when I have walked into a tack room and find myself cleaning up spilled shampoo or fly spray. The cap was not put on tight and somehow it was knocked over and not noticed. I now make sure all liquids are in some kind of container, so if they are leaking they will leak into the bucket and not the tack room floor. This may not seem like a big deal to you at first, but once you are cleaning the floor and the mess a few times you will start to understand what I mean.

- **No dirty horse blankets in tack room.** If you want to keep your tack rooms clean, then don't allow dirty blankets to be put back in the tack room once they have been on a horse. That is the fastest way to a very stinky and dirty tack room. The hair and mud will drift and eventually be all over.

- **No wet saddle pads in tack room.** I recommend having your boarders put their wet saddle pads on their blanket bar to dry. Once it is dry, then it can go back in the tack room. This will help keep the tack room from smelling bad.

- **Treats need to be in air-tight containers.** Mice are almost always present in a barn so don't invite them into the tack rooms. There is nothing worse than walking into a tack room and seeing mice poop everywhere. It is even more upsetting when the mice start making nests out of the stuffing from saddle pads and even saddles! Prevent it from happening so you avoid very upset boarders. Make it a rule to have all treats put into air-tight containers even if they haven't been opened. Mice will chew through brand new bags of unopened treats to get to the food and there is no stopping them once they realize there is food in the tack room.

- **No fresh food of any kind allowed in tack rooms.** At our barn I don't allow any apples, carrots or other perishable foods in the tack rooms at all. The simple reason is they will start to rot and smell and usually the boarder will forget they even have them in there.

- **Have a trash can in the tack room.** Make it easy for your boarders to keep things clean. Having a garbage can in your tack room will be appreciated and you will find less trash lying around.

- **Tack room rules are needed.** Having a list of rules for the tack room is important. It makes things clear and there is no confusion on what is allowed and not allowed. You may feel uncomfortable creating rules for your tack room at first, but you will quickly realize that they are needed and you will get over your fear and move forward.

Once you have established what you expect for the tack room you will soon find out that your boarders will also love having a clean tack room. Get them on board with how you want things done and you will have fewer issues. Having a clean and orderly tack room is a benefit for any boarding business and it shows your current boarders and future clients that you take pride in your barn and run your business professionally.

~39~

When A Horse Breaks Something-Who Pays?

This is a part of horse barn management that many barn owners struggle with. For some reason it is extremely hard for barn owners to ask for payment for something that a boarder's horse has broken or damaged to the point that it needs replacing. Your boarding barn is a business and being compensated for damaged property is a fair and standard practice. Don't be afraid to make clients aware of damage incurred by their horse and the cost for repairs.

After we opened our boarding barn, I really started to see how destructive horses can be. You would think that it wouldn't be a surprise at all since I had owned and boarded horses much of my life and even worked at a couple of barns, but it was and the reason is very simple. As a boarder, I never really noticed all the things the horses at the barn were breaking on a daily basis because, after all, it didn't have anything to do with me or my horse and I didn't have to fix them. It was always taken care of by the barn owner or someone who had been hired to fix everything. It was basically "out of sight out of mind" which rings true for most people.

Who Pays When A Horse Breaks Something?

When running a boarding business, you need to have it in your boarding contract that your clients are responsible for paying repair fees, including labor, if their horse breaks something. Once you open your business you are going to find yourself fixing many things from broken boards in the stalls to broken fences outside. You will have horses that will chew on everything to the point that it will not be usable anymore. You will have broken corner feeders, water tanks and even a stall door or two that need repairs due to horses kicking. Horses will get into anything they can and it will cost you financially.

There are going to be times when you don't know exactly which horse caused the damage and those are the times when you will have to eat the cost to fix what is broken.

For the rest of the times that you do know, it is the boarder's responsibility to pay for the damages done.

It is never easy to talk with a boarder and tell them that their horse has broken a corner feeder or something else and they are responsible for replacing it, but it is business. You can't be replacing everything for free or you will lose a lot of money and most business owners don't have the extra money just to give away. You need make sure the owner of the horse knows that it is not personal, but it is simply part of how you run your business.

Horses will be very hard on everything and you want to make sure you are not paying for everything that needs to be replaced because a horse has destroyed it. Have this written in your boarding contract so you are protected. Even water buckets are expensive to replace.

You should have a section about labor, repairs and replacement for damages done written into your boarding contract and make sure it is very concise. I also encourage you to have your lawyer read it over so that you have it written correctly for the state you are doing business in. When a new client comes to your barn to board and they are reading the boarding contract, make sure they understand this part of it so there are no surprises when their horse kicks a huge hole in the water tank and they have to buy a new one. I am going to be totally honest and tell you that replacing a five dollar salt block holder is no big deal, but replacing a ninety dollar water tank is painful. This is when barn management and owning a business becomes very real. With horses, expect the unexpected and be prepared for unexpected costs, but hold boarders accountable for damage caused by their horse. Boarders will respect good business practices and professionalism even if they don't like paying for repairs.

How To Receive Payment For Damages

When setting up this policy you will have a couple options for how you want to be reimbursed for damages done. Some stables will have new clients pay a deposit when they first arrive that is put into an account, and when a boarder gives their notice and is going to leave, then the barn owner will look back at all the damages done by the horse and decide if the boarder will get their deposit back or lose it to repairs. I have never been a huge fan of running our business this way, because you will have boarders that might be at your farm for years and it is very hard to keep track of something that happened years before and the client might not remember either. In some situations, it could end up causing more issues if there is a disagreement on what the horse actually did and when. You would need to be extremely diligent in your paperwork to pull up something from prior years and most people are not disciplined to manage the details over time.

I believe it is a much better business decision to bill the client for labor, repairs and replacement for damage immediately on the next month's board invoice. It is best to talk with the client when the damage happens and discuss repair options and let them know exactly what the plan is to complete repairs and the cost estimates. Let them know as much as you can about cost and that it will be on the invoice, and then there are no surprises for them. Your client might not be happy about the extra charges, but they won't be upset at you and will understand that it needs to be done. The more you communicate the better.

Be Professional And Sensitive

I truly believe most of your boarders will understand if their horse breaks something and that they need to pay for it. The best thing you can do as the barn owner is to remember that how you talk with your client about sensitive issues will make a huge difference on how they respond. They are already going to feel terrible enough and some of them will even worry that you don't like their horse because of this. Be professional, sensitive and always nice and you will be pleasantly surprised at the positive results you will have.

~40~

Giving A Thirty-Day Notice To A Client

Giving a thirty-day notice to a client is extremely emotional and from the moment you start to feel that a boarder needs to leave until you give the notice, will be very difficult. This is a hard but necessary part of business ownership. You are likely to be afraid of the unknown because you have no control over how the boarder is going to respond. When a business relationship has deteriorated, and issues are unresolvable, the client may need to leave. This situation can be upsetting and you may find yourself wondering what went wrong. It will be an emotional roller coaster until they finally move their horse and the barn gets back to normalcy.

The Wrong Way To Give A Thirty-Day Notice

I am going to be honest and tell you that I have blown it when it comes to the proper way to give a thirty-day notice. The first time I had to tell a client that they would need to leave was unbelievably stressful and looking back I did it in a very unprofessional manner. I typed up a letter and put it on the client's stall on a Friday afternoon and then my husband and I left for the entire weekend and didn't come back until Sunday night. What happened while we were gone left my barn and the boarders in a state of emotional distress. It became a barn issue instead of a barn owner/client issue. I was gone and couldn't defend myself or try to fix what had happened over a short two-day period.

Looking back, I was totally wrong in the way I managed giving a thirty-day notice. I was trying to avoid confrontation with this client and I was running away from my responsibilities as a barn owner and manager. My mistake caused additional problems and when I came back, I had to clean up the mess and decided that I would not make that same mistake again.

The Right Way To Give A Thirty-Day Notice

The right way to give a thirty-day notice is to provide a written notification in person. Is it going to be difficult? Of course it is! Asking someone to leave and discussing the problems will never be easy, but it does become less stressful the longer you run your business. Take the time to answer the questions that the boarder might have and be direct and very honest. This is your one shot to be honest about what is going on at your barn and you won't get a second chance to do this right.

Giving A Thirty-Day Notice By Email

People will ask me if it is okay to give a thirty-day notice by email. I have given a thirty-day notice by email and it has not gone well in the past. First of all, you have no assurance that they received the email. They might not check their email for a few days and if you see them at the barn you will have no way of knowing if they read it. It will become extremely uncomfortable for you and timing is important. It can be easy to misinterpret an email message when there is no personal contact and opportunity for discussion. In person is always best to keep things very clear.

Keep It Professional At All Times

One of the hardest parts of delivering a thirty-day notice is keeping calm when the boarder becomes angry with you. Maintain composure and don't let your emotions get the best of you. Just get through it and move on.

The reasons that you need to give a termination notice to a client will vary from one end of the spectrum to the other and that will regulate your emotions and how you handle everything. If you have a client that is rude and challenging then you already know that your upcoming conversation will be much more strained. If you are giving a thirty-day notice to someone who is unbelievably nice but hasn't paid the board in months, then it will still be hard but you won't be going into the conversation on the defensive.

You will learn how to talk to many different types of people and with each experience you will gain some wisdom. You will make mistakes and that is okay. Learn from them and if a next time comes, then you will know what to do differently. The best thing you can do for your business is to treat your clients with respect even when it might be very hard to do. The end results of how you handle the situation will determine how others will look at you as a professional and it will set the tone for your barn and business.

Giving a thirty-day notice will never be easy because you are asking someone you valued as a client to leave and losing their business can feel like a personal failure at times. You will learn to keep your emotions in check at least until you get back into the house. You are not alone and through all of this you will gain an amazing new confidence in what you do and how you run your barn.

~41~

Adjustment Time And Conflict Management

Many of the issues a barn manager has with their boarders come from the history a client has from previous boarding barns. Each barn does things differently and it takes a new boarder time to adjust. This is an important part of barn management that gets overlooked, but it is very crucial to a well-run barn.

I believe that if you take the adjustment slow and help your new client understand how your barn operates, the misunderstandings and stress will be greatly reduced. If you think about it for a minute, everything from the way you feed your hay to the way you clean your stalls will be a little different from the previous place for most boarders that come to your barn. For some, these differences will be easy and not difficult to adapt to but for others, the differences will be hard. Horses need time to adjust to a new surrounding and so do your new clients and if you don't allow for an adjustment time, then conflicts can arise.

What Your Boarders Will Watch For

Your new boarders will watch how you handle their horse and other people's horses. They will want to see if you lose your temper easily or neglect to follow through on things you say you were going to do. They will take note of how much hay you put in the stall or how much you feed outside. They will watch to see if you are consistent in feeding times and if grain and supplements are being fed like you said they would be. They will notice each time they come out if their horse has water in his bucket and if the water is clean. They will watch how you deal with herd management and where you place their horse. They will watch to see how you deal with horses that don't get along and if you are open to making changes in certain situations. They will watch how you make decisions depending on the weather and their horse. They will watch for a long time to see if you keep your commitments. Are the arenas dragged? Are the stalls cleaned daily? Is the hay a good quality? Do you fix things when they become broken? The list can go on and on and there will be times that you will feel like you are under a microscope.

Your boarders are not trying to be difficult. Most of the issues that come up are fear related because they have had bad boarding experiences and now they don't trust anyone with the care of their horse. It is very common in the boarding industry and it is up to you as the barn manager to earn their trust and show them that the care and wellbeing of the horse is first in all situations.

Don't Take Offense

I believe one of the reasons the barn owner/client relationship falls apart early in the relationship is because the barn owner doesn't know how to read the signs of fear. Boarders that seem overbearing and controlling might simply be nervous and unsure. People want a safe place to keep their horse, where they are going to be fed enough food, fresh water to drink and shelter. The simplest of basic needs for a horse seems to become such an issue at many barns and it should never be.

A boarder might not come right out and tell you that the previous place was terrible and the care was bad. They might not tell you that their horse didn't get fed enough or that the conditions of the facility were not healthy for their horse. They might not tell you that their horse developed nervous behaviors because of the way they were handled. Some people are very quiet and don't want to talk badly about anyone, but their concerns will be evident through their assertiveness or opinionated statements. They may use assertiveness in an attempt to convey their convictions about the care of their horse. They want to make sure mistreatment never happens again. It is your job to dig a little deeper and find out what their fears are and then you can start to ease those fears with action.

Some of my most challenging boarders were only that way because they were driven by fear. They watched how we handled the horses and did the chores and talked to me daily about how I did things and why I did them the way I do. It would be very easy as a barn manager to be either intimidated by their overly strong personality and questions or annoyed. But if you take a step back and look at the big picture, they are just looking for reassurance. You need to put yourself in their shoes for a minute. Answer their questions and be patient. Give them time to trust again and you will see a person change into a devoted boarder who will be one of your best clients for a very long time.

Sometimes You Just Need To Say Good-Bye

Most of your boarders are going to be wonderful but you may encounter a client that you just can't please under any circumstance. Even after six months at your barn they still seem to question everything you do and are creating more issues for you. Sometimes a barn is just not a good fit for someone and that is okay. There are people who have their own idea of how things should be done and will easily share that with you on a daily basis. There might come a time when you need to have a heart to heart talk with a client like this and find out if it is time for them to find a more suitable stable. Usually a boarder like this will move from barn to barn without satisfaction. I often think people like this would be better off having their horses on their own property. Try to identify this type of boarder by asking questions about their previous boarding experiences. You will learn to tell the difference between prospective clients and someone that seems unsatisfied wherever they go.

If you take the time to let your boarders adjust to their new barn home and are willing to share how you do things, you will be paving the way for a healthy, long-term relationship built on trust. Have the heart of a teacher and you will see wonderful changes in your boarders with time. Don't be too quick to judge, otherwise you might miss out on a wonderful and devoted boarder who just needed time to trust again. Remember that they are entrusting you with part of their family.

When Conflict Happens

Conflict is something that none of us want to deal with, but if you are going to run a barn with clients, then it will come with the territory. Conflict seems to be an unavoidable part of working and dealing with horse people. How you deal with conflict will determine the atmosphere of your barn. You will always have a lot to learn about resolving conflict because situations vary and can be complex. Always seek to avoid conflict because it is much easier and healthier than having to work to resolve conflict!

As a barn owner, you are going to deal with many conflicts between you and your clients. It is a part of working and dealing with people and your barn will be no exception. You will have conflicts between boarders and it will be for many reasons and sometimes it doesn't end well. The issues might be about horses that don't get along and horses that are being picked on. You might have conflicts with trainers and how they run their business.

You will have boarders that will follow the rules and some that choose not to. You might encounter a situation where a horse is hurt and the owner refuses to call the vet, and you need to decide at what point to step in and not give the owner an option. Drama and jealousy is something that will creep in if you allow it and it can ruin a barn. What about when a boarder is doing extremely unsafe practices with their horse? What about when a boarder or trainer is using extremely aggressive training techniques on a horse and other clients are calling you upset about it? Do you say something or look away? What about the client that is always late with the monthly board check? The list can go on and on and conflict management is one of the roles of the barn owner and manager.

Your Responsibility As A Barn Owner

It is your responsibility as the barn owner to deal with the issues that are at your barn. Take a positive perspective and realize there is no better classroom then your barn for learning to problem solve one issue at a time. Some of your efforts may be unproductive but you need to keep trying until you gain skills and language to facilitate conflict resolution. Your clients might not like some of your decisions, but they will respect your honesty and your efforts to make things better.

Every successful barn owner has had their share of terrible days where they wanted to quit and sell their farm. The difference is they chose to handle the issues head on and keep going. That is why they are still around and that is why they are successful. It is a journey with a great deal of learning along the way, some of it painful and some of it glorious. That is how you grow and get better at your job.

Making the final decisions for issues that come up in your barn will have an impact on you and your clients. Are you ready to stand your ground and run your barn how you think it should be run? I hear about issues at barns all the time where the barn owner is struggling to please everyone but it's at a high cost to them. The clients are not stressed at all, but the barn owner is regretting ever getting into the boarding business to begin with.

Resolving conflicts in your barn is something that becomes easier the longer you do it. The first couple of years will be the most difficult but if you stay focused and work through each problem, they soon will become a memory and you can learn to avoid conflict by preempting it. After you have been in the business for a while and refined your leadership skills, you will be more prepared to recognize the issues on the horizon even before they are brought to your attention by your boarders. That is when you will notice that the job is becoming easier when it comes to resolving many conflicts.

~42~

Handling A Boarder's Difficult Horse

It is not common, but you could find yourself in a situation where you need to ask a boarder to remove their horse due to its dangerous behavior. I have had to talk with a few boarders about a horse that bites continually or is very difficult to handle and sometimes trying to walk a horse safely can be challenging if the behaviors are bad. I have been kicked, bitten, pushed, head smacked and received rope burns on my hands from horses with behavioral issues. Some horses won't let you put a halter on and others won't let you catch them out in the paddock, which can be maddening when you are trying to do chores and get the horses in for the day. Poor behavior is something that can be dealt with, as long as it hasn't crossed the line where the horse endangers people. When the horse poses a dangerous threat to people, you need to talk with the owner of that horse immediately.

Talking with the owner about a serious issue their horse has is never easy and can go very well or very badly. No one wants to hear that their horse is dangerous or has serious issues. It becomes personal to many people and for some, it is very hard to accept. In fact, an owner can be in denial about aggressive behavior of any kind and refuse to engage in productive discussion about options. The barn owner needs to take immediate action to assure the safety of barn workers and boarders.

Have It In Your Boarding Contract!

The first and most important thing you can fall back on is a well-written boarding contract that includes a section on horse behavior. You need to have a section that states that you have the right as the barn owner to ask the owner of a dangerous horse to remove the horse within a certain number of days. This is intended to protect you, your employees, boarders, your business and, above all else, you need to have this legally defensible in accordance with the laws of the state you are doing business in. I hope you never have to go this route but the longer you board horses, the greater the chances are that you will encounter a horse that needs to be removed quickly for behaviors that are deemed dangerous.

In these situations, make sure that you have thoughtfully considered what you are going to say to the owner in advance of confronting them with the news that their horse is exhibiting dangerous and aggressive behavior that is unacceptable at the barn. This is not likely to be new news to the horse owner, but it might be distressing and create defensiveness in the owner.

Learning to talk with clients about extremely difficult situations takes time and skill. Choose your words carefully and try to encourage the owner to seek a trainer for help. If the problem is a behavior that can be modified, you need to strongly encourage them to find an effective trainer and have a defined timeframe for re-evaluation. Many behaviors can be corrected, but only if the owner is willing to resolve the behavioral problems through training.

The way some clients perceive their horse's behavior will be different from how you see their horse and you will need to be direct and clear about the safety of handling the horse. You can't control how the boarder reacts to this news but in most cases their response will be concern, distress and receptivity to recommendations to help change the aggression. Their emotions may overwhelm them initially followed by fear, anxiety, anger, dismay and incredulity that they own a truly dangerous horse and are not equipped to alter their behavior without help...if the behavior can be changed at all long term.

Talking with a boarder is never easy when the subject matter is the dangerous behavior of their horse. You are going to learn and grow through this management process and you will also learn how to talk with people under sensitive situations. You will make mistakes along the way and think to yourself, "Why did I just say that?" Don't be too hard on yourself because we have all been there. It is all part of learning to run a business and you will change how you address tough issues a few times as you experience different problems with horses at your barn. Each problem you come across with a horse will require different perspectives and you will get much better at it with time. Clients will come to understand that a boarding facility must be able to assure the safety of their boarders, workers and horses by making fair but difficult decisions when managing an unruly or dangerous horse.

~43~

Billing Your Clients

Creating Invoices For Your Clients

If you are going to board a large number of horses, then you will need to have a system in place for documenting fees and invoicing clients or you will be spending excess time doing this task. I would recommend purchasing any computerized system that helps you with business accounting and invoicing clients. There are many programs on the market and you can find one that works best for your business. You can easily keep track of each of your clients' individual expenses and have a record for the entire year.

Every part of your business, including your invoicing, should have a consistent, professional appearance. Providing invoices that are easy to understand supports your business image as that of a well-run business. This allows your boarders to keep their copies for their records. Paying the board or training bill is a private matter to most people and having a place that you can deposit their invoices is appreciated. You may not realize it but you are showing your clients respect by being discrete and they will appreciate those little details in how you run your business.

Charging A Late Fee

Have you ever had a job where you were supposed to be paid on the first of the month and your boss was continually late paying you? What about if your paycheck was ten days late? You would most likely be very upset and you might even quit your job if things didn't change. Now I want you to look at your horse boarding business with that in mind.

The option to charge a late fee is something that many boarding barns have in their contract but it is something that many barn owners have a difficult time enforcing. It is not fun at all to call or email your clients and remind them that the board is late.

It can even be stressful to charge a late fee because we worry that our clients are going to become upset with us and, even worse, they might leave our barn. If you are a barn owner then you know exactly what I am talking about. It is a very real fear that many barn owners have felt at one time or another.

Many businesses struggle with the financial impact of consistently late board payments but they can't bring themselves to directly enforce timely pay through penalties. Some clients will ignore the due date, blow through the grace period and pay ten days late without remorse. They will come to the barn, use the services and ride seemingly without a care in the world, while the barn owner was struggling to pay the bills on time. It can be very upsetting because of the lack of concern and disrespect this behavior demonstrates. The barn owner needs to realize that the problem starts with them and how they run the financial part of the business. Your clients need to respect your policies and pay on time or have a late fee charged to encourage compliance.

The fear that you will have clients that will leave if you charge a late fee is something that we create in our minds and it is not reality. The truth is, if a boarder leaves because they were upset over a late fee for a bill they didn't pay on-time, then they had other issues to begin with and you need to let them go. You deserve better for the hard work you do seven days a week to take care of their horse and if they leave, then it will open up a spot for a new client that will pay on time to board at your barn. Most late-payers do so out of habit and it does not reflect something personal or subjective, even though you may take it as a personal affront.

Once you start getting paid on-time each month, it might change how you feel about what you do for your clients and their horses. You will start to feel better about yourself and the services you offer at your barn but, more importantly, you will start to feel respected. It is all connected and even something as simple as getting paid when the board is due can have a huge effect on your emotional well-being. Take a position of leadership and charge the late fee if needed and you will quickly realize that this issue will take care of itself and will become almost non-existent.

It's Not Personal, It's Business

When you are in a situation where you need to contact a boarder because they are late with their board payment, I encourage you to keep it simple and direct. I have found that sending out a friendly reminder a day before the grace period has ended is an effective way to request payment. Make it a professionally short text or email message. If you have a situation where the person has gone past the grace period, then you need to professionally inform the boarder of the new total that is due immediately, including the late fee. Once a late fee has been added, you will find that most people won't be late a second time. You need to put your irritation aside, especially if it happens often with the same client. Once you are paid, move forward and keep the late payment problem between you and the client only.

Raising Your Board Rates And Service Fees

Raising the board rates is always a difficult part of owning a business. No owner likes to raise boarding rates. On the contrary, they worry they will lose clients because of the new prices. When rates need to be increased it is generally due to operating cost changes that make the increase a necessary part of maintaining financial stability in the business. Most boarders will understand that the costs to keep your barn operating will go up each year and you need to adjust or risk losing money. The rate increase is generally not an annual occurrence but should be anticipated periodically. Boarders might typically anticipate a rate change every other year for a boarding business, but every business will vary as they do whatever is best for their financial stability.

Giving A Two Month Notice For Rate Increases

How much advance notice should you give your boarders when the board rate is going to increase? Giving clients sufficient notice of any rate increases is important so they can adjust their budgets to cover the new costs. The change may seem minor but can be significant for many boarders as they determine how to afford the additional monthly expenditure.

Horses are hard to move and finding a new place to board can be challenging, especially if most stables in your area are full. If you have a client that needs to move due to the price increase, it can be very difficult for them to find a new stable in thirty days, as sometimes there are no good options available for the foreseeable future. This can be very stressful for the horse owner if they are forced by finances to transition to a less expensive stable, especially if they are happy where they are and do not want to move. It is important to give clients the time and respect they deserve by providing at least a two-month notice for planning, which gives them extra time to figure out their finances and, if the board has become unaffordable, it gives them time to look for a new stable. This practice shows boarders that you respect and value them as a client.

Sometimes all your clients need is time to adjust to the new prices and figure out their finances. Some of your boarders can adapt to the change without difficulty but some will continue to board by eliminating other things in their life so they can stay at your barn. Rate changes are difficult for owners and clients alike but are essential to a sustainable business operation.

One last thought—You may have a client tell you that they can't afford the board or feel your board is too expensive. **Do not adjust your board rates because you have a client complaining about your prices!** They do not know your business, your finances or your efforts to operate in a cost-efficient manner. If you have a person that is complaining, it may be best to listen to their complaints and then to let them go and move their horse. Don't take it personally because this is part of having any kind of business. The right people will find your stable and they will be so glad that you have an open stall and your board prices will be acceptable to them.

~44~

What Kind Of Clients Are You Trying To Attract?

What kind of clients are you trying to attract? Do you know what kind of clients you want at your barn? These may seem like odd questions to ask but you need to know the type of clients you want to attract so that you can develop and sustain a positive, accepting and supportive learning environment at your stable. It is very normal to have never given this part of barn development any thought, but you can benefit by thinking outside the box proactively, especially if you are in the planning stages of a new business.

Knowing what type of clients and horses would be a good fit for the type of business you have is important to the overall atmosphere and success of the barn. Equally important to understand is that what you want and what is a good fit for your barn might be on the opposite ends of the spectrum at times. Narrowing the gap can be accomplished over time if you keep your eye on your goals.

What You Want And What Is A Good Fit

If you have dreams of having a hunter/jumper barn but do not have a large enough arena with the proper footing, then you probably won't attract that type of clientele. If you live in an area where weather dictates the need for an indoor arena to ride year round, you will need a sizable indoor arena to attract clients who like to show and need to practice year round. If you want a boarding barn that caters to barrel racing and speed events, then you need something more than a round pen for practice. I hope you are starting to appreciate the realities that prospective clients face when selecting facilities that match their interests. If you want to attract trail riders that want a casual atmosphere and love obstacle courses and lots of local trails, then realize that you will need special amenities to accommodate these types of horse owners. As you develop your future plans, whether a new facility or an existing one, learn about the physical requirements and amenities that are typical for each discipline, as well as the attitudes and expectations of the riders. You need this information to determine the future direction of your business and the possibility of successfully supporting the disciplines with your facility and the amenities available. This will help you target your marketing to reach potential boarders. It will also help you develop a plan for future improvements and changes that will provide predictable returns on investment.

I have learned to be very direct with potential clients when they come for a tour and tell them what we can and cannot offer for the type of riding they do. If you don't have any idea of the clients you want to attract to your stable, then I encourage you to take some time and really think about each discipline and the requirements they typically have. There are a few disciplines that are not well-suited for my barn and it took me a year or two to figure that out. Once I did, it became much easier when someone called and asked about our facility and what we offered.

If you are building or changing an existing barn, make sure to include a budget for the purchase of some of the equipment that you would use in certain disciplines. Letters for dressage are a must if you want dressage riders at your barn. Purchasing jumps (even if it is a few at a time) will help attract people that jump. If you want a barn that caters to reiners and speed eventers, then make sure to budget for footing improvements that meet their standards.

Your Riding Disciplines Might Change
A multi-discipline barn might see a trend change in riding disciplines over the years. You may start with people who liked to jump, along with dressage riders at your facility then, over the years, experience a change to hunt seat and western riding and then a reversal back to jumping and dressage mostly due to riding trends and the influence of the trainers who practice in the area. For a while our barn was turning into a training barn with many young horses and training for hunt seat and western pleasure. When the trainer heading that program left, it opened the door for new trainers and different disciplines which worked to the advantage of the boarders and the overall atmosphere in the stable. Change can infuse everyone with enthusiasm if there is a positive and accepting environment to support change. My objective in this chapter is to get you to see that your boarding barn will go through different changes throughout the years unless you are discipline specific. Your professional direction should ideally be based on good planning and execution rather than chance.

Set Your Standards High
There is a difference between a reliable client who is going through a tough period and a client who habitually shares their pain or anger and creates a negative atmosphere in the barn. Dealing with people who cause drama in the barn just for the sake of drama and attention is not a rewarding experience.

Once you gain a reputation for managing stable dynamics to avoid drama and encourage no-drama clients, then you will be unlikely to attract the person that created drama everywhere they boarded. They usually won't come to your barn because your reputation for no drama precedes you and they know their drama will not be accepted. As the barn owner and manager, you will be the one that sets the standards for your boarders and a no-drama or low-drama barn is an enviable and marketable attribute.

If You Build, Your Clientele Will Change

Many people get into boarding horses the same way we did; they have some property with a couple of horses and they start boarding a few friends' horses. At that point, things are casual and easy until you start to dream of a large facility where you can quit your full-time job and make horse boarding a career. It happened to us and it happens often.

If you are boarding a couple of horses and decide to build a barn, you need to be prepared for your clientele to change as you develop into a bigger business. This can be difficult for the casual boarders that have been at your barn because your new business will change to include rules and many more people and horses. The change will often result in higher board rates and this can be extremely hard on the people who boarded at your place before. There is a chance that they will leave if the price increase and changes in atmosphere become too much for them to accept.

There will be a huge adjustment for everyone involved when you decide to build and become a fully operational boarding business. I encourage you to be patient and supportive with your current boarders and give them time to adjust to all the new rules and changes that are happening.

As the new barn owner, you will also experience some personal changes that you will need to learn to deal with. You will start to get calls from trainers and other equine professionals about boarding and events offered at your barn. You will talk to many new people about your facility and they may have specific requests in mind when they come for a tour. You will experience meaningful conversations along with others that will leave you feeling like you are under oath with all the scrutiny and questions. You will have conversations with clients that are intense and others that are completely casual, some that are worthwhile and others that are a total waste of time. You will have people who once boarded horses for a living and others that are brand new to horse ownership and have never boarded before. As you learn to deal with prospective clients, you will also become very skilled in providing tours and answering questions. You might even have fun as you discretely evaluate the people for suitability as a boarder–all while they think they are interviewing you!

Your Board Rate Will Attract A Certain Clientele
The one thing most new business owners don't think about is the importance of your board rates and the type of clientele that can afford your rates. The truth is, if you only charge one hundred dollars for board, then you probably don't have much for amenities and that will be great for many people. You can find many places that will have a very low monthly board rate and it will be enough to feed the horse and have shelter and water. People who have owned horses for a while know how expensive horse care can be and also know that a hundred dollars will not get you much at any stable.

If you have a small stable and just want a couple of boarders to help with chores when you want to go away for the weekend, then a small fee will probably work. You might only cover your costs, but you will have company and help once in a while when you need it. Many people will do this but you still need to make sure you have insurance and a boarding contract. Things can happen with even one horse boarded at your place.

As Your Board Rate Increases

As you build and add amenities, it is only natural that your board rate will increase. If you decide that you want to build a large facility with many extras, then your board rate will reflect those amenities and you will start to notice some changes in clientele attracted to your barn. Your clientele will change because not everyone can afford a higher priced facility and you will also start to attract other equine professionals from trainers to veterinarians. Some of your clients will become your friends but some of them will be there strictly for business and working their horses for competition. It may be strictly a business arrangement and you need to understand this and respect it. They might all be good boarders and you will definitely have a diverse group of people as clients.

Transition From The Hobby Farm
There is a transition that takes place when you go from having a hobby farm with a couple of horses to a professional boarding stable. Your relationships may change, and you may focus on business relationships first. You might become good friends with some of your boarders but not all of them and that is to be expected. Many clients will board at your barn because you offer the amenities they need to compete or show at a competitive level and that is all they want. They will come to ride and take care of business and not participate in anything else at the barn. You will find that you appreciate that they have chosen your barn for boarding and that is enough. Remember that these people come to your barn because you run a professional facility. They don't want to go to a hobby farm and you are no longer running a hobby farm. This will

become easier once you embrace your new role as a barn manager and equine professional.

The Upper-End Barn And Expectations

If you decide that you are going to own and manage an upper-end boarding facility, then you need to be aware of clients' expectations. The more your clients pay, the more they will expect for their money. People that are willing to pay a higher board rate for top quality care also expect the arenas to be dragged and the water buckets to be cleaned on a set schedule without exception. They will not accept their horses having frozen water or ice in their paddocks. It means you are going to ensure that the barn is organized and runs efficiently with safety as a high priority. When clients pay a higher board fee, they are expecting your place to offer extra care that they may not find elsewhere. I am not saying that every small place that is less expensive has care that is not as good. What I am saying is that when something is higher priced there are expectations attached to it. That is no different than when you stay at a hotel and you pay top dollar for an executive suite. You would expect the sheets to be clean and the bed to be comfortable. That upper end hotel will come with some added perks and comfort. The same will be true in the boarding world.

The most important thing to remember is that your boarders work hard for their money and they deserve to get what they are paying for. If you are going to run a boarding barn then be honored that they have chosen your barn for their horses care. You will have a wonderful opportunity to meet many different people from all walks of life at your barn. I encourage you to get to know them and their horses by encouraging open communications and being approachable. Don't miss out on the wonderful opportunities of developing new relationships that are right in front of you. Happy boarders are your best advertising!

~45~

Boundaries With Your Clients

This is a subject that is near and dear to my heart because I had no clue in the beginning how **not** having boundaries in my business could actually hurt my business. I cannot express how important boundaries are between you and your clients. Once you become a business owner, your role is going to change and the way your boarders will see you will be a huge adjustment, especially if you boarded with them at a barn before you decided to start your own business.

Most people are not ready for the change and it can be very hard on the barn owner or barn manager when they need to separate business from pleasure in relationships with boarders. Becoming a business owner is not something that everybody is cut out for, but if you are going to venture into the world of business ownership, then getting your boundaries in place is a great step forward in creating a healthy environment for you and your clients.

Figuring Out The Boundaries

Figuring out what the boundaries are for you and your clients will be something that takes time and trial and error. One of the best things you can do as a business owner is to find a mentor who has operated a business and is willing to help you work through establishing boundaries with old and new clients. It can be difficult to see what the problems are when you may be part of the problem! It is advisable to talk with someone outside the business for advice and a fresh pair of eyes on issues that you are struggling with.

I have created a list of ideas to help create healthy boundaries between you and your boarders. Most of these points have survived the test of time in business. I hope they will help you avoid problems instead of dealing with the aftermath of a barn without proper boundaries.

Creating Boundaries:

- **Sharing too much**-One of the biggest mistakes a barn owner can make is sharing too much about their financial situation with their clients. You need to remember that your boarders are paying good money to board at your barn and discussions about the business financial issues can undermine their sense of security about the future of your barn and their horse. If you are struggling financially, confer with someone outside the barn about how to manage your business finances. Think before you speak!

- **Not enough personal space**-You may be an open book, but not all your clients will be the same way. They all have a separate life outside the barn with their own problems and the barn may be their only peaceful place. If they want to talk about personal issues, then let them lead. Giving your boarders space is important and if they want to talk, they will let you know.

- **Too much personal information about you and your family**-Have you ever been around someone that talks constantly and when you see them coming, you want to walk the other way? Don't let this be how your boarders feel about you. You will become friends with some of your boarders but sharing too much about problems in your marriage or family can make your clients uncomfortable. I want you to remember that everything you talk about will reflect on the business and if you are having marital problems and you are sharing it with a few boarders, then they will start to wonder if the barn is going to be affected by this. There have been barns that have closed up overnight because the husband and wife decided to divorce and everyone had to get their horses out immediately. It happens and your boarders know this. Don't give them anything to worry about and keep it professional.

- **Stay away from gossip**-There is no way around having some gossip in a barn. If you get people together, they will start to talk and it can turn into unhealthy gossip. As the barn owner or manager, you need to avoid this type of talk. If you are just standing there while they talk negatively about another boarder, then you need to try to change the conversation to something more productive or move on. Joining in on the gossip only makes you look much less professional and reflects poorly on your character.

- **Giving your clients boundaries**-The one very unique part of many boarding stables is that many barn owners or barn managers live on site. Living on the same property as the barn itself has many advantages especially when it comes to doing chores or checking on a sick horse. It also has some drawbacks that most people would not accept in their daily work life. If you live on the same property as your boarding business, then you never get away from the business unless you drive off the property. Many of your clients will not realize they are intruding on your privacy when coming to your house for things that could have been emailed, texted or written on a dry erase board in the barn. They don't realize that you need your personal space as much as they do and it can be challenging when your life and schedule are so intertwined with the business daily.

Creating an office or place where you handle all business in your barn or stable is important, as it can help keep your home off limits. It doesn't mean a boarder can't come to your home in case of an emergency but, in most cases, they could use other communication methods to ask you about a question they have. The longer you board horses, the more you will realize that some people don't understand boundaries and you need to manage intrusive behavior. In these situations, be direct and nicely explain that from now they need to call or text when they have a question and not come to the house unless it is an emergency. You will need to be very clear and direct when it comes to these kinds of issues and you will get better at communicating it over time.

The Barn Owner's Responsibility

The barn owner or manager has the responsibility to make sure that boarders act respectfully toward each other and accept their differences. People can be very quick to judge others and that can be dangerous for your business. Behavior that isolates or polarizes boarders needs to be noticed and redirected as quickly as possible. The barn owner and manager will set the example so that all boarders feel accepted and safe. A welcoming environment for all is a wonderful marketing advantage.

You are going to have many different types of people come to your barn throughout your career in the horse industry. If you can, embrace them all just as they are. You will have boarders that will love to talk and share their life with you and others that will be very quiet and private people. Learn to listen more and talk less as a barn owner or barn manager and you will learn, over time, what type of boarders you have and enjoy them just as they are. They each will make your barn complete.

I believe that as the barn owner, you need to keep things professional always. It doesn't mean you can't go out and do fun things with your boarders, but you need to remember that they are clients and if they ever start to sense there are financial stresses, or other problems that could compromise the care of their horse, that is when you are going to have problems. You also need to remember that even though you are friends, there is a business relationship that will always be part of the equation until the day they move their horse. That business relationship cannot be compromised and it needs to take precedence in order to keep the business healthy. It's not easy, in fact it can be very hard at times, but it is important when it comes to the daily activities of the barn. Boundaries come in many different forms and it could be the barn owner crossing the line just as easily as the client. Keep yourself in check and I encourage you to have a business mentor that can help you walk through this part of running your barn and business.

~46~

Why Do Boarders Leave?

Once your boarding stable is established and you have a clear understanding of how you want to run it, your job will become so much easier. You will know what works and doesn't work for your barn and the trials and mistakes will become fewer. But as in life, there are always a few bumps in the road to keep us on our toes. When clients come to your barn with their horses, many of them will be thrilled to be there. Some of them will come from poorly run facilities where the care was not good. Others will come because your barn offers the perfect atmosphere and amenities for them. Even if you are extremely detailed in how you do things at your barn and the boarder is in total agreement, you will have a few clients that will change over time as they grow as equestrians. What they wanted for their horse may have been fine in the beginning but sometimes that changes. As your boarders grow in their horsemanship, many of them will try new things along the way and sometimes it will affect your job as the barn manager and it could affect your business if they choose to leave for another barn.

When Things Change For A Client

You will have clients that will try showing and if they fall in love with it, they may decide they now want special turn-out for their horse during show season. You might have a client that sells their horse for a more competitive horse in the show ring and with that comes different needs that maybe you can't offer. You might not have a trainer that is available for the type of riding discipline a boarder has now chosen and in that case, a boarder will leave a barn for a training barn of their new discipline choice. You will have clients that will suddenly want night turn-out if they feel they need to keep their horse's coat from fading during the summer months. You could be asked to keep a horse inside all the time because the client is now worried their horse might get hurt being with other horses. You might have a boarder that decides to put special show shoes on and now they want their horse inside all the time and your barn has always had a policy that all horses go out during the day.

There will be boarders that will follow fads and want to change how you feed their horse according to what is popular at the moment. That could include the type of hay you offer and don't offer. You are going to watch boarders grow tremendously in their riding skills and sometimes they will ask for amenities that you have never offered before. You might even have a boarder that has now decided that they prefer a different way of doing herd management and this can be true for your feeding program as well. What was once a perfect barn for them has changed and that will definitely be a difficult thing for you to deal with.

The list of changes that your clients will go through is really endless, but every change will affect you as the barn owner or manager to some degree. Some of these changes and requests will be easy to accommodate but many of them will not, especially if it becomes more work for you. Your barn might start out as the perfect barn for someone but as their needs change, they might start looking elsewhere if you can't offer what they now want for their horse. This is a very real part of running a boarding business and you will drive yourself crazy if you try to make everything perfect with every change that a client is going through. Don't go there!

You don't want to start making changes to accommodate a few boarders at the risk of disrupting other boarders. It is okay if some of your boarders need different amenities than what you offer as they pursue their equestrian goals. The best thing you can do for your business and your clients is to be honest about what you offer and if they need to make a change in barns, then wish them the very best. It is simply part of watching your boarders grow and change.

~47~

First Impressions And A Clean Barn

You don't need a new barn to make a good first impression. Each person that visits your stable will immediately start to compare it to their needs and expectations. A good first impression is not about the size of your barn or the amount of pasture you have for the horses at your place. It is not about how many riding arenas you have or accessible trails near your place. Sure, some of those things might be impressive at first, but they will quickly be forgotten if your place is dirty, disorganized and in a state of disrepair. What people will notice first and remember last is cleanliness, order and organization.

Many people around our area think that the reason we are always at full occupancy with a waiting list is because we are a newer facility and we have a large indoor riding arena. That simply is not true. Our "new" barn is now many years old, but it has been meticulously maintained and is always clean and orderly. I believe one of the reasons we are full all the time is that we pay attention to the details, do proper maintenance and take great pride in our establishment. Our boarders also participate in making our barn visits memorable by talking with visitors and sharing their experiences in a meaningful way. We can walk away from their discussions knowing that our interests will be well represented. Our boarders and their partnership is vital to our success.

Taking everything out of the tack room and giving it a thorough cleaning once a year is something your clients will appreciate.

Get Rid Of The Junk And Clutter!

If you are serious about making a great first impression, then get rid of the junk and clutter. Too many boarding stables keep junk all over the place and even in the pastures where the horses are. If you want to set your barn apart and look professional, then get rid of the junk! If you don't have a storage shed to put it all in, then at least take it out of the pastures, aisle ways and everywhere else and store it all in a place where the horses can't get to it. Have a designated place for everything so horses can't get hurt and it will make your place look bigger, cleaner and much more organized. It will give a great first impression that your barn is a well-run business.

Having brooms, pitchforks, shovels and muck buckets in designated areas creates a well-organized barn.

A Clean Barn Doesn't Just Happen

Sometimes people will assume that a clean barn is a newer barn that hasn't had time to get dirty and collect cobwebs. Again, not true! You could have a twenty year old barn and if you put time and work into keeping it clean, then it will look newer than what it really is. My husband will spend hours once a year cleaning down the cob webs and washing things that need to be washed. When he is done it makes a huge difference. We will take a blower and blow through our barn two or three times a week to get the dust and cobwebs off of everything and it really cleans it out. The state of your facility and grounds reflects on you as a barn owner.

Using a steamer to clean the grit and grime off of your stall grills will make a huge difference on how they look. Horses are hard on everything and that will include your stalls. Cleaning them will definitely give your barn a great first impression for someone that is touring your place and your current boarders will appreciate it as well.

It's The Little Things That Make A Difference

It is the little things like keeping the grass cut and the arenas dragged and fixing things that get broken that will make a great first impression and set your place apart from other barns. As people drive up to your barn, they will start mentally checking off all that they see and categorizing the pros and cons of your facility. The size of your riding arenas and other amenities might be what brought them to your place but a clean and organized barn might be the thing that sells them on signing on. If your facility is dirty and seems unsafe for the horses because you have equipment everywhere and things are broken, then it doesn't matter how nice or big the arenas are or the extra amenities you offer at that point, there is a good chance they will leave and look somewhere else.

If people like what they see they will tell other people and that is always great for your business. It might sound a little cliché but you never get a second chance to make a great first impression.

Power washing your barn walls is an inexpensive way to give your barn a facelift and will help keep your walls free from cobwebs. Using a blower will also keep the cobwebs down if done on a regular basis.

~48~

Competing With Other Horse Stables

Most business owners keep a close eye on their competition. That is a very typical thing to do and boarding stables are no exception. We want to know what other boarding barns offer for amenities and we compare prices and what is included in their board rates. It is good business to keep an eye on the competition.

You can go on Facebook or a competitor's website and look at their place in pictures and it looks absolutely perfect in every way and all of a sudden you start to feel your place is inadequate and not good enough. Maybe you start to feel your place needs to be bigger or have fancier accessories. Competing with other boarding businesses in the area is not a bad thing at all, but first you need to stop trying to compete with what the other places "*say*" they offer.

I have always believed that having a few competing boarding barns in our area is a good thing for business, as it keeps us all working harder to make our place better for boarders and horses. The other very important part of the equation is that every client is looking for something different in a boarding barn. There are many people who like a smaller stable with only a handful of boarders, while others like a large facility with a few trainers to choose from and many clinics and events going on throughout the year.

They Say They Do It all!

After many years of boarding horses, I have an extensive understanding of what it takes to keep the horses in my care safe and healthy. It is nothing fancy or magical that makes our place run well, it is old fashioned hard work and being very observant to what is going on with the horses. When you read other boarding barn websites that talk about what they do every day for the care of the horses at their barn, you need to remember that if it sounds too good to be true, it probably is! The other places just have a magical way of wording it!

You will find out what you are good at when it comes to promoting your business but the most important thing you need to realize is that if you give quality care and run an ethical business then your business will sell itself. People will talk, and they will start to see how you do things and that will be the best advertisement of all.

Smaller Boarding Stables Are Important

For some reason many people have this mindset that horse owners want a large facility with many people to ride with and lots of stuff going on. That simply is not true. We have a larger facility and there have been people who have come to our barn and have left after a few months because it was too big and busy for them. They preferred a quieter and smaller stable. Not everyone will want a large riding arena and there are many people that only trail ride in the warmer months and are just happy to come out and visit their horse and brush them for a while. Smaller stables will offer special things that a large facility cannot offer because of the size. If you are a small stable, then advertise all the advantages of a nice quiet place and the individual care that goes with a smaller barn. Smaller stables are vital to the horse industry and there are many people looking for a smaller place to keep their horse. They just need to find you and that is why a website is so important.

I believe competition is a good thing but you need to keep it in perspective and remember that not everything is as wonderful as it appears in pictures. You may have a surprise when you drive up and take a tour at a stable and realize it's not as it looked on the website. Pictures can be deceiving and words will always create a great image.

Learn from other barns if you like some of their ideas but only if they will be good for your stable. Don't make changes solely for competitive purposes because that will be a waste of your resources. Go back to your business plan to reinforce your decisions and stay on track for your goals. Stay true to your plan and your goals and your business will flourish.

~49~

Your Barn Will Have Growing Pains

Growing pains are a part of business ownership. They come in all different forms and for many reasons, so if your business is very young, then you will likely experience many of them as you figure out what works best for your boarding barn. Growing pains happen because you start out running your business one way and later find that there is a better way to do things. Growing pains happen because you decide you want to go a different direction with the horses and training program that you have set up. You might decide that you want to change how you do herd management and turnout or the feeding program and that could be a little upsetting to some of your clients. Growing pains happen because change is disruptive for your clients and when you start making changes that affect them, they can become nervous. Growing pains is rarely about growing larger.

Growing As A Barn Manager

Growing pains will be experienced the most by the barn manager! As you start becoming confident in taking charge of how the barn operates and enforcing rules, your clients may be confused by your transformation to a cordial but firmly assertive manager.

Some of your boarders may not like the new you and you will need to, once again, be patient and let them adjust. The more confident you become in how you run the barn, the more likely it will be that some boarders will resent your change because it diminishes their influence at the barn.

You are likely to experience many difficulties during the first few years as a barn manager, but things will gradually smooth out. After talking with many barn owners over the years, I have found that it is very common to lose boarders during the first few years when all the changes are taking place. It is important for you to understand that this is a business and you shouldn't take it personally. It is not easy, and it may even be painful at times while going through the changes, but it is worth it because it makes you stronger as a barn owner and manager and your business will be stronger also.

~50~

Why Your Job Is So Unique

Boarding horses for a living is a rewarding career and at the same time very unique. You are taking care of amazing animals, each with their own personalities that will have you smiling and even shaking your head in disbelief at times. Your boarding business is unique for several reasons. First of all, you will never truly be off work. Like many service business owners will tell you, you might be on vacation, but the phone is still ringing! That is very true in this business. I have never had a vacation without some work involved because my phone always rings with questions or horse concerns; it is just part of the job. The second thing is that the horses need to be taken care of every day of the year, including weekends and holidays. There will be times when you can't find employees that can work, or someone will call in sick and you are the one stuck doing the chores. It is a very real part of this business and you can't call in sick yourself! Most people who start a boarding business are just like me when we first opened. They are so excited to start their new business but overwhelmed when the burden of responsibility becomes a reality. I am here to tell you that if you hang in there and take it one day at a time, the days will become easier.

During those early years, your clients will change as you make changes to the business and there will be some growing pains. Before you know it, you will settle into a routine and your boarders will know a good thing when they experience it and they won't leave. Your turnover will be much lower, and the horses will settle in. Your herd management skills will be apparent, and you will know each horse and their personality like they were your own child. I believe it takes a couple of years through all four seasons to become comfortable with running your stable and all that goes with it.

You will always have fences to fix and things to replace that have been broken, but not every job has beautiful horses waiting for you every morning as you walk out to the barn to start your morning chores. You have a very unique job and your office is something that so many people can only dream about. Learn to take the bad with the good and find out what works best for your stable. You will become skillful at decision making and leadership skills which will be for the betterment of your entire barn and business. You will change a lot over the years and your confidence is going to grow in leaps and bounds.

Do What Is Best For You

You need to remember that your clients will come and go, but you and your business will still be there. You need to do what is best for you, your family and your business. Embrace your position as owner/manager of your boarding business and watch it grow throughout the years and you will grow too. One day you will wake up and realize that you are good at what you do and you will be glad for all the challenging times because that is when you grew the most.

You have chosen a career with many unique demands and challenges, but one that provides countless experiences and relationships. What a life to go to work each day in the care of horses and their owners! Your perspectives and efforts will determine if that life is wonderful or fraught with regrets.

Wishing you the very best in your horse boarding business and hope it only gets better over the years and, as you reflect on your journey, you can say it was wonderful and fulfilling!

Sheri Grunska

About The Author

With many years of horse boarding experience on both sides of the fence, first as a boarder and later a barn owner and manager, Sheri Grunska followed her dreams of turning open farm fields into Vinland Stables and launching ProBarn Management as a resource for other equine professionals. As an author, blogger, speaker and consultant, Sheri draws inspiration from her own experiences, building a successful boarding facility and working in all parts of her business daily.

Sheri is busy these days working alongside her husband at their barn daily along with writing and consulting, but her favorite place to be is at home with her family on the farm and keeping things simple.

Sheri's Books and Website

You can catch Sheri's blog articles every week at

www.probarnmanagement.com

Sheri has written several books about running a horse business. She has also written inspirational books for the horse lover and equine professional. You can find all her books on her website at www.probarnmanagement.com and Amazon.com.

What It Really Takes To Start And Run A Horse Business (And how to do it right the first time).

The Total Horse Barn Management Makeover (Practical business wisdom for running your horse business).

Caring For Horses With A Servant's Heart (A daily devotional for the horse professional and the horse lover in all of us).

One Horse Woman To Another (Embracing your life as an Equine Professional and finding confidence in who you are and how you run your horse business).

Made in the USA
Middletown, DE
18 February 2019